Dealing with the Dutch

DEALING
WITH THE DUTCH

The cultural context
of business and work
in the Netherlands

Jacob Vossestein

KIT PUBLISHERS — AMSTERDAM

Dealing with the Dutch, J. Vossestein

KIT Publishers
Mauritskade 63
Postbus 95001
1090 HA Amsterdam
E-mail: publishers@kit.nl

Websites:
www.kit.nl/publishers
www.landenreeks.nl
www.hotei-publishing.com
www.samsam.net
www.leespiramide.nl

First edition 1997 © KIT Publishers, Amsterdam
Eleventh revised edition: June 2001 © KIT Publishers, Amsterdam
Fourteenth revised edition: October 2004 © KIT Publishers, Amsterdam

Lay-out: Henny Scholten, Amsterdam.
Cover: Nico Richter, Monnickendam.
Cover photo: Zefa, Nederland.
Production: Meester and De Jonge, Lochem.
Editor: Shirley Agudo, Pro/PR, Laren.

ISBN 90 6832 565 5
NUR 812/ 741/ 780

Books on intercultural communication available at KIT Publishers:
Nurtured in the Netherlands, N. Sharpe
Vreemd volk, J. Vossestein
ExpatHandboek, J. Vossestein, N. Vink et al.
Zo werkt dat in Nederland, J. Vossestein
Grenzeloos communiceren, N. Vink
Een bestaan als expatriate, F. Quarles van Ufford
Opgroeien in het buitenland, E. Kunst, M. Simons,
Wereldkids, M. Zoer

CONTENTS

THE NETHERLANDS

- ● City >100.000 inh.
- ・ Other important towns: (not shown in Randstad area)
- Randstad (5 million inh.)
- <u>Assen</u> Provincial capital
- Provincial boundaries
- Rivers and canals
- Area less than 1 meter (3,3 ft.) above sealevel; without protection of dikes or dunes, this would be flooded
- Dams and barriers (Delta and Zuiderzee projects)

N

NORTH SEA

WADDENZEE

Schiermonnikoog
Ameland
Terschelling
Vlieland
Texel

Delfzijl
GRONINGEN
Groningen
Winschoten

Afsluitdijk
Leeuwarden
Harlingen
FRIESLAND
Sneek
Heerenveen

Crachten

Assen
DRENTHE
Hoogeveen
Emmen

Den Helder

IJsselmeer
Enkhuizen
Emmeloord
Meppel

NOORD-
HOLLAND
Hoorn
Alkmaar

Kampen
Zwolle

FLEVOLAND
Lelystad

OVERIJSSEL
Almelo
Twente
Hengelo
Enschede

IJmuiden
Zaandam
Haarlem Amsterdam
Schiphol
Hillversum
Leiden
Zoetermeer

Almere
Harderwijk

Deventer
Zutphen

Apeldoorn
Veluwe

UTRECHT
Amersfoort

GELDERLAND

The Hague
(Den Haag)
ZUID-
Delft
±2 m
Gouda
Europoort
Rotterdam
Dordrecht
HOLLAND

Utrecht
Lek
Betuwe
Tiel
Waal
Maas
Nijmegen
Oss

Arnhem
Wageningen

Winterswijk

Rhine (Rijn)

GERMANY

's-Hertogenbosch

Oosterschelde
ZEELAND
Middelburg
Vlissingen
Zeeuws-
Vlaanderen
Terneuzen
Westerschelde
Thom

NOORD-BRABANT
Roosendaal
Bergen op Zoom
Breda
Tilburg
Eindhoven

Helmond

Venlo

LIMBURG
Roermond

Oberhausen
Duisburg
Mülheim
Ruhrgebiet
Krefeld
Düsseldorf

München
Gladbach

Antwerp
(Antwerpen)
Gent
Schelde
FLANDERS
BELGIUM
Brussels
(Brussel)

Sittard
Heerlen
Kerkrade
Maastricht
Hills
Aachen
Maas
Vaalserberg +312 m

INTRODUCTION

The subject of this book is the everyday working culture of the Dutch. It is intended for people from other countries who have contacts with the Netherlands through work or business: incoming expatriates, business people coming here for shorter periods, and those who work with the Dutch on a regular basis, either in Holland or abroad. This book tries to be a light-hearted description and an explanation of everyday Dutch behaviour as it is observed by foreigners encountering the locals in work-related environments, whether just for a few months or for a number of years.

It therefore focuses on the Dutch system of values and norms in the present-day social and economic framework. I set the observations (printed in *italics*) of non-Dutch nationals who have already had dealings with the Dutch, in the wider context of culture and society, concentrating on the level of everyday contacts in work and business. I shall tell you what you are likely to encounter here and advise you how to avoid misunderstandings.

In previous editions I wrote: 'Foreigners working with the Dutch seldom experience problems of sloth or inefficiency, inadequate infrastructure or other logistical or "hardware" problems'. Mostly this is still true, but with long holidays, quite a lot of bureaucracy and many traffic jams, Dutch society could be more flexible than it is. People bringing their families here find the general facilities (shops, schools, etc.) excellent, although it must be said that it is neither easy nor cheap to find a suitable place to live. Of course, the initial phase of settling in a foreign country always causes some uneasiness, but once that shock is over, you will have no difficulty with matters such as these.

So what do these people complain about in relation to the Dutch? People participating in our programmes keep telling me that it is the underlying values and norms of their Dutch colleagues, counterparts or subordinates that puzzle and sometimes irritate them. For example, they mention the *directness* of the Dutch, the *negative feedback*, the inordinate amount of *rules and regulations* and their Dutch colleagues' strict *separation of work and leisure time*. On a more positive note, they are generally pleased with the *helpfulness* of the Dutch, their *reliability*, the fact that almost *everybody speaks English*, and the readiness to *compromise*.

Norms and values are not static, and it seems that in recent years Dutch society has been changing more rapidly than ever before. However, cultural characteristics and 'typical' behaviour don't change overnight. In fact, they may reappear in other forms. I have tried to take this into account, on the one hand by sketching the underlying, historical roots of Dutch culture, and on the other by bringing the picture up to date with examples of recent changes that appear to be crucial.

One widespread misunderstanding should be cleared up before we continue. So far, I have used the names 'Holland' and 'The Netherlands' as if they are one and the same, just two names for the same country. In English, indeed, they are more or less interchangeable, although the more official term 'The Netherlands' is generally used for ceremonial or diplomatic purposes. (In much the same way, the Dutch often use the term 'England' informally to refer to the United Kingdom.) However, the Dutch themselves call their country 'Nederland' and with just a few exceptions, use the word 'Holland' only to specifically indicate the most important and dominant region of the country: the highly urbanised area in the western provinces, the so-called Randstad (see map). This region is the economic, cultural and political heart of the nation and increasingly functions as one large city of some seven million people.

Most business encounters with Dutch people take place in the Randstad and this means that you will usually be dealing with 'Hollanders', people who were either born in this region or live there now. Since this 'Holland proper' exercises a strong overall influence through national institutions and the media, this book largely deals with the mentality and behaviour of people in this region. More information on the other areas of the country will be provided in chapter 12.

Thus, the following chapters focus on what one might call the 'average' behaviour of the ethnic Dutch majority in business and work. But, like other European countries, the Netherlands – certainly the Randstad area – has turned into a multicultural society. Including those from former Dutch colonies (most of whom already had Dutch nationality), over two million people from different cultural backgrounds have moved here in recent decades – now surpassing 15% of the total population. Although many have integrated into Dutch society, the mentality and behaviour of quite a few of them is not the same as that described in this book, and their presence is a hot issue in Holland. More discussion on these ethnic minorities and their position in Dutch society can be found in chapter 11.

Generalisations are inevitable in a book like this. Even in such a small country as the Netherlands there are differences in values, views and manners between various groups of the population, between generations and so on. Some of the issues related to gender and generations are discussed in chapter 10.

As for the business world, another factor is worthy of mention. The Dutch economy is open and internationally oriented and many Dutch business people have been affected by wide exposure to foreign cultures. In their working life, and perhaps in their private life, too, their mentality and behaviour may no longer be 'typically Dutch', but rather reflect a kind of international culture. Business people from other countries frequently find such 'international' Dutchmen are 'easier' to deal with than the more 'local' ones: *'The Dutch are not all the same. Are they or are they not exposed to an international environment on a more or less daily basis? If they are, then the differences tend to blend away, for instance, their need to leave the office and be home for dinner at six. If they have had more exposure to an international environment, they are more willing to stay until the job is finished.'* (Israel)

Granted, the Netherlands may have a large number of internationally experienced managers and CEOs, but such people are still a minority by far. Therefore, this book will try to prepare you for more likely – and more challenging – situations: dealing with people who behave in a 'typically' Dutch manner. Such people may be found in smaller companies that are only now beginning to explore cross-border markets, and in larger and/or multinational companies where not everyone at all levels has had business experience in the outside world.

It may seem obvious to say that Dutch mentality and behaviour will be most surprising and strange to people from vastly different cultures such as Nigeria, India or Brazil. But there is a pitfall here for people from nearby Germany, Belgium or Britain. Just because, superficially, things in the Netherlands seem to be very much the same as they are at home, neighbouring cultures may be fooled into thinking they *are* the same. With the realisation that there are a significant number of small differences after all, frustration and culture shock may hit even harder.

Throughout the book I will quote observations by people from other countries that are residing in the Netherlands, mostly for reasons of work.. I have tried to select quotes which, in my opinion, are not only fairly typical of what people from other countries think of the Dutch, but which also accurately reflect Dutch reality. At the same time I have tried as far as possible to select quotes that have something 'extra', whether in the phrasing, in an interesting point of view or in the humour .

The quotes were collected by me personally from interviews in Dutch newspapers or magazines, or made to me by participants in the training programmes called 'Understanding the Dutch' at the Royal Tropical Institute in Amsterdam.

Some remarks on the third edition   An old comment on the Netherlands (attributed to the 19th-century German poet Heinrich Heine) says, 'W*hen the world comes to an end, go to Holland because everything happens fifty years later there*'.

This may have been true around 1830, but it certainly isn't true in the 21st century. Quite the reverse. The first edition of this book was written in the winter of 1996/1997. Not very long ago, one might think – but in some respects it seems it was not only in the last century but almost a century ago! For obvious reasons, the words 'Internet' and 'e-mail' did not appear in it at all, and although there certainly were references to prosperity, it still hadn't become entirely clear that the country was heading for the wave of prosperity during which the first revised edition was written, in 2000/2001.

But waves recede and tides change. Just when the new edition appeared – shortly before Sept. 11, 2001 – the first chilly winds started blowing. Since then, the Dutch economy has slowed down considerably and come almost to a standstill, with some quarters officially in recession. After years of having the higher growth rates of Europe, Dutch figures now lag behind those in other European economies. After flying high, the downgrade has been more painful.

Another shock, headlining even outside the national borders, was of course the assassination of the controversial politician Pim Fortuyn in May 2002, the first political murder in the Netherlands in over 400 years. Occurring during an election campaign that was already fiercer than average, the killing caused a wave of emotions that, for a moment, seemed to bring the country to the verge of civil war. How could such a thing happen in a relatively peaceful and stable country with a population usually perceived by outsiders as calm or even 'cold'? We will come back on this issue.

Uncertain economic prospects and altered moods prompted yet another edition of this book. Short-term economic waxing and waning only superficially affect a nation's culture, but in the Netherlands there also occurs a more profound change away from longtime attitudes. The traditional Dutch idiosyncrasies are still there but less visible, with new elements creeping in.

Perhaps it's true that the more things change the more they stay the same. In my ongoing programmes at KIT, newly arrived foreign managers continue to express their surprise at aspects of Dutch behaviour that I had thought less common today than before. Certain mannerisms do get mentioned again and again, and when I ask if perhaps it is an older person they are talking about, they deny it: no, fairly young people did so and so, said such and such, reacted in this way or that. Apparently beneath the façade of modernity and free market principles, the Dutch are not changing as quickly as they sometimes like to believe (or fear).

Certain old-time Dutch characteristics, such as directness, critical attitudes and money-mindedness, still abound. 'New' behaviour may well – consciously or unconsciously – be a dissociation from older patterns: 'Please let's be different from our parents'. But it often strikes me how especially during a conflict, when the debate reaches a critical point, the norms and values noticeable are those firmly rooted in previous periods. Behaviour may have changed, but new norms and values do not appear to have crystallised yet.

For this reason, I have included evidence of new phenomena in relevant sections. Given the fact that, below the surface, cultures only change very slowly, I still classify seemingly 'new' behaviour into the more traditional categories of Dutch culture. Such categorising is debatable, of course, and I'd be interested to know if you disagree with my views.

What are these older categories? Well, after years of training foreign business people and other professionals in the field of Dutch culture, I have put together the following list, which forms the basis of this book:

Low hierarchy: the old Calvinistic precept that all people are equal may have worn thin by now, but the resulting ambiguous stance of the Dutch towards hierarchy, power and status still abounds.

Directness and critical attitudes: abiding by a centuries-old trait, the Dutch are usually not afraid to voice their many opinions in no uncertain terms, unless private emotions are at stake, though even that doe not always impede them. On social and political issues, the opinions seem to be voiced even more strongly than in previous years.

Pragmatism and money-mindedness: an innately functional approach to life, with a keen eye on financial aspects, is a prime orientation of the Dutch, but less so for more relationship-oriented matters.

Bureaucratic and yet tolerant: a general inclination exists towards applying fixed procedures for almost anything, yet being permissive and tolerant to other lifestyles. The Netherlands is a land of rules and regulations that, by and large, still allows people to live the way they choose to live. Or are the Dutch just indifferent?

Internationalism and openness: a trading nation that needs to face the world, and does – with bold aplomb and finesse. One needs only to witness the Dutch facility for languages.

Let me begin the discussion of present-day Dutch mentality by giving you an idea of the changes that have taken place in Dutch society over the last few years.

Chapter 1

THE NETHERLANDS: A TRIFLE LESS DYNAMIC THAN BEFORE

'You know what you have, not what you get.'
(old Dutch saying promoting cautious proceedings in uncertain conditions)

The Netherlands is a very wealthy nation that is going through a bit of a dip, both economically and mentally. But despite references to a spoiled nation, the Netherlands is a prosperous and stable country with predominantly healthy and well-educated people who are well-fed, well-clothed and well-housed, thanks to strong social structures. In general, the Dutch enjoy their work, can afford long holidays both in terms of money and time, and experience little physical threats, yet they worry that things are not what they used to be. *'Incredible, you Dutch worry about 6% unemployment. We have 12% already for years!'* (A young lady from France, 2003)

In the spring of 2000, the British journal *The Economist* declared the Netherlands to be the most attractive market for investments for the period up to 2005, stating that the Dutch economy had no evident weaknesses in its business environment. Just a few years later, the tables turned. A significant number of Dutch companies – not all of them small – are in dire straits, and unemployment is showing its ugly face to a generation that barely knew the concept. This obviously affects people's attitudes in the labour market, resulting in less risk-taking, lower demands, settling for lower salaries, and less 'perks' and bonuses. There even seems to be a return to old-fashioned frugality, with holidays shorter or closer to home, cheaper supermarkets preferred, the withdrawal of children from expensive day-care, and so on.

On a national scale, economising is the order of the day. In a rash of cutbacks, the private sector is slashing its expenses, no longer routinely financing leased cars or mobile phones for employees, for example. Government does the same, and more. *'I always admired the health care system, until they started breaking it down. Exactly that system was something America could learn from.'* (USA)

It bears saying that the term 'economising' has hardly ever *not* been used by Dutch governments, but this aspect seems to be seriously resolved, with social benefits 'frozen' and subsidies for cultural and social activities decreased or stopped altogether.

To the older generation this may appear as the sensible thing to do – the right attitude that they themselves always supported more than a 'free-for-all', but to some of the younger generation it comes as a shock. *'It strikes me how you Dutch people complain about many things while you are living in paradise. When I heard someone say that his social benefit is not sufficient, I thought this was Dutch humour. In Lebanon, such a comment could only be said in a theatre play.'* (Lebanese student in Amsterdam, 2003)

The new conditions obviously cause concern, but let's not exaggerate. After all, the Netherlands is still extremely rich compared to most of the world: it ranks fifth on the UN's Human Development Index and, at 6,5% in 2004, unemployment figures are still below those of the rest of the European Union. Consumers may need to be a bit more careful after the price increases following the introduction of the euro. Shops and restaurants may be quieter but they're not empty, and people still go on holidays and throw parties. Most Dutch people are still fairly well off, even though they did suffer losses in the stock market – the same as everyone else – over recent years, whether directly or through their pension funds. Some local observers warn the Dutch that they should not talk each other into a depression, which might then be self-fulfilling.

State finances are in fact not really in bad shape either, but macro-economists are concerned that the Netherlands' international position has suffered setbacks, such as breaking through the 3% national debt limit the EU sets to its members – a limit the country itself had always insisted upon. Yet most of the reasons an American investor gave in 1998 for his company setting up business in the Netherlands still hold: the stability of the country, the cooperative business climate, the stable currency, Rotterdam as the major gateway to Europe, the availability of a desirable site and raw materials, the modern infrastructure and the fact that English is widely spoken. But there is a certain uneasiness in Dutch business circles. Foreign investment suffers from competition by Central and Eastern Europe, the stable guilder dissolved into the 'expensive' euro, the capacity of Dutch traffic infrastructure seems to be stretched to the maximum, and even the political stability suffered a blow in 2002 with the aforementioned murder. Moreover, various scandals and less favourable developments occurred in the business world itself of recent. Dutch companies move facilities to lower wage countries elsewhere, while the country resists a labour influx from new EU member states.

Still, half of the world's multinational companies have a branch office in the Netherlands, with Amsterdam ranking high among the best business locations in Europe (albeit slightly less than before). Small as it is both in area and population, the Netherlands remains one of the world's largest importing and exporting economies. But some Dutch companies now regret certain foreign ventures, while others couldn't compete any longer and were themselves bought by foreign companies. Former Dutch steel factory Hoogovens is now merely a part of British Corus; Amsterdam's formerly independent AEX stock index became just another participant in Euronext; while the world's oldest airline, KLM, is now, in the eyes of many, little more than a working company for Air France. Ahold (food and supermarkets) is under severe scrutiny and debate. Among smaller companies there were scandals of fraud, and protests against top salaries and 'perks' felt by the public to be undeserved. Arguably, the days are past when governments in the western world looked at 'the Dutch model' for inspiration.

The Dutch miracle (*1982 – † 2002)   Until just a few years ago, the Dutch economic 'miracle' (the term was coined by US President Clinton) received worldwide acclaim. Locally known as the polder model[1], it represented a strong economy with permanent high growth, low unemployment and low inflation figures, combining internationally competitive wage levels with a good social security system. It started out as an agreement between Dutch employers and trade unions in 1982 when the economy was at a low ebb and unemployment high. Before then, Dutch politics were described by the term 'polarisation', the antagonism between employers and trade unions. The 1982 agreement called for fighting unemployment by changes in labour relations, including a shorter working week, more part-time work and, in particular, more participation by women.

After a slow start, these changes began to pay off during the 1990s. In that decade, the Dutch model became the metaphor of a stable social climate, a well-educated and flexible work force, and a favourable tax climate for foreign investors. To this day, it also conjures up the idea of negotiating and compromise between opposing parties. Seen as a successful model for restructuring rusty welfare states into flexible economies, it was first brought to international attention at the G7 Conference of leading industrial nations in 1997. President Clinton invited Prime Minister Wim Kok (representing the EU) to explain to those present this 'Dutch miracle'. Foreign delegations and journalists came to visit the Netherlands to study the 'mysterious' harmony between Dutch employers and trade unions – a relationship in which the government keeps a low profile. By the late 1990s, however, in the Netherlands itself, cracks were appearing in the model. Unions' wage demands started rising again after top managers asked for (and were given) huge salaries, or rather, huge 'perks' alongside socially acceptable salaries. Good old polarisation seemed to be back on the scene. When in 2001 the economic barometer changed from 'fair' to 'changeable' with inflation and prices going up, the public mood shifted and, in fact, the Dutch miracle was over. The related shift in the political scene took place in 2002.

At present, the Dutch parliament is no longer discussing budget *surpluses* but rather *deficits*, by slicing off budgets everywhere, preparing people for paying more for medicine, home care, education and the like, and announcing the decrease or total stop on all kinds of subsidies.

After having had the highest growth in Europe, perhaps the bad news now hits harder here than elsewhere, and analyses abound. Some economists accuse the previous government of not having economised when the big money was coming in; others point out that due to scarcity of personnel around the turn of the century, wages then went up too much for international competition. Captains of industry voice their concern as to how the Netherlands as a whole is not doing enough in the field of R&D. Trade union leaders together with *The Economist* warn how, with little government stimulus for (unpopular) science education, the country is neglecting the knowledge economy which will soon be crucial for competing in the international rat-race. In fact, in the race for 'best ICT countries', the Netherlands tumbled from third to eighth position, while it also seriously fell back in international competitiveness, from being number four in 2000 to fifteenth in 2003.

Economic growth, which hovered for several years around 4% (a high rate by European standards), came to a virtual standstill by late 2002 and remained so throughout 2003, with quarterly figures fluctuating from −1.2 to +1%. Prospects improve for 2005, but only from a European perspective at relatively low levels. In the meantime, after years of unemployment remaining below 3%, this ghost is also back in town and may stick around for some time. The first large-scale dismissals have already taken place. More often than not, unemployment is a stealing process – a few people here, some there, companies not replacing those who retire, etc. One effect is, of course, that many organisations that previously could not find enough employees – ranging from supermarkets, restaurants and hospitals to the police and the army – no longer have problems filling their ranks, but their budgets are often down. In health care, waiting lists are almost gone, and the urgent shortage of schoolteachers has evaporated, while – after government economising – the army is no longer on the hunt for personnel but instead is shrinking. One no longer hears about foreign personnel being brought here to work in IT, hospitals or construction. If foreign IT workers come to the Netherlands now, it is generally to be trained on the job for outsourcing work at the lower salary levels of their predominantly Asian home countries.

In economic life, coming down is harder than going up. The success and wealth of the past decade had their effects on Dutch society and on the Dutch way of life, and they linger on. For several years in the 1990s, consumption rose to – for this country – unprecedented levels, and was mostly taken for granted, although in this post-Calvinistic society there was an undercurrent of disapproval and distrust. Due to what seemed permanent growth, consumer trust in the economy was at an almost constant high.

Obviously, this is no longer the case. With higher premiums for pensions and social insurance, net salaries go down rather than up, and life is very expensive for all. Pressed by financial concerns and depressed by developments in the stock market, many people had to sell the shares they had bought in the booming 90s, often financed by acquiring higher mortgages based on an increased value of property. The evident losses were not always accepted and people tried to sue the financial institutions that had seduced them into participation. Such institutions cannot really be blamed, of course, for trying to win clients, and the litigation is felt by others to be somewhat silly.

Most people manage to moderate their consumption, but increasing numbers find it hard to live at a different standard of living, running into trouble and needing assistance to adjust. Young people may find that they have to curtail frequent use of mobile phones, fashionable scooters, and weekend partying in the latest fashions, and the rest may need to alter their extravagant habits as well.

While '9/11' is seen as a major cause of all this concern, many people also blame the euro which, right after its introduction a few months later, gave entrepreneurs the chance to capitalise on the state of confusion and sharply raise prices. In spite of official denials of high inflation, virtually everyone agrees that, especially in cafés and restaurants, prices went up tremendously. Now I have also heard such complaints elsewhere in the 'euro-zone', from Thessaloniki to Paris, but the fact remains that Amsterdam (as an indicator for all of the Netherlands) rose from a 40th to a 20th position in *The Economist's* 2003 cost-of-living index of 137 cities worldwide. In the European Union, only in four capital cities was life more expensive.

Previously, conspicuous consumption by the Dutch was quite often financed by overdrafts of mortgages. In the new climate it became clear how many houses and apartments were financed with borrowed money and needed to be sold. The *'te koop'* (for sale) sign is a common sight throughout the country, and many new office buildings from the 90s are now *'te huur'* (for rent). Since the 1990s more Dutch people may own their houses than rent them, but the demand for rental properties is on the rise again now that people have trouble financing a mortgage. Yet with interest rates remaining low and the mortgage interest tax deductible, the housing market did not relax as much as one might have expected; prices may have stopped going up but they didn't really go down, to the despair of locals as well as expatriates.

Although it is less easy than a few years ago, young professionals keep trying their luck at entrepreneurship. In the 1990s, many started up their own companies, upon discovering niches in the market and seizing opportunities. Many of the start-ups were either a first career endeavour or a rebound from another job. Unfortunately, many such small businesses didn't make it in the dip of 2002 and '03, so amidst growing unemployment and bankruptcies, the hunt for more secure jobs was on again. More stamina and creativity are required now, it seems, to make dreams come true, so all the better that in 2004 more people are again confident enough to set up their own businesses.

The prosperity of the 1990s has also brought about what may be some permanent changes on the Dutch economic scene. Job-hopping might not be the best move at this moment, but the days are definitely over when semi-permanent employment was the standard. More competition and financial inequality are also likely to remain. In spite of protests, a growing difference between top salaries and those at the bottom of the labour market means that the Netherlands no longer has one of the most equitable distributions of income in the world. Further, the social benefit system may not be quite as severely curtailed as the government announced in 2003, but it is definitely not the easy life of yesteryear when a job is lost nowadays.

No matter what the economy does, one last aspect that will definitely stay around is the computerisation of Dutch life. This not only applies to the work floor but also to private life. With over 70% of households linked up, Internet penetration is very high. Access to public information such as theatre and travel reservations is much easier to get online than off. Also, both banks and the tax authorities prefer people to communicate digitally. The flip side of this is, of course, an even lower level of personal customer service, an issue that many expatriates commonly complain about, as we will see. It may be a hopeful sign that one bank, after having closed many branches and dismissed front-office personnel, will now focus on more customer service.

Concerns   In the last edition, I mentioned that the Dutch saying 'The trees seem to be growing into heaven' indicates a certain distrust of a seemingly positive condition. Those who were suspicious then were indeed proven right, as we saw. But let's not be too gloomy about the Netherlands' position; everything is relative.

There may be more economic concerns than some years ago, but this still remains a prosperous country where most people say they are happy with life and where many non-Dutch people like to settle, whether as immigrants, refugees or expatriates.

In 2000, the ten most urgent problems for Dutch people[2] were: rising crime (a concern to 92% of those interviewed), the state of the environment (72%), the living conditions of people on minimum income (71%), AIDS, unemployment, the number of people on WAO (labour disability) benefit (more on this in chapter 7), traffic jams, asylum seekers (see chapter 11), rising house prices, and the national debt. In 2004, the ranking might be slightly different but the overall picture is the same; this is a fortunate country without war, famine, oppression or natural disasters.

And yet, on a more philosophical level and with varying degrees of concern, many people also notice the more negative aspects of a wealthy country. Already for years, intellectuals and church representatives have expressed their concern regarding the new consumerism, the increasing selfishness and anti-social behaviour. In her radio talks on Christmas day, Queen Beatrix regularly warns against outright materialism and egoism, against the impersonality of modern society and the erosion of traditional norms and values. Many people agree. They worry about the increase in random violence, and react with horror when they read about mafia killings, even though these rarely affect ordinary people's lives.

Manifestations of a lack of consideration for others include loud mobile phone conversations on public transport, rude street behaviour, and aggressive driving. People regret the old pastoral landscapes disappearing and being replaced by more and more highways, 'science parks' and new suburbs. Space is clearly at a premium here, and might well be the scarcest commodity in this country. Living in the Netherlands, one has to come to terms with the paradox of the good luck and comfort of living in a prosperous and peaceful country, and the concerns that there are some less fortunate aspects for society as a whole. *'I think the Dutch should watch out what all this wealth may do to them. Being rich changes people, it makes them hard and selfish.'* (Ethiopia)

In the previous edition I gave the reader some quotes by foreign observers indicating how the country is changing away from its old-time roots, losing its Calvinistic stiffness and sobriety. But it is quite fascinating to see how under the surface of technological modernity, some things do *not* change, such as the frowning on extravagance, the collective disapproval of outright greediness and materialism, the tendency during social tensions to take shelter in one's own ideological 'cubicle', the on-going dilemma between good business and shaky morals. Of the changes in Dutch society, one person said, '...*what is so amazing is that the great leap forward – or whatever you want to call it – has proved to be so much wider than elsewhere. It goes from one extreme to the other.*' (France)

The speed of change was also expressed in this quote: '*Recent developments and attitudes seem to contradict everything I always felt to be 'typical' about the Dutch.*' (Hungary) And here is a more recent quote commenting on the further change of the last two years: '*Unfortunately, my idea of the Netherlands changed over the years. Gradually I hear the same racist remarks and I see the behaviour for which I was previously scolded as an American. I saw the level of education and health care decrease and criminality rise. And I wonder: where did the famous Dutch tolerance go?*' (USA) In a later chapter we will address this question.

Uniquely Dutch?   Several of the changes, of course, are not a uniquely Dutch phenomenon, but in a crowded country with little chance to get away from it all, exposure to them may be more intense than elsewhere. The result is that many people go abroad to get away from it all, temporarily or permanently; others resist and try to be of humane use to society, while yet others turn inside themselves and develop spiritual supports. Quite a few combine these reactions. Whatever they do, of course, affects the overall mentality of society.

Outside pressures and material temptations make life in a rich country an everlasting quest for balance, which is not easy to attain for everyone. Small wonder, perhaps, that alongside successful people and the vast majority who live a very regular life, there are people in the Netherlands – as in most western countries – who turn their back on society, people with psychological troubles such as severe depression and, therefore, people who simply cannot cope. Some resort to crime or violence to vent their perceived feelings of deprivation or exclusion. Both politicians and the media in Dutch society pay attention to all this, with quite a lot of concern.

Social scientists speak of a 'fragmentation' or even an 'atomisation' of society, indicating increased individualism. Critics use the older term *tweedeling* (pronounced *tway-dayling*, meaning duality, dualism), a word referring to the split between the true participants in society and the economy, and those left out or left behind. Increasingly, this also implies knowing how to work with a computer, or not. Given the prosperity of Dutch society as a whole, the term is not the same as distinguishing 'haves' from 'have-nots', not even quite the same as 'winners' and 'losers', but with its psychological implications, the latter comes close. In one line of thought, groups left behind – perhaps financially but more so regarding opportunities in society – are single mothers, elderly people without children living solely on state old-age benefits, people with mental problems, and the homeless. It is estimated that, taken together, such groups comprise between 10% and 20% of the population. They share a certain isolation, a lack of contacts or networks, and a sad feeling that they have been left to themselves without much real support. The fact doesn't help them very much that in many countries people in similar positions are far worse off financially.

Others see the social split more between the local Dutch and the growing group of immigrants, certainly after '9/11' and – less than a year later – the killing of Dutch political figure Pim Fortuyn. In chapter 11 we will explore the origin and overall state of this multicultural society in the Netherlands, but let's address the referenced murder here and now, despite political overtones, as it has connotations to various subjects discussed later on. It was probably the only political event in Dutch society that headlined in foreign media.

The rise and fall of Pim Fortuyn   In 1999, in the prestigious Dutch newspaper *NRC-Handelsblad*, a serious intellectual called Paul Scheffer published a long article entitled 'The Multicultural Drama'. Describing the unsuccessful state of the integration of ethnic groups in Dutch society and the causes thereof, it broke through political taboos on these sensitive issues. From then on, all kinds of people felt more free to voice concern and irritation on generally perceived problematic aspects of the presence of so many migrants: crime and street violence, drug trading and sexual harassment, and disrespect of authorities such as school teachers, police and public figures. Post '9/11' when worldwide concern over Islamic-fundamentalist terrorism and extremism grew, this easily blended in the Netherlands with the rising dissatisfaction over ethnic issues, certainly when the first signs of economic adversity further tempered general optimism.

In this more critical and outspoken mode, Dutch people from relatively underprivileged areas with high ethnic presence started speaking up, publicly and emotionally voicing their opinions of the political elite. Many accused the Dutch Labour Party's establishment of not listening to them, of always having promoted the tolerant but also hypocritical policy of 'let's keep talking and maintain social harmony', of always having defended ethnic people, also when they were clearly uncooperative, fraudulent or even criminal. More and more people proved tired of the policies and attitudes of live-and-let-live, expressing fiercely negative views on the presence of so many 'foreigners'. It seemed as if the much-famed Dutch tolerance had started eroding. Public attitudes toward homosexual marriage, euthanasia and prostitution invariably remained very liberal, but the views expressed on the conditions and limitations on multicultural society were definitely not liberal at all.

In 2001, with national elections on the horizon, one very outspoken and eloquent political figure's popularity rose fast – Pim Fortuyn, or simply 'Pim' to his ardent followers. A somewhat controversial university professor and columnist, so far not taken serious by those in power, he gathered public support by proclaiming himself the voice of the hitherto unheard, with emotional debate and provocative one-liners. A loose political group gathered around him, bringing together many poor whites with some of the new rich who felt ignored by the intellectual elite. Pim gained increasing approval in many a Dutch living room as he sprinkled chili pepper into usually very quiet (or downright boring) Dutch politics. Even opponents admitted that debate was livelier than ever before. His point wasn't so much 'out with the foreigners' but rather 'enough now, let's first consolidate society before allowing more immigrants in'. Foreign media compared him to extreme right-wing politicians in other countries, but ideologically he was quite elusive, posing as openly homosexual and a *chic* intellectual rather than as a spokesman of lower middle class. Some of his views on economy and society were left-wing rather than conservative.

Although soon entangled in the chaotic politics of a party built around his ideas, a few months before the elections Fortuyn declared very self-confidently, swaying his index finger, 'I am going to be Prime Minister of this country, mark my words!'

It was not to be. Two weeks before the May 2002 elections, Pim Fortuyn was shot down near a television studio in Hilversum where he had just been interviewed. It was the first Dutch political murder in four centuries. For one very tense evening, everyone feared it was a reaction from ethnic circles, but the murderer turned out to be a stern environmentalist who opposed Fortuyn for his mockery of 'green' ideas. (In a court process dragging on for a year as the murderer refused to speak, he was finally sentenced to 18 years of imprisonment.)

Political chaos ensued. Clearly, the end of the eight-year, left-wing liberal (so-called 'Purple') coalition was imminent, but with the charismatic leader gone, the landslide victory of Fortuyn's party LPF ('Lijst Pim Fortuyn') only produced internal chaos and national turmoil. With Pim's charisma missing from new elections half a year later, most of the voters returned to the established parties, including Labour, which had found itself a young, new leader. Other parties also reviewed their leadership, and a new generation of politicians arrived on the scene. Lacking an outlet, vague social dissatisfaction went underground again. The government that followed has a moderately right-wing signature, with no socialists involved in the coalition but also lacking any of Fortuyn's radical emotionality.

Later on in this book we will try to see why even the Dutch themselves thought all these events to be rather amazing, or as many called it: 'so un-Dutch'. For the moment, let's turn back to the more economic aspects of recent developments.

More American?   Like most Europeans, the Dutch have a love/hate relationship with the United States, and they will not hesitate to vent these feelings. (For the consolation of American readers, in chapter 5 you will find out how, in Dutch culture, open and direct criticism such as this usually indicates emotional involvement and appreciation.) Quite a few Dutch people would agree that the recent changes in their own culture and society could be collectively described as 'more American', in general – more individualistic, more hurried, more commercially-oriented, and more economically-driven. Already for some decades the Dutch tend, jokingly, to see their country as a candidate for becoming the 51st state of the USA, and this feeling has only grown with the changes described above.

Americans themselves, however, apparently feel differently. In an interview with a Dutch newspaper, a top USA consultant was asked to comment on the fact that the Netherlands sees itself as 'the most American country in Europe'. All he said was, *'Hmmm? Interesting....'*, adding immediately that so does the UK. On one of my courses, an American expatriate commented, mostly referring to family life and shopping facilities in the Netherlands: *'At first, living in Holland felt like going back in time twenty years, but now after some time we like it a lot.'*

Most Dutch people would probably react to this with a mixture of disbelief and curiosity, as I did, since being called 'old-fashioned' isn't really considered a compliment. (On second thought, upon following American news, perhaps that isn't so bad...).

Despite the concerns outlined above – which are not immediately visible to newcomers, Dutch society definitely comes across to most other foreigners – *and* to some Americans – as not only modern, liberal, open and flexible, but also as humane and relaxed. When I described Dutch work ethics and regulations to an American interviewer, she reacted: *'That's exactly why I chose to live here, in spite of all the bureaucracy it cost me to legally do so!'*

Yet it's true; there are a lot of things in the Netherlands that are clearly not American – not even like the America of the 1980s. Americans themselves mention the ongoing strong family orientation in most of Dutch society, the near taboo of discussing one's religion in public, the uncensored nudity and sex on television, the wide acceptance of homosexual relationships and the relative safety on most streets even after dark. And, of course, the Netherlands in general is less geared to free market values than the USA, but that is an underlying theme of this whole book.

So, in its own way, the country is changing along with the rest of the world. Even the basic tenets of Dutch society are no longer quite the way they were – after centuries of pushing back the water, some land is now being given back to the old enemy. In the field of religion, the secularisation process has gone so far that even most native Dutch children hardly know the significance of

Christian holidays such as Easter and Pentecost. With the waning of religion and the growing influence of the market economy, the cultural differences between the north and the south of the country seem to be fading. There is even a debate regarding the position of monarchy, certainly after some recent disputes surrounding the Royal Family (ask any Dutch person for details and opinions). In another field – that of the farm – although foreigners still comment with some amazement on the amounts of bread and milk the Dutch consume, local producers see only decreasing markets for these products. At the same time – at least in the cities – vendors of ricotta, kwikwi, piri-piri, star fruit or brownies no longer have to explain their products to their customers. In another arena, even the national reputation for fluently speaking several languages needs some revision now that the Dutch learn to speak only English and no longer appear to be interested in German and French. And the old Calvinistic virtues of thrift and sobriety are hard to find these days, although some people are forced to return to them to some degree, given lower incomes and a higher cost of living.

Yet quite a bit of the old remains – if not always visible, then at least in the underlying values and the comments that people make. The generic Dutch value system hasn't yet changed altogether. This is certainly the case among the vast majority of people who do *not* work in the ITC sector, who do *not* live in the Randstad cities, who do *not* work abroad, and who do *not* fly back and forth to New York or Singapore all the time. For visiting business people and expatriates settling in the Netherlands – and they are the target group of this book – such less 'globalised' people make up a large portion of the people they will probably encounter at work and in their private lives. So let's explore the characteristics of the majority of the Dutch, and the society they created – then and now.

1. *Polder* is the Dutch word for reclaimed land, made out of water or swampland, through strict water-control. Low and grassy, mostly used for keeping cows, polder-land makes up a large part of the Netherlands.
2. Researched by Bureau Lagendijk, Apeldoorn

Chapter 2

ON IMAGES AND STEREOTYPES

*'Ah, you're from Holland? Such a nice little country, with flowers
everywhere. Pity it always rains there.'* (French lady talking to the author
on a train from Paris to Nice)
'Sex Shop Amsterdam' (name of small enterprise in Granada, Spain)
'Double Dutch' (old English expression for unclear language)

Almost everyone has preconceived ideas, frequently generated by
the media, of other countries and the people who come from
them. Even the remotest country inspires some mental picture,
however vague or stereotypical, of what it might be like. Of course,
stereotypes are not wholly representative, but they usually do
reflect certain realistic characteristics, perhaps out of context or
outdated, or stripped of their real meaning and function, but characteristics nonetheless. Accurate or not, the stereotype is what
most people start from; it colours their expectations and their initial perceptions. But particularly when we work among or with the
people to whom the stereotype refers, we gradually learn how
valid or untrue the generalisations, contexts, and nuances really
are. The same, of course, applies to the stereotypes about the
Netherlands and the Dutch.

The Netherlands is not exactly a remote country, being in the
heart of Europe, and it features regularly in the international
media. This means that different people have different images of
our country, some more accurate than others, some promoted by
Dutch institutions or media, some definitely not. Abroad, prevailing images differ widely, depending on the observer's national origins, because the way a person perceives a foreign country always
involves that person's own cultural background.

In that vein, virtually all the quotations cited in this book,
besides commenting on the Dutch, usually also reveal something
of the observers' own frames of reference. For example, the French
lady's comment above says something about France too – its relative size and climate. Opinions like this often reflect the observer's social position and the sources from which (s)he acquired the
information. It makes quite a difference whether one reads Dutch
newspapers, or has worked with Dutch people, or made several

visits to the Netherlands, or had meaningful contact with the Dutch in any other way.

Be that as it may, let's attempt to make an inventory of the most important images of the Netherlands as they surface in foreign publications and public opinion. Some of these are major factors in attracting – or repelling – incoming expatriates; others are not.

The sturdy image: (popular in geography books): a flat, wet country, most of it lying below sea level. A place where it never stops raining and which would surely be flooded if it were not for the windmills, the famous Delta Works and little Hans Brinker sticking his finger in the dyke. (In 1995 this image was reinforced by international media coverage when the great rivers in the centre of the country threatened to burst their banks and entire towns and villages were evacuated.)

The tourist office image: (the previous French lady's): a largely agrarian idyll. Charming Queen Beatrix ruling an innocent little country, much like a fairy-tale, the inhabitants of which wear wooden shoes and ride bicycles and peacefully produce milk, cheese and flowers. The residents live in old, quaintly-gabled houses along canals or in picturesque, thatched-roof farmhouses – and, of course, in this image the sun is always shining.

The cultural image: a small country with a great tradition in the arts. Famous painters past and present, with their works on display in wonderful museums; also renowned for its world-famous symphony orchestras and ballet companies, and as a good place for avant-garde theatre and modern design. Of late, it is also gaining fame as a source of great literature, which the outside world reads in translation.

The permissive, lenient image: (upheld from rather different angles by both foreign journalists and young travellers): a place where apparently anything goes. Although most of the journalists and travellers typically concentrate on downtown Amsterdam, they tend to depict *all* of the Netherlands quite sensationally as a (far too) liberal society, where specialised shops sell legal drugs and pornography. A nation that finds it perfectly normal for gay couples – officially married, of course – to obtain children by artificial insemination, and where people are helped to die by itinerant doctors legally practising euthanasia. Luckily for the Netherlands, foreigners staying a bit longer discover that much of this image is distorted, and that there is a lot more to Dutch society than meets the eye.

The humane image: a comfortable, safe haven, an idea held by immigrants and political refugees coming into Europe, linked to the permissive image above, but from yet another perspective. *'The Netherlands has a good reputation among Africans. My friends in other EU countries like to come here. It's a kind of safe haven. You don't notice too much discrimination here, but if I go to France the police pick me out immediately.'* (Nigerian asylum seeker in a newspaper interview). Dutch laws have become much stricter over the last years, to the despair of many people from other parts of the world who would like to live here because of this country's wide-ranging political and religious freedom, as well as its prosperity.

On the global scene, the Netherlands is also seen as a country that takes seriously its international obligations in providing development assistance. It not only finances international peace missions but also takes part in them, and presents initiatives in environmental and other global issues. In 2003, the Dutch contributed twice as much per capita to the EU budget as the next net contributor, while it reaps far fewer subsidies than most member states. Some local political observers sourly describe this as 'trying to be the most obedient kid in the class-room', while others applaud it, calling the Netherlands 'a decent country'.

The image of the Dutch being blunt and opinionated: (largely discussed among expatriates and hinted at in diplomatic circles): a tiny country with a big mouth, wanting to appear larger than it is, its people tactlessly expressing their views on other people's and other nations' affairs. It cannot be all that bad, given the prestigious international positions Dutch people achieved in organisations like NATO, the European Bank, the European Commission, the UN High Commission for Refugees, the International Red Cross, etc.

The sporting image: a nation of excellent football teams applying intriguing techniques. Well, traditionally, that is; they didn't win very much recently, although they came fairly close in the 2004 European Cup. Also, of course, their fans dress in bizarre orange outfits, feasting and partying, even literally painting the town orange! But the Dutch also have a good reputation in other sports such as ice-skating, swimming, tennis, hockey, and even darts, but they are not always aware of this. Dutch hockey teams may be among the best in the world, but back home they are lucky to receive more than a few minutes television coverage.

The tight-with-money image: money-minded people whose greatest pleasure is extracting every last cent out of any transaction. Many people abroad – particularly in neighbouring countries – are convinced that when the Dutch go on holiday elsewhere in Europe, they load up their caravans with food from their own supermarket rather than spend money in local restaurants. As a result, all the way down to the shores of the Mediterranean, street vendors comment (in Dutch!) on Dutch shoppers with the slogan *'kijken, kijken, niet kopen'* or 'looking, looking, not buying' ... which brings us to the final image.

The economic image: Even now that the polder model has lost its spell, the Dutch economy is still taken very seriously. Small as it is, the Netherlands is one of the world's larger trading nations. With Rotterdam being the world's busiest harbour and Schiphol a major airport, the Netherlands promotes itself as 'the Gateway to Europe'. Moreover, it is home to such a large number of globalising companies and financial institutions that it can be said to have the highest 'multinational company density' in the world. Based in a small but wealthy home market, all these companies are active in many other countries, with majority shareholdings (often acquired at a very favourable price) or even outright ownership of foreign companies.

Finally, besides large companies and banks there are scores of smaller Dutch enterprises that are active internationally. Just a few examples: the Netherlands' dairy industry, which supplies half the world with cheese and milk powder, and, less traditionally, an entertainment industry producing formats for TV shows throughout the world, plus many internationally renowned artists who record their music at Dutch studios.

While these images may be over-generalised and over-simplified, many Dutch people will recognise them. Sometimes they agree with them, although they will probably not let them pass without comment (which, of course, fits in perfectly with their image of always knowing better than everyone else).

Some of these stereotypes are quite contradictory. For example: How can such 'money minded' people put up with such heavy taxation? How can pornography be associated with wooden shoe-wearing flower growers? Where do the quaint old gables fit in with the 'legal' drugs? How can a booming modern economy successfully compete with an image of cheese and windmills? How come these football hooligans are so anti-German, although they were born at least 30 years after the Second World War?

Such contradictions, and the wide range of the stereotypes, reflect a pluriformous society that accommodates a broad variety of lifestyles and views within a very small country. When we condense them, a broad-based image emerges of a country that does not avoid challenges but is willing to try solutions that may be out of the ordinary.

This sounds rather fascinating and provocative, and it could easily evoke the idea that the Netherlands is a land of non-conformists. There certainly are such people around, and Dutch television happily presents them to an amused audience. Yet most visitors from abroad see the Netherlands in quite a different light; they see a highly organised society of great regularity, a country where public transport runs on time[1], where rules written and unwritten abound, where, in spite of all the permissiveness, most people seem to follow a set pattern of daily activities. As an illustration, a Spanish lady working in Holland exclaimed: *'Sometimes I wonder if the Dutch have blood in their veins, or milk!'*

This picture is quite contrary to some of the stereotypes – conformity rather than unconventionality, boring rather than fascinating. The Spanish lady's comment reveals something of the despair someone from a more emotional, warm-blooded culture may experience here.

And yet there *are* those sex shops, those coffee shops selling soft drugs, those social experiments, groundbreaking laws and otherwise daring solutions. And there also are those stubborn Dutch who will insist on going their own way, despite convention. The Dutch paradox, in other words.

1. This is a foreign compliment that amazes Dutch people. Not familiar with other countries' public transport, the Dutch complain that trains and buses are always late; that they never run when you need them and – of course – that they are too expensive. In defence of this Dutch view, it must be said that foreigners usually base their positive opinion on experiences in the well-serviced Randstad area.

Chapter 3

HIERARCHY AND THE
DUTCH PROBLEM WITH IT

'Geen kapsones!'
(Dutch-Yiddish slang expression, rebuking perceived 'airs', arrogance)

In an interview preceding his state visit of February 2000, French President Jacques Chirac compared France and the Netherlands. After flattering the Dutch with Latin charm by pointing out the country's strength as an economic, diplomatic and even military power, he said: *'France and the Netherlands have a lot in common. ...They are two nations with a distinct character. ...Ideas like independence, national grandeur and the respect for people and human rights are just as important to the French as to the Dutch. The French respect for identity and independence can be seen equally strongly among the Dutch.'*

While such political niceties may make some people feel good, it is not the general image that the Dutch hold of themselves. In fact, they tend to take these aspects for granted and prefer looking a little deeper into their own souls. In discussions as to what exactly Dutch identity is and what sets the Dutch apart from other nations, various journalists and philosophers came to the conclusion that at the heart of Dutch culture lies 'egalitarianism', a sense of everyone being equal from a *moral* point of view. Although there certainly are financial aspects to it, the underlying ethical principle is that everyone should have the same opportunities and that no matter what people's position in society, high or low, they should be treated equally and with fairness, and treat others with due respect as well. The major condition is low profile behaviour. If people do indeed occupy a high place in society they shouldn't openly pride themselves on it, while those in more lowly positions have the right to speak up on balance.

Principles are great, but they're not generally lived up to, and the Dutch are no exception. So in everyday reality, the egalitarianism issue is quite complex and, besides a number of subtle consequences both in general Dutch society and in the business world, it also carries a certain amount of hypocrisy. The overall effect is that the Dutch have difficulty in dealing with hierarchy, always trying to maintain a balance between being aware of the hierarchical aspects of a relationship while, at the same time, not wanting to make that awareness too obvious.

I first want to explore these general effects: attitudes towards hierarchy and excellence, the class-orientation of Dutch society, and aspects of status. It is within this context, explaining much of the everyday behaviour in work and business, on which we focus in more detail in the next chapter.

It is not easy, especially for foreigners, to notice egalitarianism as a core value right away. It lies somewhat hidden in Dutch behaviour and institutions, and it may be some time before foreigners understand its scope. What they do notice from the start is a certain lack of decorum, the casual way in which many Dutch people seem to deal with hierarchy and status, the approachability of authorities, and the do-it-yourself aspect of society. They sense, for instance, a lack of appreciation for outstanding performances, or a certain uniformity in modern Dutch housing, or a surprising degree of workers' participation in companies.

All these things can only be explained by taking into account Dutch egalitarianism. It is deeply rooted in history and, according to some observers, even in the flatness of the landscape. It has quite a few consequences for people's everyday behaviour, both inside and outside the business world. Even conduct apparently quite contradictory to egalitarianism is often, consciously or not, little more than a dissociation from this core-value. This is how one foreigner perceived it: *'If anyone here sticks out from the crowd, his head is chopped off. There is always criticism. They always tear people down; even good performance is played down. Everyone must be the same... there shouldn't be anyone brilliant.'* (Argentine) A young Dutch businessman with international work experience added: *'All this egalitarianism irritates me. We don't allow heroes or prominent people. We dare not be proud without inhibitions...except on the odd occasion when we become world champions in skating or football.'*

'Just act normal, that's strange enough' In fact, this much-used Dutch expression says it all. As an ironic comment when someone's behaviour or opinions are perceived as being out of the ordinary or overdone, it is a call for conventionality; to blend in with everybody else, conform, not to stick out. Looking at all the wealth around them, foreigners sometimes don't believe me. *'Come on, this may have been true twenty years ago, but NOW? There are seven Jaguars parked in the street where we live! OK, it's a well-to-do area, but still!'* (USA). I then try to explain that 'egalitarianism' is not directly related to people's wealth or possessions, but rather to their attitudes. It is a moral state of mind rather than some kind of communism, although some foreigners may think otherwise. One may drive a Jaguar, but when this is perceived to be accompanied with haughty behaviour, it will be duly criticised.

This may come as a surprise in a country that also has a reputation for tolerance. On closer inspection one might realise that the call for equality, for conformity, relates not so much to the behaviour or opinion itself, but to the moral stance that people might attach to it. They may be very special indeed but that should not make them feel or behave if they are superior to others. The message is: be or do whatever you want, but don't boast of it, and don't expect privileges or more respect than anyone else. Witness the Dutch advertisements on radio and TV that use actors and actresses playing cocky, elite people with affected voices in order to get some easy laughs.

Common people are the standard; public figures and the elite can be mocked. Neither material extravagances nor high profile behaviour are appreciated. On the other hand, any individual or group that is, or can make others believe he or she is, a victim of injustice – an underdog – can certainly count on a degree of support, either from other individuals or from a political party or action group. One might see Dutch society as an upside-down pyramid – the large majority of ordinary people, being middle class, are the overall norm; the elite merely facilitate them in exchange for silent acceptance of their prominent position. This is certainly the case in the public sector. A few examples are in order. For decades, virtually all houses built in cities were of the size and taste of 'average' middle and lower class families.

The Dutch tax system is meant as a kind of 'levelling device', skimming the rich, uplifting the underprivileged, bringing everyone to the middle ground.

Business tycoons, politicians or intellectual big shots are given less public attention than people representing the commonplace, such as football players, pop musicians and TV presenters.

Politicians and managers may be seen riding a bike to work, having a simple lunch, camping out or walking along the beach, just like anyone else, quite 'normal'. In the business world this attitude may be less prevalent, but it is not completely absent. A public impression of being a good family man and hardly more than an average consumer helps to make the wealth of big shots more acceptable.

An example of Dutch sympathy for underdogs in the international playing field can be cited in the 2002 World Football Championships, when Dutch people organised and financed the match between the world's two *least* successful (and obviously poor) football teams, those of the Himalayan kingdom of Bhutan and the tiny Caribbean island of Monserrat (4:0).

Formal hierarchy – the use of names and greetings In Dutch culture, first names are not immediately used on initial contact, unless the 'higher' party suggests so. For a while, people will address a new boss or business partner as 'Mr. X' or 'Mrs. Y'. When the surname is used in Dutch, the formal you word *'U'* is employed, while the use of the first name automatically implies the informal you word *'je'*. In the seventies a general relaxation in manners led youngsters to almost always use first names and 'je', even to parents, teachers and older people. When people introduce themselves with both first name and surname, others will be hesitant to use the first name right away if the other party is clearly senior in position or age. But in the workplace, after perhaps a formal start, most people will use first names and 'je', quite often also to people a few levels up in the organisation. Although in the 1980s a reverse trend occurred in some sectors of the business world, this familiarity – or lack of respect, some say – toward older or higher-level people is still present in everyday situations such as shops and public transport.

Making first acquaintances is always done with a handshake (firm but not overwhelmingly strong), as is done when meeting someone again after some time. But colleagues at work don't shake hands every day, as the French tend to do. A French lady comments: *'Here they say hello all day long, to the same person!'*

The Netherlands is a typical European culture where greetings like 'good afternoon' are frequently used, certainly to relatively unknown people, but also among colleagues. Greetings comparable to 'hi' ('hoi') and 'see you' ('dag') are only used for people one already knows or sees all the time.

The two or even threefold cheek or 'air-kissing' of the Dutch – much giggled about among expatriates – is mostly restricted to private meetings. (Be aware that there are no guidelines for two versus three kisses, and no particular order as to which cheek is kissed first.) At work this type of greeting may happen only on birthdays and special occasions like returning after some long absence, and particularly between long-term colleagues. Women kiss both sexes, men usually only the opposite sex, although in 'progressive' (not necessarily homosexual) circles, men greeting men in this fashion may also be seen.

Another strange aspect for many foreigners is that, unlike most countries, in the Netherlands you answer the telephone, both at home and at work and with mobile phones, by stating 'Met' (with) before your name: 'Met Jan de Vries', or 'Met Mevrouw (Mrs.) de Vries', either in a firm voice or a questioning one. The foreign way of just saying 'Hello?' on the phone may lead to some confusion or even silence by the Dutch person on the other end, wondering if the right number was dialled. For those who prefer not to reveal their family name on the phone when speaking from their home, using first names only is fine.

In most countries, one has a far easier life when high up in society than when one belongs to the lower levels. The higher-ups are given – or take – all the chances, get most of the privileges, and make the rules. In the Netherlands, the myth is upheld that this is not the case, and to some degree this is true. In exchange for the social harmony that keeps their privileges silently intact, the elite lie low. Anyone with authority or with exceptional talents should make it clear through his/her behaviour, between the lines so to speak, that although (s)he may have power, money or prestige, (s)he is nonetheless modest, approachable and democratic. Australians recognise their 'tall-poppy syndrome' in this.

Americans, in particular, perceive this reluctance to acknowledge winners and successes as a lack of competitiveness, assuming that such an attitude leads to mediocrity. But as a Briton says, *'The Dutch are content with being second best.'* Observers from quite different cultural backgrounds think otherwise, however. *'Every-*

body here is competitive.' (Russian businessman working in the Netherlands, speaking to young Russian managers being trained here), while an Argentinean academic researcher remarks, *'Since I came here several years ago, I have learned a lot and met many nice people, but you have to fight here to achieve something. You have to prove yourself again and again.'*

Both points of view are correct, in a way. The Russian and the Argentinean are both right because the Dutch economy, and also the sports world and academia, can hardly be called non-competitive. Yet the Anglo-Saxons have a point, too. On a smaller scale, between individual people, competition is not greatly appreciated, but rather felt to be unfriendly. Whether among schoolchildren, university students, co-workers in a company or members of a sports club, the feeling is that it is fine to try and be the best, but don't overdo it, a modest victory is usually good enough and you certainly shouldn't compete at the expense of weaker players or colleagues[1]. Perhaps this observation by a young German studying in Amsterdam may serve as a good illustration: *'Dutch students have different attitudes towards grades. The Dutch are content with a mere 5.6.* (In the Netherlands, with a 0 to 10 grading system in education, a 5.6 is the exact minimum required to pass an exam.) *Once I witnessed a guy who answered just six out of ten questions at an exam and then left. He explained to me, "I got these six questions all right, why should I bother doing the rest?"'*

This certainly seems to prove the American point of 'reinforcing mediocrity', and even among the Dutch it may cause some disapproval, but in the end the core value of egalitarianism prevailed, as well as 'the same rules for everyone' principle (see chapter 7). A student from Slovakia said in 2003, *'It strikes me at college how many people just make a mess of their studies, hanging in their chairs and not really working on their studies. I don't understand that. I know how bad poverty is, so why don't you do your best when you get the chance?'* The crucial difference is that her Dutch fellow-students do *not* know how bad poverty is. There is no true poverty, since the Dutch social system takes relatively good care of everyone. It should be added that studying at Dutch universities is subsidised and, compared to American universities, not very expensive. Moreover, a fairly wide government scholarship programme helps anyone to study academically. Yet, Dutch students complain about both the high fees and the low scholarships, not realising how lucky they are.

Academic titles and education In Dutch society the use of academic titles is mostly limited to the functional working environment and then in writing only, on business cards and letters. Using them in private life or in speech does occasionally occur, but most people find this boastful rather than respectable. Another observation by the German student quoted above: '*I find the teachers here much more approachable than those in Germany. You have to address the latter with "Herr Professor", but in Holland that isn't so. Here you can just go for a beer with your teacher.*' One more observation on Dutch education, this time from a Dutchman who grew up in Italy before coming to the Netherlands in 1965, at age 14: '*Shortly after school started, the teacher asked me a question. Automatically I stood up next to my bench to answer it. The whole class roared with laughter, and I had no clue why. Somewhat embarrassed, the teacher told me that he appreciated my gesture but that I could remain seated, since standing up to a question was not the custom in Holland.*' Needless to say, nothing in that respect has changed here since 1965.

Personal relations and price agreements The issue of competition deserves further attention. In this small country, there probably always existed price agreements and outright monopolies. Besides the obvious economic benefits for the companies involved, people in the same industry tend to know each other. As long ago as 1968, a union leader brought to public attention the network of some 200 'old' families all knowing each other personally and rotating key positions in the economy, in politics and other high places. You might see it as a Dutch version of the British 'old boys' network' or the Finnish 'sauna society'. Indeed, there are family names that keep cropping up in various influential fields already for decades or even longer.

With increased social mobility and the rise of a vast group of 'new rich', these days the Dutch economic and political elite is a larger group and less homogeneous, but the basic condition still exists. Because these people see each other on all kinds of social occasions – serving on various boards, meeting in business clubs and theatres, and job-rotating between different companies and organisations – too much competitiveness is felt to be unpleasant. There always was and still is an unspoken agreement on harmonious live-and-let-live agreements. Cartels and other non-competitive cooperation resulted, and European institutions reprimand the Netherlands for this again and again. In the 2003 process of KLM merging with Air France, one French journalist called nepotism 'a characteristic of Dutch capitalism'. That's taking it very far, but indeed, even in today's more market-oriented climate, the government organisation set up to break open such strongholds (the NMa, or Dutch Competition Authority), has certainly not finished its job. For preventing interwoven interests, double positions and other dubious practices, in 2003 a corporate governance code was introduced, nicknamed 'the Tabaksblat Code' after the president of the designing committee. In order to secure shareholder power – besides enforcing detailed publication of managers' and CEOs' salaries and bonuses, it also urges publication of all their executive functions and other board memberships. After one year, Mr. Tabaksblat said that he was reasonably content about the way the business world had put his proposals into practice. Even so, the wider public is suspiciously convinced that there is still a whole lot of playing into each other's hands going on in the business community.

Thus, public trust in the market economy is not too great. Over the last decade, various former state companies in the field of public utilities were privatised: energy, water, transport and telecommunication, often accompanied by promotion campaigns promising paradise. Now these new companies may have to face *national* competition but still have *regional* monopolies, albeit for a restricted period. So privatising the companies generally did not bring down consumer prices, and people feel that customer service has only grown worse, with inadequate call-centres and impersonal telephone tapes taking the place of 'real' service. The major Dutch telecom companies have been found to be quietly cooperating and keeping outsiders out. When it was found that Dutch gasoline prices were the highest in the EU (even before taxation), suspicions immediately arose. On more modest levels, Dutch bicycle makers have also been accused of silent price-fixing, while a group of shopkeepers (Dutch and other ethnic) in an Amsterdam street persistently protested against the expansion of a successful 'Turkish' supermarket chain. All in all, neither price agreements nor market liberalisation is met with positive response by the general public.

Resistance   For several years, a very clear example of Dutch resistance to competition was the everlasting 'taxi war' in Amsterdam, where an organisation of semi-independent taxi drivers fought the entry of other taxi companies into the market with rather unpleasant aggression. That war still continues today, but an even more serious example of anti-free market practices surfaced in 2002, when it was discovered that numerous Dutch construction firms had made silent price arrangements which cost society at large millions of euros. Officially competing in an open market system but communicating in an old boys' network, under the surface, so to speak, the companies had managed to cheat in what seemed to be open tendering for official building projects. These ranged from government offices, hospitals and university buildings to new residential areas erected by municipal councils. A parliamentary research committee enrolled public hearings of the parties involved, broadcasted live on national television, in which shady bookkeeping transactions and secretive arrangements came to light. Legally, it was very hard to prove, so most companies involved got away with reprimands and no more than some damage to their public image. In the eyes of the general public, it only confirmed that you should never really trust the higher-ups, whether in government or in enterprise.

Personal attitudes   Although top-class performers in the fields of the arts, sports and business are certainly applauded in the Netherlands, people generally think that they should remain 'human' and accessible to everyone. Remember: no airs! In other words, they should behave with some modesty, appreciate their fellow competitors and share their glory with others. Others lending assistance or support should participate in their victory, be mentioned by name, and hauled up onto the rostrum with the winner. If this doesn't happen, terms like 'swaggering' and 'arrogance' soon crop up.

The basic premise of this issue is that everyone merely uses the talents that (s)he happens to have. To have them is simply good fortune, nothing more. In the more religious past, such talents were considered to be God-given, and it was considered one's duty to use them for the benefit of all. Thus it follows that very gifted people should be grateful rather than expect applause.

(Indicative of this attitude might be the relative absence in Dutch cities of monuments to national heroes and other figures. The few that can be found were usually put up long after the hero died.)

Nowadays, with secularisation, being talented is no longer largely considered to be God-given, but rather a stroke of nature, a fortunate DNA structure, the result of good education – anything except strictly personal excellence. To me, this is proof of the not-so-individualistic attitude of the Dutch, a touch of collectivism. You may be good but remember that you owe it to others, divine or human, and never forget the context, the external factors so to speak, that helped to make you who you are, and therefore you should find a way to pay your dues. Later we will see how this works out in practice, in social responsibility, in charity work and in contributing to society by, more or less, honestly and obediently paying one's taxes.

High work morals   So, no one is essentially better than anyone else. Success should not go to one's head. That is essentially the Dutch mindset. An old Dutch rhyme, still quoted, can be translated as: *'Those who don't appreciate the small, don't deserve the large'*, i.e. gifted people should deploy their talents for the benefit of all, not just for themselves. This ingrained duty indicates, generally speaking, that the Dutch have high work morals. Being useful, in other words being active and not idling, is generally considered a virtue. If you happen to be very talented, naturally you will reap the benefits, but you should keep quiet about it and just do your 'duty'. Be equal, after all!

In private life as well, just hanging around, not doing anything constructive, is usually frowned upon, unless it is 'deserved' relaxation after some kind of fruitful activity. One can be almost certain that many of the apparently relaxed people in street cafés on sunny afternoons have just finished being 'useful' or are about to be so again soon. Well, at least *they* think so, as a result, perhaps, of being raised by parents who said things like 'hard work never killed anyone' – a Calvinistic-based creed.

Lazy?   A few years ago, an American journalist asked me, *'Are foreigners right who assume the Dutch are lazy?'* – a rather shocking question to a Dutchman. I am aware that foreigners perceive this country as a relaxed place, but I advised her to never again use this 'L-word' to a Dutch audience, because we are convinced that we work very hard. Many Dutch people assume that the labour statistics of just a few years ago are still correct, when the Netherlands had one of the highest productivity figures per hour worked. But, although I'm reluctant to admit it, things do change. To my opinion, the Dutch are not really lazy and idle, but they certainly do strive for a comfortable life. Granted, the IMF (International Monetary Fund), the president of the Dutch Central Bank and various local political figures have warned the Dutch that they must work harder if they want to keep up with international competition. But being used to long-term prosperity and having experienced the limits of the satisfaction that consumption brings, quite a few Dutch people may even think, 'So what if we're not number one? What's the point of being super rich when you don't have the time to enjoy it?'

Being contented with a comfortable life and chasing a maximum salary are difficult to combine, so – in comparison to other nations – most Dutch people work relatively few hours per year, enjoy long holidays and try to retire early, as will be discussed later. Then, when a consumer test on sleeping, executed by Ikea home stores in 27 countries, proved the Dutch to remain in bed longer than all the others, I really started doubting my objections to the 'L-word', also after some critical self-inspection – but that's another book entirely.

Yet the majority of the Dutch perceive themselves differently. In fact, when asked how you are doing, for some time it was something of a status symbol to reply *'Druk, druk, druk'*, that is, busy, busy, busy. The threefold use of the term seems to be out of fashion, and for some people, indeed, business is slower, but the word 'druk' is still often heard, as both a complaint and a self-compliment at the same time. (Significantly, the word *druk* also means 'pressure'!)

In contrast, many foreigners working here see Dutch work morals differently. *'After hearing about all these Dutch successes (in the 1990s), one expects the Dutch to work really hard. But in reality they don't; they all run home at five and, even during work hours, they're not particularly effective. So in my view they just organise the work better. They're very involved in the company, that's probably where the results come from.'* (Peru) And: *'They talk a lot, don't work very hard, but are friendly.'* (Ireland) Small wonder, for the Dutch do lead a comfortable life.

Suffice it to say that the Dutch don't necessarily work harder than other people. At best they work more concentrated. A fairly small segment of the population does work long hours, especially people at top levels, but for the rest, the Netherlands' wealth is largely the result of the country playing a vital role in the economy of the western world. Some additional contributing factors of the last decades are: more flexibility in the labour market and in the housing sector, the fairly sharp rise in population – largely due to immigration – and the integration into the labour market of hitherto 'in-actives' such as women and senior citizens. Although for quite a lot of people the profits from the increase in house prices and the stock market boom of the 90s have evaporated, they still are far from being poor. With more unemployment and higher prices the need to work harder may have risen a bit, but generally the Dutch remain a relaxed, albeit well-organised, culture.

Labour satisfaction In a representative survey of labour satisfaction, held in six west-European countries in 2000, 80% of the Dutch interviewees declared that they liked going to work, second only to the Germans who scored 86%, and way ahead of the Spanish with 57%. Only 23% of the Dutch said that money was their sole reason for working. All others gave additional reasons like contacts with colleagues, a sense of fulfilment, etc. But as you know, there are 'statistics and other lies', and indeed, in 2004, EU-wide research found, with only Italy having higher figures, that two-thirds of the Dutch wouldn't mind never returning to work, not so much to be idle but to dedicate their time to 'personal satisfaction', whatever that may be exactly…. The other one-third said that they did realise how work is essential to human well-being. For more on work incentives, see chapter 6.

So the underlying directive is to use your talents, no matter what they are. The successful and famous should only humbly accept the public attention and the privileges they are granted and not act as if they are all that wonderful. The Dutch are aware of the limits their attitude of 'don't grow too large' can set. If even *they* find the narrow-mindedness too much, they may use the term *spruitjes-lucht* ('the smell of sprouts' – a kind of cabbage). A case in point: Some years ago, Dutch parliament investigated the cost of all ministers' official cars. Many of them turned out to be more expensive than the norm set by law. Eyebrows were raised. One minister hastened to declare that his car had been taken over from his predecessor – second-hand, so to speak. Luckily, the then Prime Minister turned out to have one of the cheaper cars, well below the legal limit.... Whether cabbage smells or not, the basic idea is still: 'No airs please; down to earth in a flat country.' And don't expect others to bend over backwards for you.

Customer service? *'There is no customer service here, you need to beg for it!'* (Canada) *'Customer service is a joke in this country,'* and, *'Customer service? What is that?'* (both from the UK)

You may wonder what this topic has to do with the subject of this chapter, but bad customer service is another effect of Dutch egalitarianism affecting foreign visitors and expatriates, although they may not recognise it as such. Many of the expatriates on my courses complain of poor customer service, saying things like, *'We have been struggling for two months to get cable television installed. They keep telling us they will come, but they never do. If we phone again, they say they will put our complaint in the computer, but all that hasn't done anything so far.'* (India) And: *'In restaurants here they let you wait for ages before a waiter shows up. In shops, the personnel stand around chatting to each other, occasionally looking at you, but not coming to assist you. They may also be very busy with paper work, but not with you as a customer.'* (Britain) A young, English, marketing student told me, *'Now I've got used to it, but in the first weeks of my stay here I was quite shocked how shop personnel just answer "No" if you ask a question.'* Her fellow students from various countries all nodded their heads in recognition.

This must indeed come across to foreigners as strange (and rude, obviously) in a money-minded trading country where the provision of services produces a major part of the Gross National Product. (Banking, insurance, transport and consultancy are major economic activities.) But on such a macro-economic scale, of course, services are a product for which customers do pay. At small-scale, individual levels such as in shops and restaurants, customer service is an unpaid extra. Some foreigners add that it even works this way in their company: *'Sometimes the Dutch are annoy-*

ingly relaxed; take for instance the slow service between departments!'
(France)

Be aware that, to the Dutch, customer service has a touch of hierarchy to it. As I have illustrated, hierarchical differences are hard to accept for the Dutch, making them feel uneasy and clumsy, and for this reason many of them cannot handle true customer service, neither giving nor receiving. In fact, most Dutch customers don't like it when a shop assistant approaches them as soon as they enter. As a whole, they prefer to browse independently and simply walk out if they decide not to buy anything. As a result, good assistants – in Dutch terms – are careful to not 'jump' on customers; bad ones just let the customer wait forever and then, if requested to offer assistance, they often provide it in a rather curt way. Most foreigners, such as this American, are used to a significantly different approach. *'Customer service here is terrible. I have the feeling that it is my privilege to be their customer. The attitude in the shops is not conducive to loyalty, that's for sure. I find myself thinking, "Whew, I'll never go back there!" But then I find out that the next guy is just as haughty or rude. I'm sure that it's my fault, too. In America we believe that the customer is always right – regardless.'*

Tipping   A contributing factor to the above scenario is probably the fact that in Europe, shop personnel and servers in restaurants usually have sufficient, legal minimum wages and do not require tips to make decent earnings, as they often do in the United States. Tipping is voluntary in the Netherlands because service is included, as stated in all menus and on the bill (*rekening*). Nevertheless, the Dutch often do tip, by 'rounding up' the bill. About 5-10% is customary, but tipping is still considered a friendly gesture, not a social obligation as it is in the USA. In these days of economic headwinds, however, personnel in various businesses do complain of customers tipping less or not at all.

One more justification for poor customer service is that because of the relatively high wages to be paid, shops and restaurants employ as few staff as possible, all the more since dismissals are often a complicated legal affair (more on that in the next chapter). The effect is, of course, that at peak hours the assistants may simply be too busy to serve well. Supermarkets, less expensive restaurants, chain stores and the like usually employ young (= cheap, as wages are based on age!) assistants who do the job only temporarily and aren't deeply loyal to the firm. In family-run shops and more up-market firms, customer service is generally much better and quite personal, which again is not to everyone's liking. *The service is friendly but slow.'* (Sweden). Others are more positive: *'They are often multilingual and friendly in shops.'* (Italy) A lot depends on the customers' own behaviour, too. If they are perceived to be haughty in any way, acting in a superior manner and demanding extra attention, assistants will become obstinate. But if a customer asks for advice or help in an informal, low-key way (subtly affirming that any difference in position, lifestyle or income is purely coincidental), they will usually be met with a friendlier reaction. It isn't in everyone's character, of course, to behave as such, and I'm often blasted with 'hypocrisy' on this point, but all I can say is, see for yourself.

In essence, the Dutch try to ignore hierarchy, preferring to make it invisible. Therefore, the advice I just gave will usually also work when dealing with service personnel at work and at home, such as the computer repairperson, the plumber or the cleaning help. My best advice for fitting in is to keep a low profile.

Having said all this, we should remember that, in the Netherlands, egalitarianism is a *value* – in other words, an appreciated and acceptable behaviour. It does not mean, though, that each and every Dutch person lives according to its tenets. But if they don't, they may expect criticism. Dutch language has some twenty words and expressions for boasting and swaggering! And the norms are strict. For example, only in foreign contacts may the Secretary of State for Economic Affairs be called the Minister of Trade. When in April 2000, accompanying the Crown Prince on a state visit to Japan, the lady who then held this office behaved as if she herself were royalty, it caused embarrassed giggling from the rest of the Dutch delegation. Witness further that figures of authority, including royalty, have been fined by the police for breaking traffic regulations – and this deeply satisfies the nation. 'They're exactly like us, not any better,' they can almost be heard thinking. Remember, 'Just act normal!'

In the Netherlands, then, wealth and high status are not taken for granted. Although the first Dutch examples of houses or living areas surrounded by walls, gates and other protective measures have sprung up, many well-to-do Dutch people prefer to just live out of sight, tucked away behind trees and hedges and protected with elaborate alarm systems. Ostentatious display of wealth continues to be frowned upon, however, especially when the person involved can be classed as *nouveau riche* and is regarded as lacking in good taste.

Here's another example of Dutch dislike of visible wealth: a Dutchman who owned a Porsche (remember the Jaguar story) told a television journalist that he doesn't enjoy driving this car on Dutch highways because people with slower cars either prevent him from using the fast lane, or offer insulting gestures, making clear he shouldn't think he is any better than them. A particularly venomous comment such as *Zandvoort-chic* might be heard, referring to a not-so-posh bathing resort near Amsterdam.

In reaction, the rich and famous keep a rather low profile. Until recently, few people in the Netherlands had bodyguards, and the rich did not need to put up fences or walls around their houses. But with rumours of rising crime, and after some kidnappings and the murder of Pim Fortuyn, the days of innocence appear to be over. Politicians and wealthy people do protect themselves better these days, while the less rich simply strengthen their locks, alarm systems and insurance levels. After some cases of violence and kidnapping against wealthy families, a fashionable Dutch magazine, *Quote*, which every year publishes a list of the 500 richest people in the country, was asked to stop doing so. When it refused, its office was literally shot at, but the culprit was never found.

Let's be realistic, however. The Netherlands is still quite a safe place; granted, perhaps somewhat narrow-minded. Most people's lives are quiet and peaceful and, to many Dutch people, a middle-class lifestyle is the most acceptable state. Indeed, when passing through obviously well-to-do neighbourhoods, or seeing luxurious houses on TV, less fortunate people may well make some sour remarks rather than admiring comments. There is bound to be sheer jealousy involved, but there's always also a *moral* undertone of 'This is not quite right'. Even for the more sophisticated with 'old money', wealth and power are something to be careful with because, to the Dutch, they should be backed up by high moral standards – or at the very minimum with low-profile behaviour. *Noblesse oblige.*

Class society Truth be known. Under the surface of egalitarianism, the Netherlands is a class society after all, although perhaps slightly less visibly than other European countries due to the inherent, 'low-profile' attitudes. The fact that a person belongs to a particular class shouldn't be expressed openly, so Dutch people have become experts in interpreting the subtle signs: language (vocabulary, pronunciation, last names), dress, cultural tastes and general behaviour. Residence is, like it or not, an important indicator too. Tell me your address and I can probably tell a lot about you. Names of towns, areas, streets and (to locals) even parts of streets indicate one's particular wealth and place in society and offer a fair chance of correctly estimating the educational level, income and cultural preferences – as is the case with many other cultures, no doubt. With strong social mobility in the last five decades, there is a genuine, status-driven hunt going on for 'better addresses', partly explaining the overheated housing market so much deplored by incoming expatriates.

To foreigners from less class-conscious cultures, the Dutch attitudes on social strata may come as a shock. *'I was once refused help at a shop because the person working there did not think that I could afford a Bang and Olufsen stereo. OK, so I was dressed like a bum.'* (USA)

In a prosperous country like the Netherlands, the *middle class* is predominant by far, both in numbers and public exposure, and has a gross annual income between roughly € 30,000 and € 70,000. As in other western cultures, subtle nuances among this large group can be observed, based on differences in income and expressed in lifestyle and status symbols. Social control is quite strong in the Netherlands, and such differences are noticed and discussed, especially in the rather uniformly built 'Vinex locations' (new suburbs) where many of these people live. The way you decorate your house and lay out your garden are visible indications of income and taste, so much money and attention is devoted to them. Ever-changing fashions make such related shops busy and prosperous, with large numbers of people visiting garden centres and 'furniture boulevards' at weekends and during holidays.

Of course, there is also still an upper class and the remains of a lower one. There is hardly a true aristocracy in the Netherlands, so the upper class is mostly made up of people who have either earned their money themselves or inherited it from a successful parent. Among themselves they may make the distinction between 'old' and 'new' money, but this is not openly commented upon in public. 'Old money' often lets itself be inspired by British examples, quiet and tasteful but ever so self-aware. The same American quoted above comments, *'I realize that the "liberal" culture is sharply divided along class lines – in other words, the higher the class, the more conservative and closed-minded. It is not as liberal as I had thought.'* There is indeed a silent clash going on between the old and the new elite, between high and low culture, especially in areas where only the rich can afford to live – the ones house brokers lead house-hunting 'expats' to: Wassenaar (The Hague area), Aerdenhout (Amsterdam/ Haarlem), Hillegersberg (Rotterdam), Laren and Naarden (Hilversum). A noticeably common characteristic of these places is that they are situated on sandy, slightly higher ground, not on swampy wet soils.

But there is a lot of 'new money' nowadays, with tens of thousands of millionaires[2]. 'New money' is often characterised by rather ostentatious consumerism, including flashy cars, champagne breakfasts and other rather fancy, 'un-Dutch' behaviour. I personally see this behaviour as a conscious attempt at dissociating oneself from the norms and values of frugal parents and their old-time sober lifestyle. Originating from middle or lower class backgrounds but having the finances to imitate old money, many of the 'new rich' combine a supposedly grand lifestyle with strong social control. Intellectuals and old money tend to judge these lifestyles as lacking good taste, but the gossip press and several television programmes picture them in a mildly mocking way, ironically depicting them as 'Famous Dutch'. Some journalists speak of a Dutch meritocracy – a country led by ambitious achievers, but although there are more and more such people around, I think the basic power lies instead with the many academics with upper middle-class salaries and views who populate national and local governments and the second echelon of many companies.

Because of social mobility, the *working class* has been replaced to a great extent by people from other ethnic groups[3], although there still are some groups of Dutch 'blue-collar' workers. They mostly live in the poorer neighbourhoods around the city centres dating from the 1890s, and in the purpose-built suburbs of the 1950s and 60s meant to improve their housing conditions. City renovation has upgraded many of these old neighbourhoods, but given high housing densities plus a population that is very mixed both socially and ethnically, they are often still considered problematic to live in. Yet an American who asked me to show her a poor area in Amsterdam was rather pleasantly surprised when I took her to such a place: *'You call this a poor area?'*

Even when compared to nearby European countries, Dutch working-class areas are not in bad shape, probably due to municipal authorities providing the same services to these neighbourhoods as to more prosperous areas. Very few of them can be compared to what Americans term 'white trash' areas. With rents comparatively low, such areas often have a high density of small shops, restaurants, galleries and the like, so some of them gradually turn into fashionable and affordable places for students, artists and other less conformist people. With social mobility and 'swapping' of lifestyles, some people argue that the old class distinctions are quickly fading away.

Salaries Coming back to the subject of money, Dutch salary scales and the tax system reflect a certain drive for equality – for 'social justice' – in keeping with the egalitarian mentality. Not so long ago Dutch managers and directors earned quite a bit less than comparable colleagues in other western countries; and only in a very few countries was there a smaller difference between top salaries and bottom. After the 'hot' economy of the 90s, top salaries have risen, and both in the public sector and in business, people now negotiate quite high salaries, often supplemented with performance bonuses and stock option packages. With quite a bit of discontent with this situation among the general public, even directors and board members of larger companies expressed their aversion to excesses, or 'grabbing' as they termed it. They themselves were found to earn between € 250,000 and € 350,000 on average, a high salary by Dutch standards, but still socially acceptable.

In European perspective, salaries in the Netherlands are fairly modest, with an average gross salary of some € 40,000. The gap between top and bottom salaries is still smaller than in many other western countries. In 1997, the then Labour Prime Minister Wim Kok criticised high managerial salaries with the term 'excessive self-enrichment'. In 2004, working for a bank now, Mr. Kok agreed to quite sumptuous salaries for his colleagues, which obviously wasn't met with great enthusiasm by either the press nor party members.

This, and an argument around a foreign CEO (further detail in the next chapter) revived the whole debate on top-level remuneration. Employers pay some lip service to the critical views, but limiting top salaries seems to be more a strategic political move than a true ethical stance. Certainly, with increasing unemployment and more people in financial trouble, trade unions and related political circles disapprove of what they term 'greed' in top management. Repeatedly, they ask what managers do so much better than the employees, who suffer from price increases and very small wage rises.

The overall picture remains that the relatively narrow gap between rich and poor (or in the Dutch context: the less well-off) keeps widening. More entrepreneurial and resourceful people may applaud this, but to the wider public this is still quite undesirable and unacceptable. Fierce protest is not in fashion these days, but a certain dissatisfaction is breeding underground, as the whole issue around the rise and assassination of Pim Fortuyn indicated.

Salaries are private   Since hierarchy and material differences are hard to digest for the Dutch, most people in the Netherlands regard salaries as a highly personal matter, both in public and in private. As it is known that foreign executives employed by Dutch companies often earn quite a bit more than their Dutch counterparts and bosses, your Dutch colleagues may be eagerly tempted to find out your salary. If you don't tell them, rest assured that they will draw their own conclusions from your pattern of consumption. For the time being, both informally and at lower levels, it is a taboo to ask anyone – even relatives and friends – how much they earn. Boasting of a good salary is always in bad taste.

Taxes as a levelling factor   The Dutch tax system helps to ensure that net salaries do not differ too much. Before 2001, the top level of income was still taxed at a 60% rate, almost twice that of lower salaries. The Dutch tax system has some unique features, such as total tax deduction of mortgage interest (a long-term 'holy cow' in Dutch politics only now finally brought to careful debate), which makes paying taxes a bit more bearable for people with high incomes. In 1999 it was calculated that, in spite of the top rate of 60%, at 43% of the GNP the average real tax burden was lower than that in Scandinavia, Germany, France and Belgium. But important tax changes have been made since then. All rates have been reduced, enabling people get to keep more of their earnings and, thereby, making work more attractive. The highest rate, on income exceeding roughly € 50,000, was decreased to 52%. In order to make the whole plan budget-neutral, private wealth over a certain level remained taxable, while VAT went up to 19%. (For the peace of mind of non-Dutch readers, it should be mentioned that people working temporarily in the Netherlands enjoy a tax exemption of 30%. And for foreign investors investing in the Netherlands, the tax climate is so favourable that the European Commission has accused the country of playing unfairly in intra-European competition!)

Needless to say, quite a few people do look for ways of evading taxes. It is estimated that the 'black' economy runs into several billion euros. Foreign tax constructions may enjoy some popularity among people whose work involves activities abroad, yet one cannot say that tax evasion is rampant. Practical reasons for this may be that the well-organised Dutch bureaucracy and new EU regulations make it difficult to do so, and that a good accountant can still find interesting legal loopholes within Dutch law. Probably a more important reason is that the tax system is in accordance with the Dutch core-value of egalitarianism, which is basically considered fair and honest.

In broad outline, Dutch citizens trust their government to spend the money in a sensible way, checked by independent control institutions. In the 1990s, the Dutch Inland Revenue launched a new public approach under the slogan 'We can't make it nicer, but we can make it easier', accompanied by entertaining radio and TV spots and clear explanations of the altogether complicated system. The whole campaign was a success, even winning great appreciation from the general public. Electronic tax forms (with built-in calculations and deductions) that can be submitted through Internet have already been successful for some years and will soon be the standard procedure.

Everyone can clearly see what is done with the taxes, which are used for their own comfort and benefit, and that of others. Although in recent years government policy has encouraged a free market approach, with economising stepped up, several public facilities are still subsidised: public transport, education at all levels, libraries, facilities for the disabled, housing schemes, house rents for low-income earners, and much more. All this costs billions each year, but it is generally accepted that they are all good reasons for paying heavy taxes. Yet the 2003 government announced drastic cuts on various subsidies for cultural activities such as theatre groups, orchestras and museums.

Another major tax expenditure is on social benefits for unemployment, health, old age, etc. By international standards these benefits are quite generous, even after government economising. They are a part of Dutch culture – or should I say 'were'? For many years, it was generally felt that it's not always their own fault if people find themselves in such situations and that they should therefore be given the chance to 'act normal', too. True poverty, people not insured against illness, and blatant social injustice in general, are phenomena largely unknown in the Netherlands for already quite some time. But the mood is hardening, and acceptance of 'losers' is diminishing among the less socially inclined, certainly after reports of abuse and cheating the system.

This has always surprised foreigners. In the first edition of this book I quoted a Czech who, just before the communist system in his country collapsed, said, *'The Netherlands is more socialist than the socialist countries.'* Mentioning this quote to Hungarian and Polish course participants more recently, they agreed to the comparison between the Dutch system and former communism. The Czech added, *'The way they take care of the weak here! Take ill people for example… one may be ill for some weeks a couple of times a year – they just keep paying you. The unemployed get benefits and something extra for their holidays. It is very social here, in some respects too much, which causes people to abuse it easily.'* So far, these conditions have not fundamentally changed, so small wonder that a Turkish manager commented, *'Karl Marx would be quite happy here.'* And a German intellectual working in the Netherlands says, *'The fact that badly disabled people can get the cost of visiting a prostitute reimbursed by the health service proves to me that Holland is a very social country. …I find it unbelievably good that such a thing is possible.'*

Of course no one likes receiving the blue tax envelopes, but all in all the Dutch public feels the system is right. Most people silently agree that justice and social harmony are well worth paying for. Then we can all act 'normal'.

The historical origins of egalitarianism It is about time to look at the origins of egalitarianism – the core-value of Dutch culture. The sense of being morally equal originates from, and at the same time perpetuates, the rather flat pyramid of Dutch society. In his book *Culture's Consequences*, Geert Hofstede[4] indicates that what he names 'power distance' in the Netherlands is among the lowest in the world, only surpassed in the Scandinavian countries. Hofstede puts this down largely to the Protestant foundation of Dutch society. I agree and shall come back on this later. But many foreign observers point to even older roots. They see the Dutch natural environment as the origin of this low hierarchy. It is highly controversial, of course, to directly link a nation's mentality to its scenery or climate, but there is indeed a striking similarity – flat country, flat society. Some stress the fact that in a low-lying country such as the Netherlands, with large areas of reclaimed land, everyone is threatened equally by water. Granted, water is a very democratic element. But others object, pointing out that other regions threatened by water – Bangla Desh, the Nile Delta, parts of China – aren't equality-minded at all! The explanation, however, might be found in a related aspect: the unique social structures that the Dutch developed to fight the everlasting threat of water.

The water control boards (*waterschappen*) that still cover the whole country were founded as long ago as the 13th century and are, therefore, older than virtually all other public institutions. Since a central government hardly existed in those days, people threatened by water had to rely on their own initiative for survival. These self-help-organisations consisted of a group of farmers or fishermen who chose a leader from their own ranks and were, therefore, very flat in structure. The elected *dijkgraaf* (literally 'the count of the dyke') was in fact a *primus inter pares* (the first one among peers) that could only exercise power when high tides or threatening storms made it necessary. For centuries, all male inhabitants of the region covered by the *waterschap* had to contribute to the construction, guard and repair of the dykes. Since all had a vested interest in doing so, they contributed manpower and finance. Thus, people made themselves, so to speak, 'physically autonomous' in a structure with a very low hierarchy. Nowadays the *waterschappen* are highly professional organisations, and the *dijkgraaf* is an engineer, but he or she is still elected. Taxes are still levied from anyone living in their territory, and they are used for the maintenance of sluices, dykes and dyke roads, and for water purification.

On a more philosophical level, other factors contributed to egalitarianism. Here we come back to Protestantism. As early as the late 1300s, a religious movement, The Brethren of Common Life, in the then Catholic Low Countries called for a sober, spiritually-oriented existence rather than the luxurious way of life that had developed among the clergy. A hundred years later, Erasmus's 'Humanism' pleaded for humane, righteous and non-violent behaviour to all living souls, including animals. Ideas such as these did indeed influence Dutch Protestantism and later permeated society as more and more people received some form of general education based on them.

In the mid-1500s, Calvinism – a particularly strict version of protestant Christian faith – became the dominant religion[5]. It emphasised that all people are born imperfect, prone to sin, and that one should work all one's life on improving oneself in order to persuade God to forgive our original sin. On a moral level, disregarding one's social position, all people are equally bad – brothers and sisters in sin. In the Bible, Jesus indicates that a wealthy or powerful person can be a greater sinner at heart than a repentant thief or a prostitute. Everyone, therefore, should scrutinise his own behaviour for the flaws of sin, and work steadfastly on them. It was a call for individual soul-searching rather then for collective expressions of faith, for quiet and thoughtful thinking rather than emotional outbursts or extravagant group behaviour. Protestant religion focuses on content, on The Word of God, not on form and ritual. This can be felt throughout Protestant northwestern Europe. To this day, Calvinist churches are quite stark – undecorated and white on the inside to stimulate an individualistic mood of introspection.

All in all, one's task on earth – and toward God – was considered more important and more lasting than any worldly appearance or position. Consequently, Calvinism also stressed the need to think of others. The biblical expression of this state of mind, 'Do unto others as you would have them do unto you', can still be heard in the Netherlands[6]. It stimulates social awareness and charity, warning people for selfishly pursuing their own interests. Of course, this soul-searching also led to the scrutinising of others, to moralism, and to long and fierce debate about what then was the right attitude, the correct interpretation. This content-orientation permeates Dutch thinking and mentality to this very day.

The dividing line between Protestantism and Catholicism in the Netherlands roughly coincides with the one between the wetter and drier parts of the country – the north and the south – a rather odd connection, it seems. But I think the rapid spread of Calvinistic socio-religious equality and autonomy was related to the physical autonomy that the lowlanders had achieved with their waterworks. Let me present modern evidence of this idea. Every year on the occasion of Queen's Day, the Queen bestows various types of royal decoration on virtuous citizens (*lintjesregen* or 'the badge rain'). In April 2000, it was discovered that these decorations are awarded more frequently in the higher and drier Catholic south than in the formerly Protestant north. An odd division, it seems, but since local people nominate such citizens to the Crown, I think this proves my point. In the Catholic, less egalitarian south, people attach more importance to this prestigious tradition than people in the lower, wetter provinces up north, which were traditionally Protestant.

To finish this short historical overview of religion, let me remind you that Calvinism became a leading force in the political struggle that gained the Dutch independence from Habsburg Spain. In all but name, Calvinism reached the status of a state religion, while Catholicism had to go into hiding. Calvinism maintained its dominant position until about 1850, when a church rift divided the Protestants into two separate denominations, later followed by others. At the same time, Catholics were allowed to surface again, and were soon followed by the emerging socialist movement.

Religion remained a highly influential factor in Dutch society up to about 1960. Then social changes, which resulted in the rejection of existing power structures, rather suddenly eroded religion, turning the modern-day Netherlands into one of the least churchgoing nations of Europe – only one in four Dutch people regularly visits any Christian church these days. Except for some ceremonies such as royal weddings, religion has mostly disappeared from public life; it is a private matter now, to be discussed rather discreetly. All this is far less true for the followers of Islam, which is now the country's second largest religion, but this will be discussed in chapter 11, which deals with the large immigrant population. An American journalist comes with this view of Dutch faith: *'Christianity is still very much alive in the Netherlands, in spite of the empty churches. But faith is very emancipated here; it greatly stimulated social development. .... Even in the Christian parties, political leaders are willing to find practical solutions. Human values count more than moral commandments.'*

In spite of low church attendance, many Dutch people apparently still search for spiritual values. All kinds of Asian religions and new-age movements have followers and students in the Netherlands. In fact, the number of native Dutch Buddhists is estimated at some 120,000! Even the more traditional churches claim that youngsters, unhampered by aversion to the traditions, are expressing a new interest in religion.

True Calvinism nowadays encompasses only some 8% of the population, most of them rural, yet its concept of moral equality still permeates many aspects of Dutch society and behaviour. Religion may have lost a lot of its importance, but its related values linger on.

Now that you are aware of the general mood in the Netherlands, let's turn toward work and business and see how this affects everyday behaviour and the relationships between people at different levels.

---

1. This also relates to a certain degree of collectivism that people appreciate in their own circles. We will come to this in a later chapter.
2. There are over 80,000 euro-millionaires in the Netherlands.
3. See chapter 11.
4. Not in the southern provinces of Brabant and Limburg; see chapter 12.
5. Linguists found that in modern Dutch some 800 biblical expressions are still regularly used, but many people are not aware of their religious origins.
6. Prof. Geert Hofstede is considered the 'guru' of cross-cultural studies. He is the most quoted Dutch scientist internationally.

Chapter 4

HIERARCHICAL ISSUES
IN EVERYDAY WORKING LIFE

As we have seen, 'acting normal' is the appreciated Dutch standard. What effect, then, does this have in companies and organisations, where people have varying degrees of authority, power and status? How are decisions made when everybody is supposedly equal in theory, but not so in practice?

I am aware that to readers from other European countries and to people working in large, international companies, the general methods employed and the solutions reached, which I describe below, may not come as a surprise. But even for them, some details of the everyday working situation in the Netherlands will, I trust, be new and unusual. And in my experience, Dutch work-culture can certainly confuse people from other parts of the world and from less globally-oriented enterprises and organisations.

The previous chapter mostly described situations in private life in the Netherlands, or situations related to society as a whole. With levels of ambition and competition rising in the Dutch business world, the core value of egalitarianism may be less noticeable nowadays than it used to be, but it certainly still has its effects. Let's look first at the everyday atmosphere in the workplace and then widen the scope to look at what is behind it legally.

The general mood   Egalitarianism, or rather the aversion to hierarchy, still plays an important role in Dutch work relations. The Dutch are task-oriented, as we shall see in a later chapter and, under normal circumstances, hierarchy shouldn't play much of a role. Employees in lower positions should not be treated as 'subordinates', as inferiors who only do what their boss tells them to. Dutch employees are (usually) responsible and industrious. They like to work on tasks independently, without being checked upon all the time. Unlike workers in some countries, they will generally continue to perform just as hard even when the boss is *not* present. Everyone's contribution is considered important to the quality of the finished product and, therefore, a manager, supervisor or foreman (or woman) is expected to consult and discuss rather than order people around. By being open and approachable, superiors make not only themselves more acceptable but also the hierarchy, which is unavoidable but slightly embarrassing to the Dutch. Some humour and a personal approach also help a great deal. Typical examples of this might be company directors queuing up in the company canteen or cafeteria, just like anyone else, or gallantly inviting personnel to enter the elevator before them. (Dutch firms usually only have one place to eat for personnel at all levels. As an exception, visiting VIPs may be served lunch in the boardroom.) Moreover, few executives would openly call themselves 'director' or any similar term. Others might use the term, but they themselves would probably jokingly reply, 'Well, at least that's what they call me here.'

Superiors with such a management style – human, approachable, friendly, not merely 'using' their personnel in a functional capacity, not assuming privileges while among personnel – will be able to count on the loyal cooperation of the workforce in busy or stressful circumstances.

Dealing with Dutch secretaries   A German quote to begin with: *'Before long, my secretary was calling me Fritz. That took quite some getting used to.'*

To get the best cooperation out of a Dutch secretary – who virtually without exception will be a woman[1] — it is advisable to keep a low profile and not be 'bossy'. A good working relationship requires mutual trust in ability and responsibility, and genuine concern about each other's working methods and workload. Your Dutch secretary prefers to be your efficient window on the company and your buffer against the outside world, rather than someone who does little more than type your letters and make coffee. She wants to be proud of her job, thinking along your lines and feeling that your success is hers, too. She may be quite well-educated, regularly following courses to update her working skills.

In companies employing managers from other countries, I have heard Dutch secretaries complain about the 'aloofness' and 'arrogance' of their new foreign boss, who 'orders them around'. In order to avoid your secretary feeling this way, it's advisable to involve her as far as possible in your everyday schedule and to plan future work together. This will allow her to operate at maximum efficiency and effectiveness, so it pays off for both of you. Let her know who your contacts are and how important these are for the business. Acquaint her with your personal management style so that she can 'smooth out the bumps' if necessary. Remember that she may have been in the company longer than you so, especially in the beginning, don't be hesitant to ask her advice on issues before you take action; enquire how things are done and how to approach people in the most effective way. It wouldn't even be a bad idea to check what her views are on the workload of the coming week or so. It was found that authoritarianism ranks high among Dutch secretaries' irritations with their bosses, along with poor planning and lack of consideration. To ensure smooth cooperation, some openness about your family affairs and private interests is important and, generally, this will be reciprocated. It reinforces that both boss and secretary are equal human beings. Hopefully, your secretary will also treat any lower-level administrative workers in the same way as she expects you to treat her. But for some people, especially foreigners, this is going too far: *'Why do I have to go down on my knees here to get support from the administrative staff? I don't like to play equal!'* (UK) To that I say, there is no real need, but it certainly does help! And by the way, in the Netherlands, April 15th is 'Secretary's Day', which you might want to remember by giving flowers.

The 'OR' Dutch directors and general managers are quite aware of the limits that 'moral egalitarianism' sets on their exercise of authority. Since their staff and personnel are usually well-educated and aware of their importance to the company, they demand – and get – a say in its affairs. Dutch employees will speak up when things are not to their liking, in minor as well as decisive matters. Equal rights and respect for all levels of the workforce are reflected in the phenomenon of the company council, quite normal in Europe, but not quite as common in other countries. *'I admire your law on company councils. By American standards it is unbelievable that a representative body of workers can criticise the management and stop certain decisions.'* (USA)

In the Netherlands, every company with more than 35 employees is legally required to have a workers' council (abbreviated 'OR' and pronounced 'oh-air')[2]. Under normal circumstances this system of company-democracy generally functions quite well. Members of the OR are elected by their fellow-workers every couple of years, and the employer is legally obliged to allow them to be trained for their council activities during work hours. The OR will defend the workers' position of course, but since the general well-being of the firm is also in their interest, it is usually felt to be unwise to totally block unwelcome company policy, while management may also try to avoid setting up the personnel against itself.

Trade unions play a role in the background of the OR but are not directly involved. Currently at about 25%, unionisation in Dutch industry is fairly low, although it is somewhat higher in the education, health care and public administration sectors.

To the last American quote my editor added: *'Well, in a company without a labour union, that is'*, which reminded me to mention here that labour unions in the Netherlands are not organised on a company-basis but usually per economic sector, e.g. metallurgy, hotels and restaurants, or hospitals, thus joining hands for (potentially) all workers in related companies or organisations. Under Dutch conditions – remember the polder model discussed in chapter 1-, unions are not really the fierce opponents of employers as they can be in other countries. Given the fact that they meet one another over all kinds of negotiations, people on both sides of the table know each other personally. Also, the political parties representing their ranks on both sides – perhaps finding their government candidates among their allies – may well need each other in the next coalition government, so open animosity would not be wise. But a bit of political tumult is needed of course, so afterwards, to the press, terms like 'dismay', 'bewilderment' or 'incomprehension' and the like will be used in an attempt to look resolute. This is not denying, of course, that the points of view can greatly differ, that negotiations can be tough and sometimes don't succeed for quite a while! But in the end, some sort of agreement is in everyone's interest and all parties' final goal.

At department levels there are what the Dutch literally call 'work-discussions' (*werk-overleg*), or regular team meetings to discuss work progress and new projects. On a more personal level, 'performance-talks' *(functioneringsgesprekken)* are held, individual evaluative talks in which the lower and higher-level employees can *mutually* vent their comments regarding each other's performance, general behaviour and attitudes. Wishes and decisions on new tasks and projects can also be discussed. A short report is then written and signed by both participants who each keep a copy, and one more copy is forwarded on to the personnel department.

The result of all these talks and agreements is that, in most Dutch companies and institutions, there is a constant flow of information on policy, planning, procedures and results – and this flow is not only from top to bottom. Obviously, these procedures are not to everyone's liking because they distract from the day-to-day tasks involved in running the business, and there is much criticism about the quality and length of all these papers and meetings. Some expatriates complain: *'They are trying to be efficient, but things take forever.'* (Great Britain)

But when all is said and done, such reviews are generally seen as a good thing for all involved. The involved parties know where they stand, and most people are convinced that they have a positive effect on the way the company functions – as well as on everyone's position within it. Foreigners are not always impressed. *'I find it hard accepting the collective decision-making. It only causes delay, after delay, after delay. There are meetings on everything here. And people have a say even when they have no information to add at all.'* (UK)

CAO Egalitarianism is also reflected in labour conditions as well. As in most western European countries, people at middle and lower working levels generally come under what is called a Collective Labour Agreement *(Collectieve Arbeidsovereenkomst* or CAO, pronounced 'say-ah-oh'). Larger companies have their own CAO; smaller firms in a particular branch have a joint one. The CAOs are the outcome of annual or bi-annual negotiations between the employer(s), the trade union representatives and government officials. It regulates issues such as safety, holidays, clothing, working hours, etc., but most of all, of course, on wages and salaries. The CAO is valid for all workers, including non-union members.

Although agreeing to the CAO offers workers greater security and protection, it takes away their individual right to demand other 'perks', but companies are free to offer more than the CAO requires. Obviously, the CAO system decreases competition between workers, which is incomprehensible to some foreign (especially American) managers, but the point is that it satisfies the Dutch need for fair treatment and equal opportunities. Especially to the older generations, competition is an unfriendly term, and they tend to see the CAO system as the positive outcome of old-time social democracy, and of their solitary struggle for better working conditions.

For a long time now, trade unions have turned down management proposals for payment by performance since that would stimulate competition between workers – a scenario not desirable to more egalitarian-oriented workers' organisations. In 2000, 48% of workers interviewed were in favour of some method of payment by performance, with just 20% adamantly against. In that year's CAO agreements, about 40% of Dutch companies and organisations had already included arrangements for some degree of differential payment on top of the basic salaries. This makes it likely that, sooner or later, this system will be introduced elsewhere, but it will not be without resistance. In a radio debate on this issue, people wondered how it would work out in non-profit sectors such as health care and education, where quality should come before quantity.

In the booming economy of the 90s, more and more young people gave up CAO security in exchange for higher wages and other attractive working conditions, resulting in decreasing numbers of people working under CAO agreements, or belonging to a union at all. Now that the tide has changed, people are taking fewer risks. The economy dictates which influence will prevail in the long run: the increased entrepreneurial mood of young professionals or the striving for safety under CAO conditions.

Being in charge   In Dutch companies and organisations, the general mood is that whether boss or worker, we are all human and we all do our best. As a result of workers' input through the OR, people at all levels have a high degree of responsibility and involvement – at least they are supposed to. Power games or compulsion are therefore unusual and unwanted. Dutch managers and supervisors are not in a position to shake their fist and say, 'I'm the boss, this is what I want done, and all of you must just get on with it!' In interviews carried out in August 2000 on the expatriate website Expatica[3], Dutch people with working experience in the

United States called the management styles there 'dictatorial' and even 'militaristic'. I have heard similar strong terms during my research visits to Dutch expats in very different continents. Jokes such as those by Dilbert saying 'Opinions ignored here' are not, for the most part, transferable to Dutch working conditions.

In the Netherlands, bosses and managers are expected to gain authority through their expertise and clever strategies, not as the result of power games. Anyone attempting to 'play the big boss' would first be met by giggles of disbelief at such outlandish behaviour ('What on earth is the matter with *him* this morning?'). If he or she persisted, individual workers or even the entire department would fiercely protest at such 'authoritarianism'. If the conflict is structural, employees will immediately involve the OR, of course.

Saying that authority depends on expertise sounds as if a person in charge should know everything and, of course, that is not the case. Already for decades, Dutch education has focused away from students knowing hard facts and learning things by heart – on having the 'right' answer always at hand. Rather, it has tried to stimulate students to be interested in things, to formulate good questions and then to be creative in finding answers to them, through books, people, the Internet, or other sources. This is reflected in a Dutch manager's attitude that telling someone 'I don't know, but I'll find out for you' does not lead to loss of face. They *will* find out, either themselves or by asking other people, and then come back to you with the answer.

In line with worldwide developments, the ideal Dutch manager is not seen as a general in command, but as an inspiring leader who gives direction and vision to a team consisting of highly involved professionals who, in return, are also supposed to come up with creative and productive ideas. The manager should supervise the overall line and give protection to the team – that is how 'expertise' should be defined here.

Granted, this may be many a company's ideal, but reality isn't always perfect. In the Netherlands, as elsewhere, there are still 'bossy' bosses, conceited dictators or self-willed loners, and managers who are better at talking than at listening. But they are rare on Dutch soil, and given the outspokenness of many Dutch workers, chances are they will be met with more bottom-upwards resistance than they would be in many other countries. (Therefore, probably, agricultural and construction companies are known to happily employ workers from eastern Europe and elsewhere, because people with other cultural backgrounds will not speak up as easily as Dutch workers do – all the more so since many of them work illegally.)

Teamwork   Dutch people may be fairly strong individualists, but at work many are quite good team players. Given the degree of job security and the Dutch task orientation, most people are quite involved with both the company and their job. Moreover, with competition among individuals not much appreciated and many companies using matrix models, people tend to work together quite closely, sharing knowledge for the benefit of the team and the company. You are supposed to give the best insights from your particular angle, and not protect your ideas just to climb higher than the others. The idea is that excellence will show itself anyway. A disadvantage of strong team cohesion may be that when a problem arises, it's no one's responsibility in particular, leading foreigners to say, as I heard: *'I don't think the Dutch are good at problem owning!'* (USA)

OR involvement   When companies hit hard times, as some are doing now, with a tougher personnel policy inevitable, management must – and will – involve the OR in discussions on the right policy. It would also be wise to explain the difficult situation directly to the workers, asking for their cooperation in solving the problems in an atmosphere of mutual trust and loyalty. Working together with the OR, management will attempt to soften unpleasant but necessary measures. There have even been examples of employees working extra hours without pay to help the company survive. If cutting down the workforce is inevitable, a shorter working week for everyone rather than dismissing people may be an option, or instituting 'natural discharge', a gradual process in which people leaving are not replaced by new personnel. It may involve early retirement for older or ill workers, outplacement facilities for people leaving voluntarily, and 'golden handshakes' for higher management (Note that there is a difference after all!). Finally, if all these measures fail to overcome the company's problems, mass dismissals may only take place after consultations with the trade unions involved, followed by legal approval.

When the going gets rough, many companies and organisations in the Netherlands – more so than in other countries – involve external trouble-shooters, advisors and *interim* managers to solve conflicts and restructure things. This is booming business, since outsiders can more successfully implement unwelcome top-down changes than people from inside a company, no matter what their position. On individual levels in recent years, various kinds of coaching have become a somewhat fashionable instrument in helping higher personnel to improve their functioning, with the possible result that they may decide to move on or make a major break in their career. Several managers who lost their jobs have decided to assist others by setting up coaching services.

Transparency   Until recently, organisational reshuffling rarely led to any individual being publicly admonished, let alone punished. In Dutch culture, seeking the source of failure in procedures[4] rather than in individual actions is generally preferred – in other words, through an analysis of how people and organisations function, and then restructuring.

These days, however, public scapegoating of top people does happen more often, both in business and in government. But even then, those held responsible for the problem are removed as elegantly as possible, with golden handshakes, or moved to more neutral positions as 'advisors'. Some foreigners living here are alarmed about the way this works. *'Time and again in the past few years, my jaw has dropped as I have watched corrupt or incompetent officials step down after their misdeeds have been found out, without having to face prosecution, as high functionaries are not even brought to book for gambling with public funds.'* (USA) Yes, in a small-scale society such as the Netherlands, striving for harmony may lead to such protectionism.

In the next chapter, on directness, it will be discussed how openly admitting some error or wrongdoing is felt to be a good way of making up for it. But against the backdrop of egalitarianism as a strong value, there are certainly also complaints about 'class justice' sparing big shots. In spite of all this, Transparency International listed the Netherlands in 2003 as the world's seventh most transparent (so perhaps seventh least corrupt) nation. This position fluctuates only slightly over the years, in spite of some cases of large-scale fraud.

Of course, people at lower levels bitterly comment that the big-shots all cover up for each other, as they do in all countries, but such storms usually blow over. Only a few individuals who have been truly exposed for malfunctioning have chosen to leave the country, at least for a period of time. Some have given interviews or even written a book explaining their actions or defending their views.

The general trend in recent years, as elsewhere, has been a flattening of organisations, a breaking up into smaller, semi-independent departments that have more autonomy in deciding their own affairs. Workers' involvement has thus been reinforced rather than diluted. This was especially so when many of them owned shares in their company, but such 'people's capitalism' lost its glamour with the stock market drop. However, the search for good managers is not over, and companies still offer bonuses both to attract such people and to keep them. In fact, more and more foreign CEOs are involved in the Dutch business world. Over the years, golden handshakes as a device for getting rid of not-so-effective managers have become heavier and heavier, but just like salaries, their levels tend to be hushed up. Nowadays, the Code Tabaksblat urges publication of top salaries, bonuses and other perks, and the press is also keen to uncover such privileges.

CEOs and bonuses   In the 1990s, the holding company of a large Dutch supermarket chain expanded quite sensationally into foreign markets, becoming a major player in the USA, Latin America and South-East Asia. Without using names, suffice it to say that it was a popular investment object for the enormous Dutch pension funds. However, things went wrong: In one of their American chains, fraud was discovered, resulting in a great loss of both prestige and actual market value to the holding company. In order to get the company out of dire straits, a top executive from abroad was hired. The board and this CEO agreed on remuneration which – including various kinds of bonuses – hit the € 10m mark. Even under more favourable economic conditions this is an amount unheard of in the Dutch context, where even top salaries used to be moderate, but this occurred amidst news of mass dismissals and with the holding's supermarkets losing customers to cheaper shops. In reaction to general protest from the public, from pension fund managers, small shareholders and customers, and with a consumers' strike against the super-markets threatening, the foreign CEO merely commented, 'I'm worth it', which is not a wise thing to say in the Netherlands. As turmoil continued, he gave in, settling for a lower amount. The supermarket chain tried to convince the public of the CEO's capability in leading the company back into a better position. But after some time he took on a new board membership in a firm in his homeland, giving the irritated public the impression that he didn't even have to work all that hard for his millions.

Further, the holding's 2003 annual report made it clear that it rewarded all of its CEOs with millions of euros. Again, the Dutch public's dissatisfaction with 'big business' became evident. The supermarket chain had to launch a major price decrease to regain lost customers. Later, the CEO more or less admitted he had not quite realised the sensitivity of payment issues in the Dutch cultural context. (Perhaps he didn't have time to read this book.)

CEOs, then, are no heroes in Dutch culture. In fact, they are met with some suspicion, and even disdain – what a boring life they must lead with all those meetings and grey suits! The top salaries that have become fashionable in big business, and to a lesser degree also in the public sector, are hardly accepted by the wider Dutch public. With some sarcasm, journalists point out that such sky-high demands are always defended with references to remuneration levels in the USA, but never to those in less competitive economies. Occasionally, protest by shareholders and television viewers has some effect, but with big business being a rather aloof abode, enormous salaries still occur, as do handshakes for which the word 'golden' may be an understatement.

In response, the people receiving those top salaries complain that attention should be paid to the Netherlands' international competitiveness rather than to individual remuneration.

Dismissals   Most people definitely don't get a golden handshake for being made redundant or 'fired', but even so, Dutch regulations in this area compare very favourably to many other countries' regulations – from the worker's viewpoint, that is. While there is definitely more flexibility these days, sacking employees is still not a straightforward procedure in the Netherlands; Dutch law as a whole still reflects the country's egalitarian values. Through the CAOs, Dutch labour legislation strongly supports employees and protects those in vulnerable positions from injustice and arbitrariness. Only in a few specific cases (bare-faced theft, an outright refusal to work, violence) may employees under CAO be sacked on the spot.

There usually is a two-months term for discharging people from their job, and workers will fight their dismissal in court – backed up by free legal assistance and/or trade union support – if only not to lose their right to unemployment benefits. Since Dutch law almost automatically considers the employee 'the weaker party', judges often tend to take their side by prohibiting dismissal or by granting them some kind of compensation. For people not covered by a CAO, dismissal is of course less complicated, since they chose a higher risk job. Given these conditions plus the tendency to avoid really aggressive competition, making a Dutch organisation 'leaner and meaner' is not all that easy.

One last aspect of dismissals: when organisations need to trim just a few people, the principle of 'last in – first out' is usually applied. This may of course result in a relatively older staff which is not only more costly to the firm but perhaps also not quite on top of the latest technologies or, according to some, even less ambitious than young people. Therefore, plans are to allow companies to categorise personnel into age groups and only then apply this principle, thus keeping younger staff on board also.

Résumés (Curriculum Vitae)   The Dutch preference for low profile may also be apparent when people are hired. Most Dutch people will not include every last detail about their studies and work experience in their curriculum vitae, thinking it may look boastful. They just briefly list their qualifications and experience, expecting the people carrying out the job interview to read between the lines and pose questions for further details. Foreigners accustomed to more confident or extensive résumés may think little of such an application, while their Dutch colleagues may consider the person well worth interviewing. Vice versa, the Dutch tend to consider full-blast résumés as unrealistic and unsympathetic, so the reaction is often 'Don't invite that person!'

Dutch understated self-presentation may also occur during a personal interview. Some Dutch educational institutions have started teaching students and the 'long-term unemployed' how to place themselves better in the market by writing an eye-catching résumé or speaking more confidently. A course leader of one such program comments, *'For my students, this kind of self-promotion is not easy. They are not used to it; it feels contradictory. "Am I now supposed to tell how good I am?" they ask me.'*

Flexibility Dutch companies and the government have worked hard at creating a more flexible labour market. Since dismissals are often complicated, lengthy and costly procedures, companies are careful in hiring people on a more permanent basis. The resulting 'slim' organisations are characterised by a high degree of automation and computerisation, with negative effects on customer service.

Temporary workers are brought in to bridge peak periods. Hired through 'temp' agencies, they can be dismissed far more easily. The proportion of 'temp' workers in the Netherlands is one of the highest in the world, since related part-time work is also popular (see chapter 8). This was one of the pillars of the polder model and will probably remain popular among both employers and employees. Temporary employment agencies (*uitzendbureau*) proliferate. They started decades ago as pools of administrative workers, but by now they can also provide computer experts, interim managers, and so on. The legal and tax position of temporary workers is strengthened by permanent work contracts with the *uitzendbureau*, while the actual work is carried out in client organisations. Some firms in this successful business arena have expanded to neighbouring countries, where attempts to copy the Dutch polder model resulted in the creation of a more level playing field.

All in all, Dutch labour legislation is gradually changing, as younger generations with a different system of values move up in the business world. In line with the rest of the western world, flexible work schedules and greater differences in salary are increasingly being considered normal and accepted. The traditional concept of material egalitarianism seems to have been weakened. But the non-material attitude of 'Just act normal' is still with us, as I hope to make even clearer herein.

Stakeholders, shareholders and 'responsibility management'
Related to egalitarianism in the Dutch business world is also the

fact that stakeholders' value (rather than just shareholders') is taken seriously by the wider public, the media and some critical investors themselves. Capitalism all right, but one should invest not solely for the purpose of making a quick profit but also be alert to the position of workers, the talents of the managers and the interests of clients, contractors and other parties involved. Many Dutch people find this the preferred, decent attitude. A quote from a British executive with wide experience in working internationally: *'The big difference is that* (name of his company) *and its activities are truly a part of this society. In many countries where I've worked, in a few discussions you could convince people of the use of your plans ... Here things don't work that way. You have to deal with the polder model, with a series of organisations, the environmental movement, and politics. You're being taken through all of society, so to speak – a difficult but fascinating process.'* One particular version of this may be the trend toward 'ethical entrepreneurship' or 'responsibility management' that is discussed and attempted in various Dutch companies. Copying American examples, many now have 'mission statements' to describe their usefulness to society, and 'codes of conduct' in which they – largely with an eye on critical consumers and the media – declare that they are aiming for production processes which are not harmful to the environment at home or in faraway countries. They promise to neither employ child labour nor impose abusive conditions on adult workers, and not give in to corruption or other questionable practices. (It needs to be said that, operating worldwide and out of sight, not all Dutch firms live by such lofty principles.)

Clearly, stakeholders are an issue, but shareholding is more widespread, albeit differently than before. Around 1995, with a booming economy and an increased 'Americanisation' of Dutch society, owning shares and playing the stock market became a widespread phenomenon. Driven by bank advertisements, media hype and the rumour mill, many people tried to make quick profits by buying and selling shares, quite often with borrowed money and probably not caring much about any stakeholders. Many fell flat on their face in the 2001 stock market slump, not 'sitting still while they were being shaved', as the saying goes, but forced to sell in order to pay their debts and loans.

This confirmed some Dutch people's idea that trying to 'get rich quick' by playing the stock market is an unwise and somewhat immoral speculation to be frowned upon. Yet also now, even the most critical Dutch people are deeply into the stock market, since their pension funds are among the world's largest investments, as we will see later.

Representation   By Dutch standards, people don't act 'normal' all the time, certainly not when they want to make a good impression. With the growing importance of public relations, perhaps in imitation of the American style of business, the issue of representation gained enormous attention in recent years. Offering a 'skybox' evening in a football stadium to favoured suppliers, clients and customers, or a VIP treatment at a cultural or sporting event became a popular way to bind these people[5]. It is a faster method than the more personal but time-consuming ways in which business people in other cultures entertain their contacts. Showing their guests around a city, for example, would make Dutch business people very impatient, while entertaining them at home is an unusual privilege in a culture with a strong separation between work and private life, as we will see.

On a more common level, the following American observation is interesting: *'I am absolutely amazed to see how much money Dutch companies spend on lavish brochures, business cards, office space, art for their walls – and parties! Wow – you don't see that in the U.S.'* Although not as prevalent as before, PR policies indeed provide advertising agencies, graphic designers, printers and distributors with many a customer. But don't think for a moment that Dutch companies spend such money frivolously. The cost-effectiveness of any campaign is carefully worked out beforehand, and if not lived up to in terms of expectations, they are quickly reduced in scale or abandoned altogether. Some firms even use this aspect in almost empty advertisements to emphasise their low prices.

Customer service, once again   Several of the circumstances mentioned above also negatively affect the degree of customer service. In the public sector, especially, it is difficult to reach people during lunch or coffee breaks. Colleagues in a particular department may choose to all have a coffee break at the same time, leaving no one to answer incoming telephone calls. The rationale – perhaps logical but nonetheless arrogant – is: 'We are entitled to it. If it's really important, they'll phone back'...

which is true, perhaps, but luckily, the Dutch usually take short lunch breaks (see chapter 6).

Another noticeable problem is that when you phone an organisation, it may take ages before you are connected to the right department. Often you will have to work your way through automatic answering procedures telling you – in Dutch only! – to dial '2' for this information and '3' for an answer to that question. And when you finally get through to a live human being, to your enormous irritation the phrase 'one moment, please' usually signifies a five-minute wait at least. Obviously, employers don't like this, and sometimes organise customer service training programmes for their employees. But after initial improvement, matters usually return to 'normal'. An article in a Dutch newspaper gave the following hint: phone at 8.05 a.m. so that you are the first caller, or one of the first, and if you have to wait too long, dial again but change the last three digits, so as to reach another department in the same organisation which may then connect you to the right person. In private companies, telephone service is usually a little better than in public organisations, but even there it is often far from perfect.

This chapter discussed various aspects of hierarchy and equality among the Dutch. When people feel equal, they will tend to speak frankly, and that's exactly what the Dutch do. Their straightforwardness is the subject of the next chapter.

1. See chapter 10 on gender issues.
2. For detailed factual and legal information on Dutch labour regulations, please refer to 'Employers and Labour Relations in the Netherlands', a publication by the Dutch General Employers' Association AWVN. An update is underway, and they also provide courses on the issue. They are in Haarlem, tel. (+31) (0)23 - 5101 213/215, website www.awvn.nl.
3. www.expatica.com.
4. More on this in chapter 7.
5. See chapter 8.

Chapter 5

DIRECTNESS AND CRITICISM

'Straight through the sea.'
(Dutch expression in praise of directness)

No doubt about it, the Dutch have a reputation for being very direct in their speech and their approach – witness the curt answer 'No' in some shops. On this matter, the reactions of foreigners participating in my 'Understanding the Dutch' course range from the positive term 'confident', through rather neutral terms such as 'straightforward' and 'very honest' to the less positive 'abrupt', 'blunt' and 'rude'. People from abroad are usually shocked by the directness at first but, after they have been here for awhile, many come to appreciate this directness. Of course it also depends on what they are used to in their own culture.

To be honest, most Dutch people are not even aware of such directness. They feel that since all people are more or less equal, so are their ideas. In Dutch society, everyone has the right to say what (s)he thinks, no matter the social position, so opinions are easily voiced. In working life and general society, most people have a rather functional approach to others: you want something; I can provide it. Both of us are here to do a job; you are a customer, I am a vendor. Personal characteristics don't matter too much in such a transaction and, therefore, 'neutral' relationship. Content please, not form. Yes is yes and no is no.

Any personal aspect such as mutual fondness or humour may be a pleasant extra, but is not strictly necessary to do business or to carry out a transaction. (This is probably one reason why foreigners complain about a certain 'coldness' in the Dutch.) So in the workplace not much attention is paid to outward signs of respect. Even when others are around, people speak up to their superiors and feel free to disagree with them – unless it's on sensitive personal issues. The words 'yes, but ...' are fairly standard in most Dutch conversations. *'It seems quite normal here to strongly disagree with your boss!'* (Britain)

Provided that opinions and comments are given in a calm, rational way, they are also listened to – although they are certainly not always accepted. But sanctions are not likely to follow, although you may be frankly criticised in return! Superiors cannot really put someone down for merely stating an opinion, and although it happens sometimes, of course, people are not supposed to use others as stepping stones. That would be considered unfair; one's *own* performance should be the only criterion.

Being straightforward is one thing, expressing real opinions another. In some cultures, people prefer voicing disapproval with terms or euphemisms such as 'not very good' or 'interesting'. In the case of the Dutch, criticisms are barely concealed and rarely expressed in euphemisms – good is good, bad is bad. This direct manner of expression can shock people who are not used to it. It is usually the first thing that crops up when I ask my target group here for their observations on the Dutch, quite irrespective of which country they come from. An observer from Australia: *'They make you feel that your choice of paint colour is stupid.'* And one from Britain: *'British people will not say what they think, except to very good friends. Here in Holland it may happen that someone asks you: "Why is your hair so long; why do you wear that tie with that shirt"? I wouldn't be surprised if they told me: "What an awful tie you're wearing"! We British always worry whether we are doing the right thing, whether we are behaving properly. Dutchmen don't.'*

No, we don't. In fact, we prefer honest criticism to flattering compliments.

Context   A better understanding of this explicit criticism requires some explanation of the structure of society and the Dutch way of making decisions. Given the socio-ideological pluriformity of the country, there is rarely a majority opinion on any issue, and even if there is there will always be factions or individuals with a mind of their own. A BBC film aptly described the Netherlands as *'a society of little boxes in a land of little squares'*.

No 'little box' has absolute power, so any decision, whether in companies, Parliament, the Town Hall or a local volleyball club, involves debate and then compromise – water in the wine. If people don't clearly put forward their ideas, preferably backed up with sound arguments, those ideas will not be reflected in the final decision. So opinions are expressed loudly and clearly, especially if they do not concern private emotional matters. And people may not give in until the final compromise is reached: 'They stick with their views.' (Russia)

The Dutch are also not afraid to make rather caustic comments to other groups in society, to those with other lifestyles. Among Fortuyn's political following, this version of directness even intensified, inspired by his slogan 'I say what I think and I do what I say'.

Such harsh Dutch judgements often come as a shock to foreigners, either because they are accustomed to more political correctness, or because they thought that the Netherlands was a land of sweet tolerance to other people (see chapter 8). But people here are used to it; it's a mutual thing, and since no one has a majority anyway, in the past such comments never had much real consequence. Nonetheless, this may be changing now, as we will see in the chapter on multicultural society.

Overleg　Somewhat surprisingly in this land of compromise, the Dutch word *compromis* is not to be heard or read that often in everyday life. The word used much more often for the process of reaching a compromise is *overleg*, translated as 'deliberation'. This word suggests a time-consuming activity and this is usually so; on important issues *overleg* can take weeks, and every step taken can produce new ideas for the parties involved and another reason for getting together again. This explains many of the infamous Dutch meetings about which quite a few expats and visiting business people grumble. Then, when the inevitable compromise is finally reached and put down on paper, with everyone's carefully thought-out arguments, an *'overeenkomst'* is reached – a word which, interestingly, not only means 'agreement', but also 'resemblance', 'similarity' or 'conformity'.

In the process of *overleg*, and in Dutch society as a whole, any fanaticism is frowned upon and even condemned. In companies and organisations, managers fanatically defending a certain point of view must have both very strong arguments and a good deal of personal charisma – remember the Dutch tendency to use the words 'yes, but'. Convincing people is a far more effective management tool here than power games.

Fairly typical of the somewhat detached manner of speech is the fact that, in debates, Dutch politicians use terms such as 'dismayed', 'alarmed' and 'perplexed' without their face indicating any of these strong feelings. The main exception here was the late Pim Fortuyn, who not only had a certain charisma but also a rather theatrical way of stating his opinions. Not used to that demeanour, his debating partners didn't quite know how to handle it, and I strongly suspect that the people who enjoyed watching him do this on television wouldn't appreciate such behaviour from a colleague or a friend.

Critical attitudes and strong opinions, then, are usually clearly expressed, but preferably in a rather non-emotional manner. Large parts of the Dutch population find a short and unequivocal word quite enough. For example, the words *fout* (wrong, mistake) and *waardeloos* (worthless, useless, lousy) are used to give feedback, even among colleagues and friends. But few people feel hurt by them. Well, if they're Dutch, that is…

Rude words   *'The Dutch curse a lot.'* (UK) Considerable numbers of people, and not only youngsters, use obscenities (mostly three-letter words in Dutch) to express dislike or a negative opinion. Native English speakers are often shocked by the frequent use of English four-letter words that, being in a different language, don't sound quite so crude to the Dutch. (By the way, every nation has its own hang-ups; in the Netherlands, 'cursing' implies using blasphemy rather than sexually-oriented words, which are considered 'uncivilised' only.)

Even when no rude words are used, Dutch opinions may come across very direct and strong in themselves. Yet the speaker only feels (s)he is being honest with you. Part of the misunderstanding also stems from the use of language. Dutch has several terms to 'soften' opinions and requests *(maar, toch, even, gewoon, een beetje)*, but by themselves these words don't carry much meaning, and many people don't know how to exactly render their idea when speaking English. The result is often that a comment or opinion sounds far more blunt than the Dutch speaker intended it to be.

Rude words are rarely used in business, but critical attitudes do prevail. Your Dutch counterparts will inspect any proposal or performance in detail, ask questions, and give their straightforward, honest opinion. This leads people who are not used to such directness to call the Dutch 'opinionated', 'arrogant' and 'judgmental'.

'At college they often tell me: "Gee, I didn't know Germans could be nice!"' (German student in Amsterdam). This remark of course sounds tactless and undiplomatic to non-Dutch people, but remember, one is free – even expected – to return exactly the same type of remark. It is up to you to develop similar frankness. The Dutch might then describe you as being 'straight onto the man', which is a compliment on your honesty. *'There is an obligation to have strong opinions.'* (Poland)

As a matter of fact, after a while quite a few foreigners begin to appreciate Dutch directness. It may not be elegant, but at least *'you know where you stand'*. Not only criticism is voiced in direct ways, but also 'good advice'. This may not always be welcome, but the Dutch will feel it really is best for you. A language teacher from Trinidad said, *'In my early days here, the most shocking thing to me was the directness. But after 18 years in Holland I know that when they say, "Ann, run!," I'd better run.'*

More on Dutch English   Many people are quite impressed with the Dutch ability to speak English, but native speakers of English should realise that, as with any non-native speaker of a language, Dutch English is seldom 100% perfect. A book on this issue introduced the term 'Dunglish'[1]. Linguistic misunderstandings may easily strengthen a native English speaker's impression that the Dutch are blunt or arrogant. A good example is the subtle difference in meaning between 'to propose' and 'to suggest'. A Dutch manager found his British colleagues irritated when innocently he used 'proposal' (a rather compelling offer) when he had actually meant 'suggestion' (a creative idea as good as any other one). Another example: tram conductors in Amsterdam often have to urge the public, entering at the back of the tram, to move forward to allow more passengers to board. As a courtesy to tourists they repeat themselves in English. In Dutch, one can omit the word 'please' without sounding really rude. But a harsh *'Move to the front, everybody!'* through the loudspeaker may sound quite abrupt to the non-Dutch.

Suffice it to say that the Dutch speak their minds. Unlike people from, in particular, Asian cultures, loss of face is of little concern to many of them. *'Especially the directness of the Dutch was new to me, but I have got used to it by now. ... As soon as I'm back in Japan, I switch*

to the norms of politeness that prevail. There, if I don't agree with something, I don't say: "No, you are wrong," as they do here.' (Japan)

You ask a Dutch person for his or her opinion and you get it,
clearly stated, no obscuring or disguising for the sake of politeness. The Dutch are programmed this way all their lives, but many
foreigners perceive such directness as hostile and unfriendly. A
German made an interesting point: 'Why do the Dutch keep saying
"heh?" after each statement?' The answer may be that they are unconsciously gauging whether the person they are speaking to supports or opposes their opinion.

But here we come to a paradox: the Dutch will only treat you in
this way if they take you seriously, if they feel you to be close
enough, in the same 'little box' as they are. So, strange as it may
sound, directness and criticism mean appreciation and belonging.
They infer that you are 'one of us', that we accept you as an equal.

If people don't feel this connection, they will critically observe
you but not say much. After all, in Dutch society, one should leave
other 'little boxes' alone: 'live and let live'. But here in our box, we
must strive for perfection and help each other to do so. The logic
is: how can anyone improve if they overlook their imperfections?
So the Dutch tell each other exactly what they think those imperfections are.

Indirectness, and keeping criticism at bay   In
contrast, some foreign observers don't agree that the Dutch are
direct. As illustration, they produce examples of colleagues beat-
ing around the bush and avoiding outright statements: *'They are
not so direct when they have to say "no".'* (Taiwan) The situations
mentioned all had to do with emotions, like the fear of jeopardis-
ing one's job or of disturbing harmony with close colleagues.

You might say that the Dutch tend to be direct and even judgemental with whom they consider to be insiders – their peer
group, the people they truly feel equal to. They feel that outsiders probably don't quite understand or even know all the factors playing a role in the issue anyway, so their judgement is less
relevant. Being task-oriented rationalists, the Dutch will then
explain and defend their views, which leads foreigners to observe
that the Dutch cannot take criticism very well. *'The Dutch don't
take responsibility for failing; they always come up with external reasons for not performing well.'* (USA)

Yet, self-criticism is also appreciated, whether toward a group or an organisation or at strictly personal levels. Probably a leftover of the Calvinistic guilt-ridden past, self-criticism at work seems to be waning in today's more market-oriented mood, but in private life and at organisational levels it still goes on. Admitting your mistakes or a gap in your knowledge is a sign of strength and self-knowledge, of 'character', rather than a weakness or something to be embarrassed about. If necessary, companies or government departments will also admit their mistakes publicly, albeit sometimes reluctantly. But, to the Dutch way of thinking, it helps to prevent protest and overcome damage done.

In the political world, there have been soul-searching parliamentary debates on what went wrong in certain scenarios. Examples were the 1992 Amsterdam plane crash, the Dutch peacekeepers' involvement in the 1995 Srebrenica drama in Bosnia, the 2000 Enschede fireworks explosion, the 2002 Volendam New Year's fire, and the government's ethnic integration policy from the 1960s to the present, examined in 2003. Just about all the people involved in such scenarios must describe their 'doings' in detail, 'with bare buttocks', as the Dutch say, and the various authorities shouldn't 'keep anything under their hat', in other words, hidden from the public. But again, all kinds of circumstantial factors are taken into account, and rarely is any individual found guilty of illegal acts, let alone punished. 'They did their utmost under difficult conditions.' In a small society such as the Netherlands, being publicly called to account is considered quite a punishment in itself.

In the previous chapter we saw an American's indignation, but it all depends on where you come from. *'I appreciate the critical attitude of Dutch society. I like the way the media tackle touchy subjects, how they sometimes attack one another and how the authorities are open to the public. That is a good element in democracy.'* (Nigeria). As I mentioned in other chapters, in recent years both the business community and the political world were not always found to be quite so open, but those are exceptions and, once discovered, the cases are fully exposed.

Tell me what's wrong!   In Dutch culture, imperfections are a challenge, something that must be overcome by stubborn hard work. 'It *must* be perfect!' An observer from Iceland said, *'Dutch people are nice, but they criticise other people too often and too readily.*

Even when they discuss a (sports) match they won, they will constantly talk about the five minutes that things went a bit wrong. I don't know whether this is because they all know how to do things better, or because they just want to fuss.'

In relation to this, the Dutch will analyse anything new. The good aspects are quickly taken for granted. 'Perfect? OK, no longer interesting, let's go on looking for *im*perfections.' These will be pointed out immediately and discussed: *'When you go to a concert or a theatre here, immediately afterwards everything is analysed, verbally cut to pieces.'* (Ireland)

Now you should not think criticism is always given in such a serious way; it can also be wrapped up in jokes, irony or sarcasm. Self-mockery and self-irony are also greatly appreciated, as a humorous kind of self-criticism. Projecting yourself as small or making your performance relative is in line with the issue of equality, and helps to make great achievements more palatable to the Dutch. The Dutch verb *relativeren* is often used. It means making things relative, seeing them in their proper perspective, not only in black and white. One might even see this as the verbal expression of the Dutch need for egalitarianism: avoid extremes; try to find the middle ground. This becomes particularly evident when a Dutch person receives a compliment. In line with the widespread critical attitude, compliments are not easily extended, since perfection is distrusted. In fact, too many compliments tend to make people uneasy and, even if they are not met with disbelief, the receiver will usually wave them aside, or self-mockingly 'make them relative'. In most cases *prima* (fine) will do. Superlatives like 'terrific', 'great' and the like are met with some suspicion and should be reserved for very special occasions only. A businesswoman from Hungary dryly observed: *'Good news is not welcomed here.'*

Perfection is merely everyone's duty; working on *im*perfections is one's real task in life. 'So tell us what's still wrong, please.' The Icelander went on: *'They need to have a problem. If they don't have one, they'll look for one, because with a problem you can discuss "How are we going to solve it?"' *

Task-oriented and serious Overall, the Dutch are task-oriented. What matters is that the product, the performance, is improved. Managers, as well as most of the other personnel, feel involved in their job and their company, so whatever changes are proposed they want to know: 'Why, what is your argumentation for this?' They will ask critical questions, think it over, give direct feedback and go on discussing it until an agreement is reached between all the parties involved. *'In the short time I have been here, what I have learned about the Dutch is that they are very straight, very much to the point and are always asking "Why?". The other thing is that they are eager to share their ideas, their brainpower, their thoughts.'* (Director of a large American company)

'You can tell the Dutch they are wrong, but you have to come with arguments why you think so. They are all professionals, but they're also careful. Give them your opinion and perhaps it may take six months, but they will come back on it by e-mail.' (Russian businessman)

In their strive for perfection, the product, or if need be, the whole organisation, is verbally dismantled into its smallest components. Anything faulty is openly discussed, taken out and replaced by a better version, and then it's all reassembled – new and closer to perfection. Companies, ministries and organisations are restructured all the time, roads are under constant repair, houses are redecorated, office furniture is changed, computer systems are updated, and new rules are made. ('Change management' consultancy and training programmes for both managers and employees often accompany such reorganisations. The Dutch management-training sector is well-developed and thriving!) And then once things are improved, 'let's not spend too much time congratulating ourselves but get back to work; there is more to do.' Quite a bit of time may be lost on this re-organising, but that only seems to bother foreigners. *'They question the why but not the what.'* (Britain)

This may all sound rather gloomy but, although the Dutch are serious, this doesn't depress them – it's a challenge. Colleagues who have just critically discussed their common performance may go and have a pint together afterwards (but just one, as we will see). Discussion may go on at the bar and no one is offended. Although the Dutch may not show it, they quite enjoy this 'working on improvement'. They talk about it, long and thoroughly, even intensely, but rarely with dramatic gestures or in very loud voices (remember: *'milk in their veins'*). Such dramatic behaviour would undermine the speaker's point of view rather than strengthen it. Well, there are exceptions like Pim Fortuyn, but for the less charismatic the dictum is: 'Not too many emotions, please, and no superlatives.' *'Sometimes the Dutch get on my nerves; their mentality is so different from mine. They are very reliable but terribly serious, so down to earth and cold. They observe life with their brains; everything goes according to the rules. I miss the Czech openness and spontaneity, the gaiety. Dancing and singing doesn't come easy to Dutchmen.'* (Czech Republic)

Organised emotions   Maybe the Dutch are generally a little shy and uncertain because, in spite of the Czech comment, many Dutch people do dance and sing; it's just that they need a good excuse, a reason, and, outside of the shower, they don't like doing it alone. Witness the fact that there are some 20,000 choirs in the Netherlands and many vocal festivals, choral singing competitions and even mass choirs. Many a song is also sung during football matches (although they sound terrible). As for dancing, every town has its discos, dance parties and dance schools. But the Czech is right in the sense that all this is not spontaneous; virtually all of it is organised. People singing on the tram or dancing in the street will receive curious looks or even frowns and hisses to stop it. Street musicians require licences from the local police. So spontaneity is not really appreciated. Only on weekend evenings when, as everyone knows, quite a lot of alcohol has been drunk and people feel they have a good excuse might one come across crowds of people singing and dancing.

The same manner of 'organised emotion' is true, by the way, for serious events. Most foreigners cannot understand the language, but Dutch people often tell the most personal and sad details of their lives in certain TV programmes, whether of a sensational or a more serious nature. In recent years, silent walks to commemorate crime victims with flowers and candles, and signing condolence registers on the Internet have become accepted expressions of grief. Cynical observers comment on the superficial character of such hyped-up collective events, where a certain political correctness also plays a role.

As you can see, dancing and singing, or other expressions of emotion, don't come easily to the Dutch, certainly not in working hours. In public, most of the time, Dutch people come across as serious, earnest-looking and concentrated, joking and smiling only occasionally. In Asia, a vague smile seems to be the common, socially acceptable expression, while Latin Americans have no problem in hugging each other freely. North Americans frequently burst into big smiles and free-rein laughter, and sometimes even engage in group hugs or collective shouts of enthusiasm. This would deeply embarrass the Dutch. For them, a calm, collected manner, a hushed voice and restrained physical movements are the norm, at least in public. The *modus operandi* is to fulfil your task, work hard and concentrate, even when enjoying a hobby. With a well-developed sense of duty and responsibility (and technology to assist), the Dutch are approaching the highest productivity in the world. Luckily for them, they have long (paid) holidays. *'The Dutch are serious and they take everything seriously. You must be careful with jokes; they may easily get it wrong. This serious attitude is good for business; Dutch people are good at that.'* (Nigeria). And: *'In my experience, the Dutch are not capable of not taking things seriously, no matter what you say.'* (British philosopher Roger Scruton, as heard on Dutch TV).

But everything is relative. A Finnish friend of mine once described the Dutch to me as *'real southerners'!* In spite of all their seriousness, the Dutch are apparently quite happy. For several years they have scored very highly in a Europe-wide survey on contentment with life. Consistent with the directness issue, you can be sure that *when* they smile, they mean it: *'I like the way they smile here,'* a Tanzanian commented. And to my relief, a young Ukrainian management trainee said, after working for one month in a Dutch company, *'You really can learn a lot from the Dutch people. They are unique in questions of cooperation, timing, humour at work and work organisation... You meet a lot of nice people here.'*

Occasionally you will even see Dutch people being very enthusiastic ('going out of their roof' is an expression for this), usually in the company of friends or relatives. In public, it takes a 'valid' reason, ranging from football matches through to Queen's Day and stag nights, and almost certainly a drink or two (or ten)[2]. The result is not always pleasant to witness. (Like me, you'll probably prefer to avoid football stadiums and their environs on match days!)

On the job, what counts is that the product is improved and the target reached. The constant striving for perfection is a (subconscious) part of Dutch upbringing. Most people deal with criticism and the lack of compliments in a somewhat detached manner: 'This here is me and that over there is what I do, so feel free to shoot.'

Conflicts Sometimes, of course, people do become hurt or angry. If 'talking it over' no longer helps, there are various other calm solutions in Dutch society: the people involved can simply ignore each other, or if regular encounters are unavoidable, superiors can reorganise work to keep disruptions to the absolute minimum. In the average Dutch mind, there is no need to get excited about things, let alone violent. On a more collective scale, the same applies. *'In other countries, conflicts easily escalate. Here, people stay calm. The company council, the trade unions and the company directors make decisions in relative harmony.'* (Switzerland) And a less positive view on the same, from a diplomatic source: *'The Dutch always strive for unity and harmony (in Europe). You will just not allow conflict. We Brits don't mind conflict. Something is the matter, but we'll solve that.'*

This constant striving for harmony, for solving conflict by way of discussion, was at the basis of the polder model. Although that is basically over now, labour disputes and strikes are still exceptional in the Netherlands, and much less time is lost to them than in most other European countries. Collective labour agreements often include no-strike agreements, or strictly defined conditions to the ones that are allowed. Strikes may only take place *after* serious negotiating has failed, and by court permission. Only then will trade unions support the strikers and pay their wages.

'Wildcat' strikes, which are unlawful and not backed by the unions, do take place occasionally, but as the strikers then have no income, they never last long. Sometimes brief ('pinpoint') actions take place, especially in public transport, but these are usually met with public disapproval. Whichever tone the actions have, new negotiations are bound to follow. In fact, merely threatening to strike can sometimes be enough to bring a thaw to frozen negotiations. Strikers marching in masses and waving protest banners are a rare phenomenon on Dutch streets. A strike in the Netherlands generally features a union leader addressing a tumultuous crowd of people wearing bandanas or T-shirts with a pre-printed union slogan. Depending on the season, this takes place out on the street or in a congress hall. They may shout the word *actie* (action!), but skirmishes and further emotions are rare. Needless to say that with economic trouble, the tendency to go on strike is on the rise, but the recent past has brought companies and trade unions closer together than in most countries.

In business and in government, the usual reaction to important and controversial problems is to have a 'working group', a 'committee', a 'commission of wise people' or some other forum to discuss the issue at hand and find harmonious solutions. People on such committees are carefully chosen to represent various views on the issue involved. The overriding conclusion is that solving conflicts or problems in the Netherlands just takes a lot of talking, so 'Please have your opinion ready, and state it, clearly!'

Decision-making *'It's unbelievable how often the Dutch hold meetings. Where do they find the time? And yet they don't discuss very well, because people always want to be nice to each other.'* (Germany)

Long discussions have always been part of Dutch culture. Historians say this country was always ruled by committees and through meetings. In the old days, public debate was often religious in nature[3]. Nowadays it is on politics, random violence, new legislation, immigration – anything, anywhere ...over lunch, at parties, in cafés, at campsites ...and on television, of course. Compared to American talk shows, Dutch talk shows are, again, quite serious and lack glamour. During such a debate, on TV or elsewhere, one may see quite earnest faces, both among the speakers and the public. But at the same time, such debate is rather fun to the Dutch – *serious* fun. It's like a game of chess, thoughtful and precise, everybody calmly waiting a turn and yet highly involved and alert. Reflecting the Netherlands' social pluriformity, widely differing points of view may, and will, be expressed, so it can take quite some time before any conclusion is reached. It should come as no surprise by now to hear that the Netherlands has many political parties and their debates take up much time, sometimes lasting into the wee small hours. *'I think the Dutch urge to have meetings comes from the need to avoid conflict and to take decisions in harmony. But I have learned to be alert. For hours and hours they talk in circles but when you doze off, they suddenly reach a decision in thirty seconds. And then it is irrevocable.'* (Britain)

There is a good side too, however, as expressed by this Frenchman: *'Yes, decision-making in Holland takes an awfully long time, but everybody is heard in the process and once the decision is finally taken, all seem to recognise their point of view in it somehow, so they will implement it.'*

And that is exactly what counts to the Dutch: everyone consulted and involved ...harmony safeguarded. This happens at all levels, including the way in which the government deals with private enterprise. The same Swiss quoted above observed, *'The agreements that (Dutch) enterprises have made with the government are unique. In every other country, environmental laws are dictated by the authorities, which then evokes resistance from the companies involved.'*

It would be a little too optimistic to think that such agreements are always met with general approval and enthusiasm, but all in all, yes, the Netherlands is a country where things are talked over and compromise reached. In a small nation, this is essential for maintaining social harmony and getting people to work for the common cause. 'Compromise at all cost.' If extra costs are needed to satisfy all parties (provided their arguments are sound), so be it. *'I was impressed with the Dutch culture being oriented toward cooperation and finding compromise, which resulted in the Delta project and the wealth of the country as a whole.'* (Ukrainian management trainee, after visiting the huge sea barrier for which a very expensive compromise between safety and the environment was needed and achieved).

Moralism   After centuries of deep religiousness, a measure of moralism has crept into Dutch criticism. Wagging the forefinger has become a recurring phenomenon: 'You are wrong!' People may even say this literally. Although unpopular, this attitude is widespread, both within the country itself and – sometimes coming as a shock – in international dealings, too. Dutch government functionaries have had the honour of being told by foreign hosts (behind the scenes, usually) that it would be better if they kept some of their opinions to themselves. Some painful incidents have occurred. At a conference on the international image of the Netherlands, a former (post-apartheid) South African ambassador said, *'The pointed Dutch finger is well known throughout the world. In the pursuit of human rights ideals, this attitude must be applauded, but sometimes this judgemental attitude should be expressed more carefully.'*

Companies, too, can be accused of misdemeanours such as polluting the environment, investing in undemocratic countries, or using dangerous materials. In the past, demonstrations, boycotts and even some violent protests followed. Nowadays, if an accident occurs during the production process, the company concerned will immediately publicise it and offer extensive apologies and promise to improve their production methods, rather than wait for the public storm to break. Such action is appreciated, and has the advantage of stifling much of the potential protest.

In spite of the continuous struggle to achieve perfection, there are still imperfections, of course. Expatriates often complain about government bureaucracy, slow service, short banking and shopping hours, unclear procedures when service people such as plumbers and electricians come to their homes, and poor service facilities for working women (see chapter 10).

The Dutch themselves may complain about all this and much more – plus the weather, of course. You may have to get used to welcoming phrases such as 'Terrible weather today, did you get very wet?', and to unexpected summer heat in buildings that are not air-conditioned. *'The Dutch have everything under control, except for the weather. So that becomes a topic of general conversation.'* (Nepal) But complaining should be seen as a national sport. A Dutch man or woman with nothing to complain about would be an unhappy person indeed.

Backgrounds   We will now turn to some historical backgrounds to Dutch outspokenness. Directness is, of course, more than just a language thing; underneath it lies an attitude. Protestant religion, besides stressing one's duties to live a frugal and productive life, emphasises the importance of 'the Word'. From the beginning this led to taking the Bible quite literally, and to sharp distinctions between God and the devil, good and bad, right and wrong, us and them – in other words, to thinking in sharply dualistic categories. In the Calvinist society that much of the Netherlands was until the 1960s, emotions were restrained and spontaneity was frowned upon; singing was restricted to church services and birthday parties, and dancing was considered sinful.

But like other holy books, the Bible can be quite paradoxical, and this has led to a multitude of interpretations from individual believers and various denominations. 'A nation of church ministers', as the Dutch themselves say. Even today it is still normal in

Calvinist households to privately discuss and judge the sermon after attending a church service.

Although for centuries the Dutch Reformed Church was the major church, there were always internal and external debates and struggles going on, and these often led to break-away denominations – from the early 1600s up to as recently as 1944, and even a minor one in 2003. Over the years, all kinds of religious interpretations have been debated, sometimes bitterly. In trying to make their point, debaters put forward what they hoped were well-considered arguments, while voicing 'rational' and very direct, moralising criticism of other parties' points of view. In my view, the roots of Dutch directness and judgemental attitudes lie in these everlasting religious debates.

Democracy There is more to all this, however, than just religious pluriformity and debate. Dutch directness also springs from great self-confidence and, again, the relatively low hierarchy. For over 200 years – until the changes inspired by the French Revolution in 1795 – the country was a federal republic that had emerged out of the 16th-century uprising against Spanish rule. Under the banner of Protestantism, which gave them support from the rank and file, local nobles and merchants aspired to political and economic autonomy from foreign rule – and won. In other words, the Dutch republic was a kind of 'self-made' country. People felt that they themselves had appointed their leaders, unlike the absolute monarchs who ruled in neighbouring countries. Since adherence to strict Calvinism coincided with great prosperity, the Dutch felt that they were under divine protection. Other countries' admiration of the republic's democratic institutions contributed to a sense of moral superiority, shared by all.

The republic was pluriform from the start; no group could really impose its will. Whether the topic of conversation was interpretations of the Bible, overseas trade policy or new laws and taxes, everything was discussed and differing views had to be accommodated somehow – by compromise. A few more authoritarian periods ended in riots and upheaval. Authority was all right as long as the public felt it to be ordained by God; then they obeyed.

A more recent large-scale questioning of authority occurred in 1966, when general dissatisfaction among the younger generation brought down university deans and city mayors. Amsterdam, addicted to the drug of freedom, played the leading role. With one or two exceptions, these social changes happened fairly peacefully, but only after very long discussions indeed. However, there was a new element – a good deal of mockery and laughter. This was the ideology of the youth movement: playfulness, fantasy, 'down with all those serious and solemn autocrats'. This was the generation that had been brought up with the funny books by children's author Annie M. G. Schmidt and the TV shows they inspired. A former schoolteacher, Schmidt advocated a mild 'naughtiness' in children, autonomy from adults who pretend to be stern and ever strict but are hypocritical and childish themselves. The books of this beloved and ironic grandmother-figure have been published in translation worldwide, but for those who do not know her work, perhaps the title of a posthumous collection of her writings says enough: *'Never do as your mother tells you!'*

More humour has come into Dutch public culture since the 1960s. Irony, satire and self-mockery became part of political campaigns and social movements, even of advertising, and this is appreciated by the public. A very popular art-form in the Netherlands is *cabaret*, a kind of one-(wo)man show with a mixture of laughter at the pomposity of the 'authorities', bits of philosophy, a song here and there, and lots of mockery at the Dutch themselves, including the audience. The rather ironic comments on other social groups that we mentioned previously also appear in this art form. At times, the cabaret participants explore the limits of taboos and political correctness by exposing hypocrisy on sensitive issues like racism, discrimination and religion. Over the years, this has caused several minor scandals, with some people writing critical letters to the press and others defending whatever stance had been taken. But once again, remember that criticism here is appreciation in disguise!

Inspired by such entertainment, Dutch television commercials also tend to use humour and mild social criticism, several of them winning awards at international festivals.

To summarise: the honesty and effectiveness of criticism and outspokenness in Dutch culture is considered far more important than the status of either the speaker or the person commented upon. As long as basic standards of common decency are respected, virtually anything goes – as long as it is likely to lead to some improvement. Other people's right to think in their own way should be respected, and harmony should be maintained. But Dutch standards in this area may still surprise people from other countries, causing a difficult debate in an increasingly multicultural society, as we will see later on.

1. For an extensive overview, see *Dubbel Dutch* by Kevin Cook, Kemper Conseil, Voorburg 2002.
2. Over recent years, several fatal incidents of alcohol-related 'random violence' have caused great upheaval in Dutch society.
3. In the 1600s, half of all the books published in 'Holland' – and there were many – dealt with religion and theological debate!

Chapter 6
PRAGMATIC, RATIONAL AND MONEY-MINDED

'They do everything at the most convenient time.
...They are practical; there's nothing that can't be arranged...and everything
here is done with one eye on the diary.'
(Portuguese singer Fernando Lameirinhas in a song
on the Dutch: *Os Holandeses*)

'Dutch disaster relief is very well organised and efficient,' observed a
Belgian news reporter a few hours after the tragic Enschede fireworks explosion in May of 2000. It's fairly typical of the Dutch:
'There may be a great deal of emotion and political uncertainties
involved, but first let's do what needs to be done; let's remain
practical.' (Some time later, of course, people complained that it
wasn't all that well organised. But they were Dutch...)

Without a doubt, the Dutch are pragmatic people, with a highly
developed sense of realism in combination with down to earth-
ness. Dutch art reflects this attitude. In the 17th century, artists
such as Rembrandt and Vermeer painted common people engaged
in their everyday activities, and in the 19th century Van Gogh
painted poor peasants. In the 20th century, Mondrian became
famous for his colourful grid patterns, which could be interpreted
as abstractions of the Netherlands' man-made, rational landscapes
with flower bulbs and canals. The Dutch art scene has also produced a number of surrealist painters who do not leave out a single leaf of a tree, or one feather of a bird. But these are not taken
as seriously by art critics and professionals of Dutch design who,
in contrast, consider extremely basic functionality a sign of good
taste. Even in Dutch homes and hotels, you generally find modern,
clean design rather than frills.

In literature, too, the Dutch seem to have more of a turn for
prose than for poetry, and their prose is usually realistic, expressing everyday concerns, rather than fantasy. In recent years, 'con-
fession literature' has become quite popular. As its name suggests,
this type of literature describes true but mostly unspectacular
events in the author's life, often in great detail.

A Russian translator has a rather poetic theory: *'Dutch people*
have to consider every step they take; otherwise they run into a wall, a
fence, and a corner. They are forced to be concrete, and they actually like

the concreteness produced by their lack of space. But at the same time they want to break out. Look at all those canals in Holland, they fade away into endlessness.'

Indeed, the Dutch like concreteness, and they are good at it. In line with the inclination to task orientation, they tend to focus on content and purpose. At work, the issue itself is always more interesting than the people involved. No nonsense, 'just act normal and be useful.' Practical aspects, such as time schedules, prices, and other concrete conditions are dealt with in great detail verbally, on paper and in action. In Dutch society in general – outside the immediate circle of one's family and friends – this rather functional approach to other people – rational and unemotional – prevails. This is especially striking to people from cultures where such a brain/heart separation is not so strong – remember the Spanish comment on 'milk in their veins'. It may lead the Dutch to overlook 'external' aspects such as personal contact, prestigious appearance, ceremony and circumstance. Typically, when in 2003 Amsterdam lost some ground in the European City Monitor (a listing of European cities' attractiveness to foreign investment), the researching agency (real estate broker Cuishman) commented that the city hadn't kept up too well its contacts with companies already investing.

Granted, the Dutch do tend to get down to business without allowing much time to get to know their counterparts. Within minutes they will zoom in on the purpose of the meeting, the qualities of the product involved, the details of the transaction. Sometimes even fellow Dutch people find this approach too hasty, calling it 'invading the house with the door', i.e. battering the door down rather than looking for the key. Yet it is done all the time, certainly among people working together every day in an office. Not consciously impolite, people can be so task-oriented here that they simply forget that the last time they saw you was yesterday and not five minutes ago: *'Hey, about that proposal you mentioned...'*

In business encounters of all kinds, the Dutch want to get 'past the post' as quickly as possible. Small wonder, then, that after the initial personal contact or round of negotiation, further steps may well be made by telephone or through faxes and e-mails. To business partners from more relationship-oriented cultures, this approach can appear to be impatient and unsophisticated, maybe coming on top of irritation about Dutch directness. *'The Dutch have a trading mentality; they want to see results immediately.'* (Pakistan). And: *'Dutch people have too much of a business mentality.'* (Iran) And at smaller everyday levels: *'In shops the Dutch behave as if to say "if you don't buy it, don't even touch it."'* (Spain)

There is a tendency, then, to go for easy quantity rather than for more time-consuming quality. Luckily, the Dutch make up for this by being trustworthy and punctual in their follow-up. A common compliment heard is that the Dutch are trustworthy in their commitments and agreements. Promises are taken seriously; they will not be made for the sake of politeness. A promise is an unwavering commitment and a test case for personal integrity, so small wonder they are most always followed up. When the tables are turned, the Dutch are obviously quite indignant when the other party doesn't act likewise. 'They say yes, but they act no!', a rather inexcusable contradiction to any Dutch person.

In their leisure time the Dutch are quite fond of philosophising, but during work hours they do not appreciate vagueness, 'castles in the air', or talk that they consider is not down to earth or relevant. The Dutch appreciate a clear vision, and that vision may be quite creative or idealistic, but in the end it should lead to practical, measurable effects. An American businesswoman boiled it all down with the term 'Newtonian', meaning analytical, rational, calculating, unambiguous, 'brainy'. It implies facts and figures, measures and weights, statistics and computations – calculating probability and estimating outcome. Behind it lies an appreciation of a rather strict separation of emotions and rationality. The rather positive Dutch word used for this serious attitude is *nuchter*, (pronounced 'nurkhter'), meaning 'matter-of-fact' but also 'sober, without alcohol'. Later on we will see that there are a lot of *nuchter* people in the Netherlands, in every corner of society.

But all this rationality obviously has its drawbacks, too. A Dutch business consultant who worked in the US comments: *'The Dutch carefulness has its advantages but also its disadvantages. It goes at the cost of speed and the willingness to experiment. I am convinced we could make more of it if we let ourselves be guided more by passion and intuition rather than this rationality again and again.'* Such a change of attitude is hard to achieve, and there may not be the American speed here of coming into action (easily felt by the Dutch to be brash and inconsiderate), but still some foreigners do notice experimenting and unconventionality among the Dutch. '*This country has guts, a vision. That is what made it present in the world, present everywhere, I find this very much "Holland". No other country this size would even think of building an island in the sea for making a new airport. OK, the plan didn't materialise, but that's not the point.*' (Belgium)

A lot depends on the scale of the observations and also on the arena in which one functions. Vision also plays a role in Dutch companies. Companies and managers with a clear vision – and the skills to communicate it – gain respect from their employees, which translates into support and enthusiasm if properly transferable into pragmatic actions.

Achieved status   Rationality and pragmatism have other effects, too. In more relation-oriented cultures, business people may like to position themselves by hinting at their good education, their prestigious family background, their power as a boss, or their good relations with politicians. This approach doesn't appeal much to the Dutch; it makes them feel uneasy. In fact, they tend to find such positioning and posturing irrelevant and a waste of time, probably even pompous, cocky and slightly corrupt. Such overtures will weaken your image rather than strengthen it. It is the *product* they are interested in, the transaction, the successful business deal. If your product is good and the price is right, they'll be happy to trade with you.

In Dutch business culture, one's own performance is the criterion that counts, not any assets one might have inherited. Things may be different in private life, but at work one's status should be achieved, not acquired. Using family backgrounds, friends in high places or other forms of patronage to make your way to the top is disapprovingly called using 'a wheelbarrow', i.e. someone else's relations. This is not always easily distinguished from networking, which certainly has its place. One effect of this reliance on self-struggle is that well-to-do people in the Netherlands may prefer to keep their children on rather tight budgets, for example, while they are students. In this way, they are not spoilt but have to fight for themselves and, thereby, grow strong. In a more extreme example, the small aristocracy – recognisable to the public by very long family names – usually choose to shorten their names in public so that they do not stand out.

In business encounters with the Dutch it is therefore advisable to stick close to the current concern. It would benefit you not to dwell on ancillary subjects such as history, philosophy, or the wonderful architecture of the city, certainly not before the negotiations are finished. A short, pleasant side remark is more than sufficient. Further, don't spend more than the absolute minimum amount of time on your personal background, and only casually mention any prestigious contacts outside of business. Of course, most Dutch people are polite enough to go along for awhile, but they will probably be wondering why you are bringing up all these extraneous things …you're here on business, aren't you? Otherwise the sour comment might be: 'Fried air' – a slang expression denouncing pompous talk or useless objects.

So, within minutes of beginning your meeting, present your product or service, speak of its qualities, stress its usefulness for the customer, bring out the prospectuses, ask the other party's specific needs, show them how you can meet these needs, answer their questions and mention the price. Your Dutch counterpart will not say it out loud, but will probably be thinking, 'This is the right person to deal with – clear and direct, coming to the point!' And don't be surprised or dismayed by critical questions. Remember that to the Dutch nothing can ever be perfect!

Don't think, however, that the Dutch shrink from philosophical discussion, debate or having fun. They like these things, of course, but it is generally felt that they belong outside of business hours – afterwards at the golf club, at a company reception, or in the break of a management-training programme, for example. As the expression goes, 'Business comes before the girlfriend'. Status and hierarchy are quickly considered rather irrelevant 'girlfriends'. When visiting factories of a Dutch company in a tropical country, I was told how local workers were surprised to see their Dutch managers rolling up their sleeves when a machine broke down. Not afraid of getting their hands dirty or oil stains on their clothes, they did the job that 'needed doing' rather than losing precious time by getting the person whose job it really was. When it comes down to it, be equal and be pragmatic!

Waste not!   An important part of the pragmatic approach to business is, of course, money. The Dutch proverbially take the Scots as examples of tightness with money, but the Scots, and people from many other countries, point to the Dutch as classic examples of stinginess. English language has long had the expression 'going Dutch' (more on this in the paragraph on page 107), while Belgians, in particular, tell quite a few jokes about the tight-fisted Dutch. The following quotations are from another perspective: *'It is striking how there's always a price tag attached here. In Holland, people immediately ask what things cost. Whether it is the shortage of prison cells, a new railway line or a UN-building in The Hague: "How much will it cost?" That is a kind of stinginess you also meet on a small scale.'* (Germany) And: *'Sometimes I find the Dutch very, very mean. I sometimes feel they're only thinking of money and how to save it.'* (Norway) Foreigners from various countries comment with dismay on the fact that in department stores and railway stations they have to pay for using the toilet. My defence, that at least those toilets are kept clean, doesn't seem to console them. (I was happy to find out that one often needs to pay for this service in other countries as well, such as Germany and Switzerland.)

Company hospitality   As many expatriates discover, the Dutch can be pragmatic to the point of being rude. Let me give the following illustration. Some years ago, I worked with Belgian people whose Brussels branch office was in the process of being merged with the Dutch office to form a common Benelux-office of their American-owned firm. They had arranged accommodation in a rather splendid city centre hotel for my colleague and me. When we thanked them for this, they told us, *'We always arrange that hotel for guests, also for our Dutch colleagues when they come here, and they appreciate it very much. But when we come to their out-of-town office in Holland, they make us stay at this nearby motel....'* I'm not sure if I succeeded in convincing these Belgians that this had perhaps more to do with pragmatism than with stinginess.

It is true that the Dutch are money-minded. Seven centuries of trading must have penetrated the national psyche. The act of negotiating and getting a better price represent fun to the Dutch – very serious fun. When I asked a group of expats what they thought was the most striking aspect of the Dutch, one German immediately said: *'business attitudes!'* Places like auctions, flea markets and second-hand shops are popular for satisfying this need. Over the last 30 years, 'Queen's Day' (April 30) has been celebrated with a kind of public garage sale on the streets, and most people love to participate!

Some nations may challenge fortune by gambling; in contrast, most Dutch people prefer safeguarding the future by steady saving and bargain chasing. Saving is still widely popular and always has been. The large Dutch banking sector rests on capital accumulated in the past by frugal citizens and merchants. In the 17th century, Amsterdam was one of Europe's main financial centres, and it ranks today as fourth, preceded only by London, Paris and Frankfurt. Given the low interest rates in recent years, people now prefer to invest their money in real estate. Earlier wild adventures in the stock market had to be paid for dearly, so most people now choose the old, solid funds represented on the Amsterdam Stock Exchange, the world's oldest! The total amount of Dutch savings and investments runs into inconceivably large figures. In spite of the great wealth, old habits die hard. The Central Bank calculated that the Dutch still save more of every rise of income than Britons and Americans. This is not true for everyone, of course. During the prosperity of the 1990s, many people got used to spending, with consumption often based on re-financed mortgages. Now that the boom is over, quite a few such people run into trouble, having to sell their houses and, increasingly, also having to change their whole lifestyle, perhaps with the help of specialised budget control agencies. With the price increases related to the introduction of the Euro, many people economise on household expenditures, on holidays and on weekend activities – as supermarkets, hotels, restaurants, cafés and travel agencies duly notice. Some economists say this negatively affects the attempts at economic recovery.

Government economising   Wanting to prove to taxpayers that it spends the tax revenues wisely, the Dutch state has been vigorously economising on all kinds of activities ever since the 1970s. The 'General Chamber of Audit' is an important government body in this matter, and after the presentation of new government policy every September, the ministries must account for their actions and financial policies.

The money-snake may bite its own tail, however. Due to years of economising on academic studies, the Dutch health care system, once one of the best in the world, is now jeopardised by a serious shortage of doctors and specialists. The technological standards are still excellent, but there is a serious waiting list problem. Similarly alarming stories can be heard about vocational training and other types of education, where large classes, overworked teachers and too little personal attention for increasingly problematic children are widespread. Beyond health care and education, the integration of ethnic people into Dutch society – a related and hot issue – is also hampered by decreasing government funds. Also, cultural life (theatres, music venues) is threatened by subsidy cuts. Yet, with the decrease of the welfare state and the increase of free market principles leading to lower taxes, it looks as if government economising is here to stay.

Pennywise Not only do the Dutch save money in bank accounts or through share portfolios, they also do it in smaller ways. When you shop in a Dutch supermarket, the cashier may routinely ask you, 'Do you have a bonus card? Do you save air miles, stamps? Do you participate in our saving scheme?' Trying to bind increasingly opportunistic and less loyal younger customers to their brand with discounts, air miles and saving funds is a popular ploy of supermarkets, department stores and petrol stations these days. Other retailers have customer cards entitling the holder to reductions and special shopping evenings. But the traditional savings stamp is also still around; older generations were accustomed to cutting out and saving small gift coupons from products such as the most famous brand of coffee, and some people still do.

In all cases, the motivation is the same – to feel that you are being a smart consumer by saving money! Whether small-scale in private life or large-scale in the business world, the Dutch clearly like to bargain. In reality, it's a sport, and one expects the opponent to be equally cunning – and one is proud to win. Again, the task at hand is the whole purpose, and any hurt feelings are mere side effects. An old complaint about the Dutch, made by an English observer who apparently struck bad luck both at work and in private life: *'In love and in commerce, the fault of the Dutch is in giving too little and asking too much.'*

Although the Dutch may not exactly take this as a compliment, they would probably think, 'Too bad for him, he should have bargained better!'

In the Netherlands, one's profits – like salaries – are a well-kept secret, but many people may mention a good purchase price as proof of their trade skills. This not only occurs in business but also privately. Large expenses are carefully considered beforehand – in government, in business and in the home – and bargaining is to be expected. So, in the unlikely event that your sales price is quickly accepted, you are surely selling too cheaply!

Following the biblical advice on 'using one's talents', however, Calvinism taught that profits should not lead to aimless enjoyment. Loans and credits for frivolous purposes were also frowned upon, let alone gambling of any kind! In short, one should save and only spend what has already been earned by virtuous hard work. The message was – and to a surprisingly great extent still is: 'Do not borrow money; always pay cash.' Today, withdrawing money from cash points is more common than using cheques or credit cards, to the dislike of some expatriates. The banks stimulate this and 'tele-banking', of course, since it costs them less. This also plays a role in relation to e-commerce, because so far this has not become as popular here as one might expect. As a rule, Dutch people don't really trust e-commerce very much, doubting whether it is safe to pay electronically by credit card, and wondering if the product will be all that they say it is. Despite that cautiousness, e-sales are rising.

The cash orientation may have resulted from worldwide Dutch trading through the ages – in regions outside any banking network, thereby stimulating immediate payment in cash or kind.

Generosity   Yet there are paradoxes even when it comes to money. In contradiction to its reputation, this nation that eagerly accumulates money and saves it, can also spend it just as easily on other than itself. Dutch expenditures on international schemes such as development cooperation, relief funds, UN peace missions, ecological projects worldwide, and so on, represent one of the highest percentages of gross national product in the world. Privately, too, the Dutch raise large sums of money in televised fundraisers for all kinds of charities. Local and international charitable organisations raise enormous amounts of money. It should be noted that over a certain amount, such gifts are tax-deductible, but that only stimulates more generosity. By the same token, collections on the streets, although not deductible, usually raise quite a lot of money. *'Yep, the people in general and the companies are tight with money. But of course, there are exceptions to every rule – some of my colleagues and at least one friend are far more generous than anyone I've ever met.'* (USA) A lady from Mauritius, having lived in the Netherlands for some twenty years, told me, *'I have come to the conclusion that the Dutch are not stingy after all. They just hate to waste anything.'*

'Waste' – that is the key word. Traditionally in line with Calvinism, as we have seen, one did not spend for enjoyment; one saved or re-invested. Still today, if the Dutch find an expense to be necessary, useful, or well worthwhile, they will spend; if they find something to be luxurious, extravagant or superfluous, then they don't. This is reflected in advertising, where a low price is often more strongly stressed than aspects like quality, technical specifications, status or usefulness. Only in ads aimed at the top levels of the market is the price argument less prominent.

Money is not the sole incentive   Although salary and other financial 'perks' are important incentives for Dutch managers and employees alike, many people try to find a working environment that offers more than just good material opportunities. They also seek personal fulfilment, self-development and a sense of usefulness to society or the world. Many Dutch people value these things more than an absolute top-level salary. Even in a slower labour market, companies might consider what distinguishes them from their competitors, e.g. what can they offer as an extra motivation; what is their mission in the world or their contribution to a better planet? What do they have to offer to young employees in the way of intellectual challenge?

Of course, with the general prosperity and relaxation of moral attitudes since the 1960s, spending has become easier for the Dutch. With ongoing low interest rates, Dutch households currently have more loans for immediate consumption, but the average family debt of some € 4,000 is low from an international perspective. By and large, the Dutch are still great savers, certainly more so in harder times. The extensive and internationally successful Dutch banking and finance sector is based on large amounts of money tucked away in bank accounts, and in property. With stock markets hardly moving, shares are of course less popular than some years ago.

The Dutch like to 'keep an apple for thirst', as they say. The privatised government workers' pension fund (ABP) is one of the largest investment funds in the world, quite disproportionate to the country's ranking in the world population. But pension funds also suffered from the 2001 stock-market slump, and there is some concern about future generations' pensions, especially since the Netherlands' demographics will reduce the number of active people in the labour market.

One might wonder what the point is of all this money-mindedness in a country as rich as the Netherlands. The expression 'going Dutch' and the one on 'love and commerce' (both British in origin) are some 300 years old. Thriftiness is a trait deeply rooted in the Dutch character, and it is fairly obvious that it can be traced back to Calvinist sobriety. This also manifests itself in the attention paid to the environment where 'Don't waste!' is the creed. Besides national policies on this issue, most individual households contribute by separating paper, glass and organic waste, an initiative stimulated by TV and radio spots saying: 'A cleaner environment starts with yourself.' Over 90% of all glass and paper is recycled in the Netherlands today, and the recycling industry has grown tremendously. There are even street receptacles for old clothes and shoes. Not everyone is environmentally conscious, of course; some people still litter the streets and dump rubbish, even in areas of natural beauty, but this is very much frowned upon by most others.

Consuming less   Wealth and conspicuous consumption are not to everyone's liking. A number of people in the Netherlands consciously refuse to live conspicuous lifestyles. Whether for environmental reasons, in solidarity with the poor in the Third World, as a protest against 'over-consumption', or in combination of these things, such people may opt for less income and a simpler life. A few abandon their often well-paid careers, seeking ways to make what they see as a more useful contribution to society. They may look for jobs in health care, education or social work, either part-time or as a volunteer.

One couple proudly calling themselves 'the Misers' even began publishing a magazine for like-minded people called

(in Dutch) 'Enough – The Non-Glossy Lifestyle Magazine'. It offers
tips and hints on how to lead a simple but healthy and pleasant
life, with articles on such topics as recycling, vegetarian cooking,
do-it-yourself, how to adjust to a sober lifestyle, how to react to
hostility or misconceptions from the outside world, and so on.

These largely practical attitudes of the Dutch are in line with their
sense of equality and their general directness in conversation. The
religiously inspired sobriety of yesteryear is becoming a thing of
the past. Nonetheless, there are still a number of somewhat
ascetic aspects to Dutch culture, in spite of all the good life found
in cafés, restaurants, amusement parks and on the party circuit, to
name a few. It takes generations of new attitudes and habits to
change a precept so ingrained, but it is slowly transforming.

Food A good example of the previous discussion is food. Some
foreigners – depending on their origins – are enthusiastic about
Dutch food, particularly the fresh vegetables, hearty soups such as
erwtensoep (pea soup), dark bread, and the variety of milk and
cheese products. But they generally share a complaint about meat
in the Netherlands. *'You Dutch seem to care more for saving money
than for quality. It is hard to find a good piece of meat here, and fruits
and tomatoes look very good but are not tasty. I generally notice that the
Dutch don't seem to ask for good quality, so the shops don't supply it.'*
(Belgium) And from a more strongly Latin country: *'You Dutch don't
find food interesting; for us Italians it is much more important. Put five
or six Italians together – serious business people, good friends, whatever
– and in no time they will be discussing food. Not the Dutch, they have
other ways of enjoying themselves.'* (Italy)
Traditionally it's true – food is a topic that relatively few Dutch
people bother to discuss. In a way food was (and in some circles
still is) seen simply as the fuel necessary to keep you fit to perform
your duties – so, from the Dutch standpoint, there isn't really that
much to talk about, is there? In their own defence, the Dutch may
point out that they have a long life expectancy, generally enjoy
good health and, on average, are now –officially! – the world's
tallest people. So it follows that their food and eating habits can't
be all that bad, but this functional approach to food will, of
course, only corroborate foreigners' ideas about Dutch attitudes
toward food. And in households, indeed, more and more ready-

made food and take-away dinners are consumed, especially by 'yuppies' and 'dinks' ('double income, no kids').

In recent years, however, the Dutch have started to appreciate good food more and more, and several Dutch restaurants have been awarded the famous Michelin stars – some with even the maximum of three. In fact, quite a few people have made cooking – both local and more exotic 'slow food' – a hobby. Nonetheless, foreigners living here are not impressed. Based on observations in company canteens and 'snack bars', they conclude – wrongly, I must say – that deep-fried, high-cholesterol snacks are 'traditional Dutch food'.

Dutch traditional food   Let's take a look at Dutch eating habits and what are the traditional foods found in the Netherlands. Dutch weekday dinners are usually brief and simple and eaten at around 6.30 p.m. The standard traditional meal – typical home fare hardly ever served in restaurants – often starts with soup, followed by a rather small portion of meat with rich portions of potatoes (boiled, fried or mashed) and one type of vegetable. The meal is rounded off by a simple dairy-based dessert like yoghurt or custard. In winter, rich stews with sausages provide energy for cold days. Today, however, such standards are becoming more and more rare with younger generations as more intricate recipes fall by the wayside in favour of either pre-cooked supermarket dinners, or Thai and Italian food.

Most foreigners aren't too enthusiastic about Dutch traditional food – if ever they get to taste it – but quite a few people appreciate the dark brown bread, even when they think Dutch meals do focus too much on bread. Dutch pancakes, pastry and cookies also have foreign admirers.

However: *'Lunch here is like a second breakfast,'* some people comment on this generally sober meal, which basically consists of different sorts of bread, thinly sliced meats and cheese, and milk. For extras, a bowl of soup, a hot snack, a salad or a piece of fruit may be eaten.

In general, long meals are considered a waste of time, so it's hardly a surprise to learn that Dutch business people have the shortest lunch breaks in Europe. Their concept is that there is always work waiting, so there's no time for a long leisurely meal. In company canteens one can observe people from all levels of the company (though not usually at the same table) eating a quick, simple lunch of sandwiches routinely brought from home – maybe only buying soup, a hot snack or milk. Not only schoolchildren or factory workers but also people in business, banking and government can be seen carrying lunch boxes from home, in line with the Dutch character of practicality, thrift and a refusal to play into hierarchy or status. Working lunches are usually even more Spartan. *'Dutch lunches during meetings consist of soft bread and milk.'* One last complaint: *'There are no pub visits here during lunchtime.'* No, definitely not for alcohol, which is prohibited during work time.

All the same, it wouldn't be fair to think that the Dutch are unable to enjoy good food. Every city has a variety of restaurants that are well frequented by more than tourists alone. On the home front, many Dutch people take pleasure in good cooking and enjoy preparing extensive dinners. Yet it is still uncommon for most people, especially outside the Randstad, to have dinner in town more than perhaps once a week, or to prepare a four-course meal at home. As in many cultures, busy family life and evening obligations often preclude this as an option, as we will see later on.

Since the 1960s, eating out is no longer exceptional, but given the decidedly sober nature of their cuisine, the Dutch tend to prefer more exotic and other ethnic food. In fact, truly 'Dutch' restaurants are a rarity. Cuisine from the four corners of the world can be sampled in all the larger cities and, when people are invited for dinner, chances are that a foreign recipe will be chosen rather than a Dutch one. Nowadays, supermarkets not only sell traditional Indonesian ingredients, but also Thai, Indian, Mexican and others. Large numbers of Turks, Moroccans and other nationalities live in the Netherlands, and food from these countries is widely available in 'ethnic' shops, also appreciated by quite some local customers.

If a Dutch business partner does take you out for dinner, be prepared that things may not always go in the way to which you are accustomed. *'They kept us sitting at the table all evening, while we were still jet-lagged!'* (USA). Be aware that, in the general European tradition, eating out is an event that can go on until late at night and is usually accompanied by 'meaningful conversation'. In the Netherlands, as in much of Europe, eating out is a pleasure that is not to be rushed.

Here are some other complaints that I hear regularly: *'There is only mineral water available in restaurants, for which they charge you.'* And: *'I was surprised that dogs are allowed into restaurants here. I have two dogs myself, but in Japan that's not allowed; they find it unhygienic. ...But I have to say that dogs here are well-trained. They don't bite, they don't bark and they don't make a mess.'* (Japan)

One final cause for complaint is that although smoking in restaurants and other public places is no longer officially allowed, with the general Dutch casualness regarding the law, in many places this is ignored, certainly when the restaurant caters to a more artistic or intellectual crowd, it seems. Rather than risking an unpleasant discussion, you may prefer to take a table near the door for better air.

'Going Dutch' For those not familiar with this term, the English expressions of 'going Dutch' and 'a Dutch treat', both imply splitting the bill in a restaurant, with each party paying his or her own share. The sour undertone is said to originate from long-forgotten Anglo-Dutch hostility in the 1600s. Judging from foreigners' comments, I have the impression that this custom is diminishing, yet this quotation from the same German observer mentioned above is fairly recent: *'You go for dinner somewhere and afterwards all expenses must be calculated ..."He drank one beer more..." Terrible!'*

Is it really that bad? I'm afraid that the Dutch will not agree. They 'go Dutch' when they feel equal, when differences in position or income don't play a role, if no special event is being celebrated and no courtesies whatsoever are necessary. Such a 'non-occasion' is apparently what the German observer witnessed. And incidentally, people making a fuss about one extra beer – and they do exist – are also frowned upon by the Dutch.

In the first edition of this book, I offered this quote from an American: *'I like the smallness of things in Holland. Everything is small here, even the sky-scrapers.'* And probably a little less appreciative perspective from Iran: *'Everything is small here: the shops, the refrigerators, the houses, the toilets, the showers.'*

Well, things are changing; a desire for bigger things has clearly come about. Keeping up with the international Jones's – creating bigger companies, demanding bigger salaries, bigger cars and even bigger buildings – seems to be the current trend. In the footsteps of Rotterdam, both Amsterdam and The Hague are constructing mini-Manhattans.

In smaller businesses outside the large cities, low profile and old-time simplicity are still appreciated. But in the internationally-oriented big business that many readers may encounter, things have changed. Traditional sobriety has been shaken off in this age of wealth and globalisation and, although people may have to be a bit more careful right now, the tendency toward luxury has definitely caught on with handmade suits, expensive cars, antiques, designer clothes and furniture, world-class office buildings with state-of-the-art architecture, etc. Elsewhere you will find what might be described as 'elegant low profile'. And although things may look, and be, expensive these days, it is considered better taste to spend the money on technical quality and careful design rather than on ostentatious details. The remnants of Calvinism?

Well, the enormous salaries and bonus packages some CEOs negotiated are anything but a remnant of Calvinism, but the widespread indignation over them was a clear reminder of where this country comes from. Significantly, however, the protests didn't change anything in the companies' generous policies.

Also breaking with national tradition, some Dutch designers and architects are producing truly non-conformist and extravagant creations. Striking buildings are springing up among otherwise boring suburbs, and there is a burgeoning market for ultra-modern furniture and household articles. Several young, avant-garde Dutch fashion designers are enjoying great success – even in Paris – but the clothes they design, of course, are worn almost exclusively at flashy, jet-set parties. Still, Dutch design isn't usually focussed on glamour. 'Humour is typical of Dutch designers,' says Italian design expert Giulio Cappellini, 'just like their sensitivity to what consumers want and need. They don't just do things for themselves; they really consider the consumers. And they also have a keen eye for detail.'

The more middle-of-the-road Dutch public have mixed feelings about glamour and elegance. On the one hand, their low-profile pragmatism leads them to disapprove of, or even mock, other nations' lavish architecture and stylish fashion, ostentatious street life and highly emotional nature. But it doesn't take a psychologist to see that, at the same time, they envy such 'joie de vivre'. This is why so many of the Dutch eagerly travel to such high-culture places, happily joining in with the local way of life.

Recent (and unusual) hot summers brought out this other side of the Dutch character. An American friend of mine, back in the Netherlands for the first time in several years, noticed the many convertible cars that have suddenly appeared on the roads. *'In this climate?'* she asked dubiously. Yes, people driving convertibles here would like to believe that this is a Mediterranean country. Similar disbelief can be expressed about the growing number of sturdy Jeeps and Land Rovers in a flat country with about ten miles of dirt road which, for environmental reasons, are closed to motorised traffic anyway. Further, there is no deep snow to tread through here.

Despite such examples to the contrary, pragmatism usually rules. A Dutch scientist jokingly raised the following thesis: *'European unification may take a long time as long as Italian raincoats are elegant and Dutch ones waterproof.'* A lady who returned to the Netherlands after living abroad for years adds, *'It's hard to stay elegant when it's raining and there's gale force seven!'*

Expenditures for pleasure is a bit less among the Dutch nowadays, but people who are perceived as underprivileged 'victims of circumstances' can still count on help from the Dutch public. Even animals, landscapes and some inanimate objects can also benefit from assistance here. Whether sports projects for the disabled, campaigns against child labour in faraway countries, the survival of environmentally vulnerable nature here or in the South Pole, or the repair of dilapidated museums in countries even Dutch people rarely visit, Dutch support spreads far and wide. Such support is given both through private donations and by government financing, and deeply satisfies the Dutch. How useful!

Of course there are the critics who point out that assistance is given on the condition that at least part of the money is to be spent in the Netherlands, or that the rain forest just saved may be the travel-loving Dutch person's next holiday destination. But such suspicious views receive far less publicity.

Backgrounds and counter currents   Dutch expatriates living in the tropics tend to romanticise the laid-back pace of life there with references to the ever-warm climate. The Netherlands is not the tropics – no one needs to tell you that. With the environmental conditions here, i.e. the constant struggle against water, hard work and forward planning are critical, particularly so in the past, but still also today. Having won this battle (so far), as a whole the Dutch are self-confident about this ever-present threat, with an optimistic feeling that they have their fate in their own hands, and can exercise a positive influence on life and society if they only 'try hard enough'. Generally speaking, Dutch people don't harbour gloomy feelings about life, and there is no Dutch equivalent of the Portuguese *saudade* or any other type of fatalistic outlook on the human condition (although international terrorism is also a concern to virtually every Dutch citizen, of course). One might even speculate that this self-confidence also explains the waning of religious faith in recent decades.

After its birth in late medieval northern Italy, Renaissance thinking – with its appreciation of rationality, individual achievement and practical experimentation – soon reached the trading cities of Flanders, with some influence farther north. During the civil war against the Spanish, Flemish Protestants – many of them merchants – fled north, bringing the Renaissance way of thinking with them and greatly enhancing northern entrepreneurship.

The 17th-century wealth of the Dutch republic stimulated scientific experimentation, and the many Dutch inventors of those days included the engineer Stevin, the mathematician Huygens and the physicist Van Leeuwenhoek. The Republic also produced famous maritime explorers and cartographers. At that point, rationalism took hold in the Netherlands. The French philosopher Descartes came here seeking the political freedom to write on this theme, producing works that would not have been tolerated in his own country. Together with the rationalist philosopher Spinoza and the lawyer Grotius, these (and many more) people, analysing and attempting to overcome the problems of everyday life, contributed to the economic and political needs of the Dutch republic.

Throughout the centuries, the high average level of education of the people of the Netherlands stimulated an unemotional, pragmatic approach to life, and this conviction ensured that such a life led to social and individual well-being. This is still true today. By tradition, the Dutch mind-set is geared for rationality and clarity. The tendency to categorise and define the countless phenomena in life is a general human need, but the Dutch seem to take it quite a bit further than many other cultures. Expressions of this can be seen everywhere – in architecture, dress, working methods, and the landscape. In general, the Dutch are not very good at dealing with ambiguity and ambivalence. They like clear definitions, categories, straight lines, and sharp divisions between this and that. There's actually a Dutch word for it: *hokjesdenken* or 'thinking in boxes'. It does have a tang of disapproval to it – a suggestion of petty-bourgeois attitudes – but the phenomenon itself is widespread. In spite of the paradoxes that people from other countries note in Dutch behaviour and society, the Dutch perceive themselves as 'logical', 'clear', and 'unambiguous'.

Even so, there is a trend towards irrationality, emotionality and 'non-box thinking', even in management, where training bureaus offer seminars and programmes on how to bring about and handle 'irrational processes', which supposedly stimulate creativity, innovation and, therefore, profit. And among the general public, Fortuyn's political movement, as well as the emotional reactions to crime and even the sentiments of 'reality TV', are felt by some to be signs of increased sensitivity, less cold rationality, and more outspokenness.

This counter-movement has a history of its own. Mondrian and Rietveld are known for their cubist styles, but ever since around 1900, intellectuals and artists in the Netherlands have also rebelled against too much rationality and 'squareness'. Several painters and authors moved from (super-)realism to surrealism, while architects started breaking away from straight lines and box-like buildings. Significantly, a famous Dutch short story[1], published in 1931, describes a drab society where a dictator orders that everything be square. In the end the people rebel and demand a return to roundness.

Later, with some success, the 'youth revolt' of the 1960s and 70s tried to break open the clearly-defined 'boxes' in Dutch society and the Dutch way of thinking (much like the youth in the US using the word 'square' to indicate everything they opposed!).

Social pluriformity and non-conformism increased with mass prosperity, resulting in more and more 'box-crossing'. Many people wanted to, and did, break free from old conventions and restrictions, whether social, political or economic. This obviously confused and irritated more conventional and older people. Also, new conventions quickly replaced the older ones, with almost just as much pressure.

In the previous edition, I wrote that the trend would probably increase under the influence of the non-linear virtual world of Internet and the CD-ROM. But a counter-trend seems to have set in, due to increased social insecurity, with a call for more order, strictness, rules, clarity and control. That brings us to the next chapter.

1. *Blokken* (Blocks) by F. Bordewijk (1931).

Chapter 7

PROCEDURES AND PLANNING

'Governing implies foreseeing.'
(Dutch saying)

A finely tuned machine *'The Dutch have a very clear idea of how they want to arrange society, but they're very modest about it.'* (USA)
Most non-Dutch people see the Netherlands as an orderly country. Indeed, with its long, straight ditches and canals, rectangular fields and neatly laid-out suburbs, the landscape does look organised. Thanks to the soft subsoil, even the electricity cables, which in many countries are carried across the countryside on ugly pylons, are tidily buried underground. Roads have orderly shoulders, traffic signs indicate not only towns but also children's playgrounds, and built-up areas have clearly defined limits and do not gradually fade into the surrounding countryside.

Society, too, gives an impression of being highly organised: the trains generally run on time[1], you can practically set your clock by the weekly refuse collection, and essential services such as water, gas and electricity rarely fail. Whether one appreciates this or not depends on personal taste, and probably also on one's experience back home. Two comments: *'There is a certain order in Holland that makes things easier. Society functions well and is also quite stable. If the government changes, nothing else really changes. This order leaves you free to develop yourself the way you want to.'* (Chile) And from another side of the same continent: *'Even inside the house everything goes on schedule: dinner at six, coffee at seven. In Surinam we eat when we're hungry and we drink when we're thirsty.'* (Surinam)

As a whole, the Netherlands can be seen as a finely-tuned machine where rules and regulations, permits and prohibitions, time schemes and spatial planning all contribute to keeping the economy running smoothly and to promoting the well-being of the 16 million people who live here. But such intricate machinery is delicate and vulnerable: if one thing goes wrong, a chain reaction of other events follows. A single road accident can cause traffic jams for miles around, a delayed train might upset the rail network over a wide area, and a bulldozer digging in the soft soil can damage electricity cables and bring an entire town to a standstill.

The Dutch may be pragmatic but they are also careful and process-driven, tending to think twice before jumping into action. The idea is that everything can be under control and 'makeable' if you just try hard enough. But the drive to perfection combined with pragmatism may lead to all kinds of exceptions and specifications. This explains the bureaucracy in which 'special cases' such as expats and other foreigners (together with former Dutch citizens who are no longer in the system) can easily be stranded.

Bureaucracy in a lenient society Foreigners sometimes see Dutch society as an amazing mix of personal freedom and official bureaucracy. The freedom issue will be discussed in the next chapter, but first I want to look at the bureaucracy in Dutch life.

One complaint that expatriates frequently make concerns the *red tape* they have to face when applying for residence and work permits, when exchanging their driver's licence or taking an exam for a Dutch one, or when requesting that electricity, gas, cable TV, etc. be connected. But once they settle in, it may not be so bad after all, as an Australian pointed out: *'There is a lot of bureaucracy, but it seems to work here.'*

Indeed, the Town Hall, the 'aliens police'², service companies … even banks and estate agents all require paperwork, and it is frequently necessary to make several visits to their offices during often limited working hours. People tell me of frequent 'Catch-22' situations where getting one paper is not possible without the other and vice versa. Birth and marriage certificates must be sent from the home country and translated by an authorised translator if they happen to be in an unknown language. Assistance from the relevant company's personnel department helps, but cannot prevent all the inconvenience. Companies are now pressing the authorities to speed up the procedures for admitting badly-needed workers from abroad, but with only limited results in these days of increased safety checks on migrants and travellers. Even in an economy requiring foreign expertise in some fields, a foreign manager pressed for time does not take precedence over an asylum seeker who is not even allowed to work. The same rules apply for all: 'Draw a number; wait your turn; come back next Friday, please.'

On top of all this, quite a few people who are unaccustomed to the system become irritated by functionaries such as bank employees or shopkeepers answering '*Dat kan niet*' (That's impossible) if they request some transaction apparently out of the ordinary. *'Any question I seem to ask is responded to with the words, "No, that's impossible."'* (USA). Quite a few people perceive this as hostile. Now this may be cold comfort, but usually it isn't blunt unwillingness. The Dutch, being 'Newtonian' and taking things literally, will respond to *exactly* what you asked – that particular option. Not very customer-oriented to begin with – and perhaps unaware of your unfamiliarity with Dutch ways – they will let *you* come up with an alternative, to which they will again reply 'yes' or 'no', 'possible' or 'impossible'. The correct translation of a Dutch 'no' or 'impossible' might read: 'I'm sorry, but we don't have that particular version (colour, shape, size, solution, procedure) right now; why don't you try next week, or see my colleague around the corner.' Admittedly, this is easier to accept when searching for a tin of peas than when applying for a residence permit.

Another Dutch word that also puts foreigners off is *verboden*. When speaking English, most Dutch people will translate this word as 'forbidden', because the two words seem almost identical. In fact, what they actually mean is the less harsh 'prohibited'. This linguistic error may easily irritate English native speakers, reinforcing their concept of the Dutch as blunt. I can only suggest that you try your luck with bureaucracy elsewhere in the world, and then come back here and try again. Red tape in a foreign country is always harder to handle than in one's own country – and certainly for first-time expatriates this can be exhausting. But even when taking this into account, the Dutch 'impossible' still sounds rather forbidding, and occasionally it is meant to be. Foreigners wonder what the reason is behind this Dutch drive towards seemingly constant registration and control. Before going into that aspect, we will explore the implications of the issue a little further.

Expatriates may not realise that they are not the only ones who run up against Dutch bureaucracy. Even the Dutch themselves were shocked when it became known that details of the average family are registered in over 900 computer files. Quite a bit of it is voluntary, of course – at auto service stations, supermarkets, banks, insurance and health organisations, service suppliers and

Internet providers, as examples. But the Town Hall, a wide range of government institutions, tax and social benefit authorities, your employer and many other institutions also 'keep track of you'. Small wonder that a law on privacy explicitly forbids all of these computer files being linked. Judging from a number of hilarious cases of insurmountable bureaucracy – where linked computers might well have come in handy – the law seems to be working. Later on we will see how the Dutch can accept such apparent shackles on their precious freedom.

Freedom and equal rights for all Dutch law reflects the basics of Dutch culture: it is equal for all, it has an open eye for anyone in underprivileged positions, and it follows strict rules. So the law tends to be on the side of weaker parties, such as employees (rather than employers), house renters (rather than owners), and victims rather than culprits. But with its legalistic and 'correct' approach, Dutch courts sometimes evoke public irritation. Lack of hard evidence and illegally obtained material have even allowed terrorists-beyond-any-doubt to be released; tiny procedural mistakes have led to obvious criminals being set free; and the psychological circumstances of the accused can lead to sentences which – in public opinion – do not at all reflect the atrociousness of the crime. Moreover, legislation is not always up-to-date in the face of social changes such as rising violent crime, multicultural diversity, or all kinds of digital sophistication and high-tech developments. But the law is the law in this procedure-oriented culture, albeit that the small scale of the nation also creates quite a few unwritten laws, which are much harder to recognize for outsiders.

Economic control In the economy too, rules, regulations and norms abound and there are controls in place everywhere. Weights and measures, licences and qualifications, percentages and time standards, quantity and quality – they are all controlled and registered, by officials who are rarely corruptible and do strictly administer the letter of the law. Besides ISO-norms and the like, there are strict regulations on the ecological, legal and taxation aspects of work. Needless to say, labour conditions are highly regulated too: safety and hygiene, time limits on working with computers or driving trucks, quality standards and ergonomic aspects of machines and furniture. The height of office chairs, the time spent behind the computer, noise levels, air quality – these are all prescribed and checked. A researcher discovered, for instance, that Dutch office workers have more direct daylight on their desks than many of their colleagues elsewhere. Such is the labour law.

Employers often despise all these regulations that indeed protect the workers but also cause hindrances and bureaucracy, so the laws are quite often eluded, especially by smaller, less visible companies.

All in all, setting up a business in the Netherlands is not an easy endeavour, neither for foreign companies nor for the Dutch themselves. In recent years the process has been somewhat simplified, and self-employment is stimulated by agencies helping new entrepreneurs to deal with the red tape. In spite of less rules and restrictions, starting your own company is still a complicated procedure and many new small businesses fail – and not only because they misread the market. Given the emphasis on the correct diplomas and, therefore, the proper knowledge, it is not easy for people to move from one line of business to a completely different one here. Since people are supposed to be experts in their fields, bankruptcy is considered downright embarrassing, making it difficult to regain the trust of investors. Sadly, the number of bankruptcies is quite high these days.

Young people may prefer the relative safety of being an employee as opposed to being their own boss. There are few fields left, however, where there are no legally laid-down regulations. Even hitherto totally 'free' professions such as the real estate business have come under official supervision, requiring licences and being subject to quality controls.

But, as the Dutch found out, the act of 'deregulating' services, which were under stricter state control before, isn't always advantageous. There are plenty of general complaints about prices going up after privatisation, about businesses using recorded messages with impersonal instructions ('dial 1 for this and 2 for that') rather than a compassionate human being on the other line, about deteriorated transport services (if not discontinued altogether), about the limited opening hours of post-office counters, about the increasing difficulty of cashing money inside a bank office rather than from an ATM outside, and many more aspects.

Rules on building   Foreigners notice a lot of uniformity in new Dutch suburbs. These days, industrial and office buildings look very much alike all over the world; to many people's dismay, the Netherlands is no exception. But many newer residential areas clearly show that there are limitations to the degree of imagination that both architects and homeowners can apply to buildings. Obviously, there are budget restraints and a large number of technical qualifications to consider, but that's not the whole story. You may own a place, but strange colours, designs totally out of keeping with the rest of the area, and other too fanciful creations are neither allowed nor appreciated in Dutch society. To keep things in line, architects have to present their plans to a municipal 'aesthetics board' consisting of colleagues, local politicians and interested citizens. If their designs are too 'loud', the creators may be told to go back to the drawing board. Likewise, homeowners are obliged to obtain permission for any and all additions to a house, such as a balcony, extra room or rooftop extension – even a garden shed. If they don't, authorities are very likely to tell them – in court, if need be – to remove it, regardless of how much the homeowner has spent on it.

Comparing this to the haphazard architecture in his own country, with some appreciation an Egyptian called this Dutch policy: 'regulated privacy'. You can generally tell when crossing the border from the Netherlands to Belgium which country you are in merely by observing the architecture of houses!

Only in fields such as ITC and the arts, as it happens, can the limits of totally free enterprise be fully explored. Non-Dutch people are usually flabbergasted to learn that even the establishments in the Red Light District are regularly checked under the health and safety regulations and that prostitutes are obliged to pay taxes accordingly, as are the 'coffee shops' that sell cannabis (both discussed in the next chapter).

'Control freaks'?   Coming back to more familiar terrain, when dealing with the Dutch in business and after working hours, you will soon find that most of them are very 'precise' people. They handle things with great concentration and a keen eye for detail, applying regulations and procedures consciously (on paper) or unconsciously (with time, daily activities, etc.). They themselves use terms like *Pietje Precies* ('Peter Precise') for individuals who overdo it, while some foreigners call the Dutch 'control freaks'. Others appreciate this trait. *'Everything here is based on time. Two o'clock is two o'clock, not earlier, not later. I like it; it's easier. You know how things will go and you can plan your day better.'* (Zambia)

Many non-Dutch nationals observe that there are fixed procedures, apparently, for just about everything – that there seems to be little room for improvisation, for simply taking life as it comes. Not everyone, including me, likes this regularity: *'I feel Holland to be cramped, claustrophobic. Everything is cultivated, over-organised. You can't lose your way, even in a forest here you keep seeing signs like: "To pancake restaurant turn right."'* (South Africa).

At work, too, the Dutch are highly structured. Time arrangements and planning are important, verbal and written agreements should be followed up, written rules applied, and details not overlooked. In negotiations, the Dutch have a reputation for arriving well-informed, and they expect their counterparts to do the same! Some comments from widely different cultures: *'If something is not written down on paper, it doesn't exist in Holland.'* (Spanish director of an art organisation).

'In my country (Cambodia) most things are verbally agreed – in talks. Here everything is put on paper and planned long beforehand. Then you start working. And if you don't meet the planning, you have failed. In other countries they think: tomorrow is another day.... The culture around meetings here is quite strange to me. They hold meetings on every subject and everything is discussed ten times over.' (Cambodia).

A Russian businessman working with Dutch people in Moscow adds, *'Compared to the Dutch, Russians seem to me rather less organised and purpose-oriented.... It is more likely that a Russian would behave in unexpected ways – positively or negatively – than a Dutchman.'*

More flexibility Some years ago an American complained, *'Many organisations here are rigid. They are old and structured and it is very hard to change anything in their procedures. It is very difficult to convince people to change.'*

Without pretending that *all* organisations have now improved on this point, it should be said that things have generally changed for the better, especially in the business world. In the face of increasing competition on the European and global scene, many companies have restructured. 'Become flatter and more flexible' is the message. (In government, deregulation is also taking place, although some say it could still go a lot further.) Moreover, a more market-oriented and flexible younger generation is gradually entering the business world. So things do change, but people from American-style countries with even greater flexibility may still perceive Dutch companies and the labour market as quite rigid. A remark by an American in my course: *'They must follow the structure. There is no creativity; they don't ask for anything.'* But also a Turkish businessman perceives a lack of creativity, adding, *'There seems to be only one way here – the way they first learned.'*

Local people may not be in agreement with this, but these observers have a point. When the Dutch have a problem, their natural reaction is to change the procedures, not the personnel (remember they are hard to dismiss). The result is that, after a long process in which the pros and cons of every proposal are carefully debated, those same people will be applying new procedures instead of the old ones. These new procedures are intended to make things better, and one can only hope that, in reality, they are indeed more efficient than the old ones. This may seem quite contradictory to the pragmatism described in the previous chapter, but the Dutch see it differently. By thoughtfully creating the structure of an activity – taking into account all possible unexpected circumstances – they feel that they can create an optimal setting for its actual functioning.

Inefficiency   In the chase for perfection, new procedures or computer systems can bite their own tail, however, such as creating new kinds of bureaucracy or causing even less customer service. A few examples:
• Applying high-tech procedures in order to attain economies of scale, replace costly personnel or reach efficiency, but reducing customer satisfaction and taking the soul out of business;
• Organisational restructuring that mostly pleases the consultancy firm involved;
• Creating inefficient trends, like decentralising in this decade, back to the former mode of centralising in the next …and then the pendulum may swing again, each phase creating its own bureaucracy (but also jobs, of course);

- Although computer-generated, of course, scrupulous book-keeping makes Dutch companies three times slower than American companies in publishing their annual figures, which obviously does not stimulate fast reactions to changing market conditions;
- Lack of coordination between different departments that are all immersed in their own procedures, e.g. opening road surfaces over and over again for pipeline and cable repairs required by different municipal departments, and other incompatible systems between semi-independent departments that need to cooperate.

Meetings An American in my course said quite some years ago, *'In the company where I work, I exclaimed, "For heaven's sake, let's stop talking about it and DO something!"'*

I wasn't around of course, but I'm sure the Dutch looked up from their discussion with some confusion as to what this man was talking about. They *were* doing something, something very useful! Surely they felt that thoughtfully talking over the problem would serve to avert potential mishaps – so they were, in their minds, being very productive. To the Dutch, 'talking' is not totally different than 'doing'; it is an important and integral part of it. Foreigners constantly complain to me that *'all these meetings keep them from working'*. That's where the deep misunderstanding arises since, to the Dutch, meetings *are* work. In a good meeting, the ground is set for the actual job – all its implications for everyone involved and every department affected …input and output, all possible objections, the worst-case scenario, etcetera.

Therefore, Dutch meetings are highly structured, with fixed agendas. In other cultures, people may come to agreements and decisions over a good lunch or while chatting in the corridor, but in the Netherlands it is carried on in sober meeting rooms, over coffee and water. Someone is appointed to chair the meeting, and sometimes an extra 'time-watcher' is designated. The minutes of the previous meeting are briefly discussed before new points are raised. Minutes of this meeting are taken and will be distributed and discussed at the next one. This is the ideal, preferred way to the Dutch – orderly, democratic and, they are convinced, leading to greater efficiency. In a way, meetings are viewed as a scale model of reality: 'Let's talk it over before we actually do it, so that nothing can go wrong.' They are seen as boring but effective.

While meetings themselves follow fixed procedures, they also tend to produce *more* procedures in order to satisfy the various views given by the participants. As a result, it may take quite some time before compromise is reached. Dutch meetings can last a long time. In broad perspective, the higher the job and the larger the organisation, the more time is spent on meetings. In firms directly geared to production and marketing, this amount is generally lower than in companies serving the public more indirectly. Yet on average, it ranges from some 20% of a manager's work time in smaller companies to 50% for CEOs in larger ones. A researcher calculated that meetings cost the country some € 14,000 million a year. But they lead to more or less harmonious work relations and give some egalitarian status to the individuals involved, i.e. 'We all matter!'

In recent years a speedier decision-making process has come to be appreciated and stimulated, especially in 'fast' sectors like ITC. But in more traditional industry, many non-Dutch people think that decisions still take far too long. In spite of what the Dutch see as more efficient procedures, apparently not much has changed. People from various other European countries keep making observations like: *'Isn't it all too democratic?';* *'They like to discuss for hours.';* *'Consensus is time-consuming.';* and *'Each discussion is a real meeting with an appointment and a kopje koffie (*cup of coffee*).'*

As indicated by the latter quote, the Dutch tend – when speaking English – to call any kind of get-together a 'meeting', from a friendly talk between two colleagues to rather tough negotiations with an external party. After all, they are meeting someone, aren't they? When speaking Dutch, however, people tend to use a wider variety of terms to indicate the exact nature of the occasion.

Generally speaking, the Dutch feel that this all leads to good end-products, solid quality standards and satisfied workers who feel involved, but outsiders may be shocked. *'There are so many procedures; to me they are a stumbling block. There is not much give and take here.'* (Singapore) On the contrary, there *is* give and take, but it all happens during those meetings. The real negotiating takes place *in* meetings, not beforehand in the corridors, although alliances, of course, may be sought there as well. *'In meetings, there is endless talking from everyone, with no clear ends or actions.'* (France) All I can say to that is, 'But *we* have very short lunches!'

Further, the procedures of Dutch meetings can be confusing – to the locals as well. Topics may reappear on the agenda several times, for example, and real decisions may be postponed. Given the importance of teamwork, all participants usually stay present throughout the entire meeting, since they may bring forward a new and relevant aspect of an issue that isn't their concern as such.

In spite of perhaps long discussions, the participants *do* have clear ends in mind. It may indeed take a long time to reach, but the eventual decision should be optimally satisfying to all parties involved. Much depends on the discipline of the participants and the particular chairperson. If the parameters are not strict enough, topics may take far longer than expected and resolutions will have to wait until the next meeting. Given the often outspoken opinions, it may take more than one meeting before everyone is convinced that this or that compromise is the most acceptable. The Dutch may use the word *masseren*, i.e. 'massaging', for this slow process. Even when a decision is finally made, people coming up with new arguments can reopen the whole discussion. *'We reached consensus at the meeting, but the next day an e-mail was sent saying that they disagreed.'* (US businessman). One Dutch person must have been thinking: 'Wait a minute, we forgot to take into account that ....'

Time and agendas   *'The Dutch are perfectionists; they are too strict in their demands. I also find them rigid in their dealing with time. To them it becomes an end rather than a means.'* (A Pakistani exporter to Holland)

Yes, the Dutch are rather strict about time. With mobile phones there is no excuse for not calling if you are likely to be delayed. Five minutes late for a personal meeting is no problem, and ten minutes is excusable, but more than that calls for an explanation. In the past, the reason was more likely to be that 'the bridge was open'; nowadays it is traffic jams or train delays. By the way, arriving early is not much appreciated either and the Dutch will just make you wait, since this is a typical example of a 'monochronic' culture, meaning: one thing at a time.

Below the very top of the company, the time allocated to a first business meeting is usually one full hour. But every minute you are late means one minute less of the time that your counterpart allocated to you. When the hour is over, it is over. Other people, who have come to discuss other subjects, will probably be waiting to see your counterpart. 'Monochronic' people are not very good at combining two things at once, unlike those from 'polychronic' cultures such as the Latin world, Africa and the Middle East.

Two different things or two different people at one time make the Dutch uneasy and irritable, in their private life as well. The good thing is that you get your counterpart's full attention when it is your time. During your meeting, other people will be kept away and telephone calls may be put on hold. So, among themselves the Dutch will say things like 'Ah, good, you're right on time!' At some deep level it satisfies the Dutch to be on time or to have things ready at the time appointed or planned. Calendars and clocks play a major role in Dutch society, as do daily agendas.

Virtually all Dutch people, starting when they are still school-children, carry their agenda – a diary or organiser full of scheduled meetings and appointments for both business and social engage-ments. Few things in Dutch life, whether at work or at home, hap-pen without consulting the agenda. 'You want to see me now to discuss a proposal? In half an hour I can spare a few minutes. …Ah, you need longer than that? Wait, I'll just check my agenda.' (Behind this is the absolute resolution to avoid overtime and be home early, as we shall see later.)

It wasn't quite this bad some twenty years ago, but since then, everyone's life, it seems, has grown into a carefully managed time project. *Druk-druk-druk*, remember?

As a result, just about all companies and organisations provide courses on time management, and many people are obliged to work with electronic agendas in their computer. Another common measure is the precise notation of the time a task was started and finished. This system has extended from paid-by-the-hour profes-sionals such as lawyers and consultants to other jobs and levels in corporations. Such consciousness of time increases people's feel-ing of being pressured, of course, and you will often hear com-plaints of 'stress', exacerbated by this inherent constraint. (More on stress later.)

Time schedules are also strictly adhered to in general society. Coming back to the issue of customer service, one should count on shops and public facilities punctually following their posted business hours. Don't think for a moment that you will get in five minutes sooner, for instance, even when the shopkeeper or official is clearly there already. *'In my country, when you smile through the window, they will open up for you again!'* (Ukraine). In the Netherlands your smile needs to be exceptionally warm because shops opening late or early risk a fine! And if you walk into an office or a shop two minutes before closing time, don't expect the clerks or assistants to fall over themselves to serve you. The shops know the rules, the workers know their rights, and private life is sacrosanct (see chapter 8). If you're late, it's *your* problem.

A Dutch-Turkish journalist described how her British-Turkish husband became doubtful about living in the Netherlands. In a shop for household appliances, they were about to make a very large purchase, but the computer system was down, so the procedure for ordering large items was done by hand. It all took very long, and the couple still needed to buy food before the supermarket closed, so they suggested coming back in ten minutes. The salesman refused this because procedures require that for large orders the customer stay around. In the argument that followed, the salesman shredded the ordering papers and sent the customers off. Procedures before service!

Now this may be an extreme case, but also within companies and between departments, there usually is little customer service – our democratically decided procedures come first, and only then your needs. The Dutch reluctance to 'own a problem' (or even worse, ignorance of this concept) may lead to passing on the issue from one desk to another, driving not only the Dutch people up the wall but certainly foreigners, and provoking 'Catch 22' remarks.

Overtime   *'The Dutch don't like to work very hard; they never work longer than required.'* (Japan) – yet another quote referring to perceived laziness among the *druk-druk-druk*s. Especially at lower levels, it's generally true that people do not work one minute longer than required – work should be done by 5 p.m. But indeed, during those working hours, the Dutch do work quite hard, are quite focused, and normally only take short breaks.

Although the '24 hour-economy' is sometimes promoted, in reality the Netherlands has a 12-hour economy, from 7 a.m. to 7 p.m., and for individuals it is a lot shorter. Shopping hours are limited here, especially when compared to non-European countries, and most people stick strictly to their eight-hour workday. Again, workers are very well aware of their rights and duties. High work ethics and responsibility make them work hard (yes, including those meetings...), but a high appreciation for leisure time plus strong family-orientation mean that most of them stick to the official working hours. 'Face time', the phenomenon in some countries of staying at the workplace just to please the boss or impress colleagues, is almost non-existent in Dutch firms.

Overtime is also not popular, not even *paid* overtime. Senior managers, of course, often work 70 or 80 hours a week or more, taking their work home and carrying notebooks and laptops so as not to lose a single valuable minute. But the habit of requiring administrative or blue-collar workers to work overtime should be kept to a minimum. With flexible work hours in many companies, employees start the day somewhere between 7 a.m. and 9 a.m., and finish accordingly.

If overtime cannot be avoided, the CAO will order that it either be paid or compensated for by additional days off. In organisations forced to make strict economies, payment for overtime might be out of the question, and workers may receive many days off as compensation; however, they may, in fact, have no time to enjoy them. In response to that problem, some commercial firms have now introduced a policy of 'buying back' these holidays, in order not to lose necessary work time.

Stress and burnout   In spite of the Japanese viewpoint expressed above, the Dutch do suffer from stress, and a great deal of it, both at management levels, and among ordinary employees and private entrepreneurs. An estimated 11% of the workforce suffers from stress and burnout (the Dutch use the English terms), and so it is considered a very serious issue. Consultancies organise management workshops and there are even TV programmes that try to assist companies, organisations and individuals in preventing and dealing with stress. Ads in Saturday newspapers promote places such as abandoned monasteries, back-to-basics nature clubs and trendy health resorts as opportunities for people to 'get away from it all'. All in all, stress-related businesses are booming.

Dutch disease?   One could design a stairslike scheme of increasing work pressure as perceived and discussed by the Dutch, but it would not always convince foreigners. *Druk-druk-druk* is still quite a positive concept – a challenge and even a bit of a status symbol. But if this condition lasts too long with a person, it might lead to feeling *stressig*, meaning 'quite nervous', which after some time may lead the worker to report to the doctor as being *overwerkt* ('over-worked'). Probably a short holiday will be advised and taken.

When *stressig* becomes permanent stress, more serious measures may have to be taken, either on an individual basis or – if more people at one location are affected – within the organisation itself. Otherwise the more serious condition of *overspannen* ('overstrain', akin to a 'nervous breakdown') may set in, triggering interrupted work for lengthy periods of time – even up to a year – and probably necessitating a 're-integration program' afterwards. As anywhere else in the world, the final stage of burnout may cause some people to break off their careers, perhaps inciting a whole new phase in their life, even in terms of their private relationships.

The WAO[3]   Stress, burnout and other related disorders, both physical and psychological, are the main reason for *'going into the WAO'* (pronounced way-ah-oh), i.e. reaping the Labour Disability benefit. This benefit, granted to people officially reported as 'sick' for over one year due to work conditions, entitles them to 70% of their last salary for a maximum of two years. Already for many years now it has been paid out annually to numbers of workers ranging between 600,000 and (to err on the cautious side) 990,000. In a labour market of some eight million people, the present number is around three quarters of a million – some 9 to 10% of the workforce – but keep in mind that, in the Dutch system, this figure also includes the severely disabled, those people who could not possibly work if they wanted. Moreover, not all of them are 'in the WAO' one hundred percent. Similar benefits are known in other western European countries, but due to different definitions, international comparison is difficult. Some say the percentage of the Dutch workforce receiving such a benefit is the highest in Europe; others argue that when strict definitions are applied, the Netherlands is not doing any worse than other western countries. Even so, it remains a highly controversial and touchy issue. Set up in the 1970s for strictly work-related illness or injury, WAO has developed over the years into a major 'escape route' for any worker who is medically diagnosed as being 'unfit' for work, whether physically or psychologically. A broken limb, a chronic ache in the lower back, RSI (mouse arm), ME (chronic fatigue) ...they all count. Serious attention is also given to psychological problems – for example, for train drivers who suffer emotionally from people committing suicide on the tracks, or for ambulance personnel confronted with atrocities.

So the numbers of people on WAO remain high all the time. Now before you start thinking, 'The Japanese person was right, they *are* a lazy lot,' remember that in a society where work is highly valued, most people would consider being 'in the WAO' embarrassing. Many people in this position become the object of other people's disapproval, and it often leads to them suffering from low self-esteem, a sense of uselessness or depression. Thus, being 'in the WAO' may make matters even worse and lead to people joining the 'long-term unemployed' faction – a fairly constant number of some 200,000 people, so it's in everyone's interest to avoid that scenario.

In the past, employers speculated on the low work ethic of some Dutch people. At times the WAO system is abused by quite healthy people, of course, some of whom work 'black' or 'under the table' and therefore untaxed, in addition to receiving the disability benefit. Reversing the charge, trade unions point out that it also offers employers an easy way of dumping difficult-to-discharge and expensive personnel. The WAO makes it possible to let difficult or surplus workers go on medical grounds, costing the employers little money since the workers and the state mostly fund the benefit. Whatever the truth of the matter, every time the number approaches the million mark, alarm bells ring in The Hague. Reluctantly admitting that much sick leave always indicates deeper problems within a company, revised plans, projects and policies are launched in an attempt to reduce it. Re-examinations and criteria are made stricter. Companies are sanctioned for letting workers slip into the WAO, and offered a bonus for employing people who are receiving it. As a result, part of the cost is now being charged to employers. Further, there are government proposals to abolish WAO altogether and separate – by 2006 – benefits and conditions for long-term, fully disabled people from partially disabled and temporary cases.

The reality is that some of the Dutch work hard and would like to work less, while others don't work at all and would like to. The misbalance between actives and inactives is widely discussed, but so far policies on the issue have not changed drastically. Also caused by an ageing population, this 'hidden unemployment' is seen as a reservoir that should somehow be tapped, with medical checks and criteria for WAO benefits made more strict. But this will not be easy, since a shortage of doctors makes careful re-assessment of inactives difficult, while not everyone in the WAO is qualified for the complex demands of the present-day labour market. And, of course, a large number of recipients of the benefit are really ill, while others, after years of inactivity, may now lack the discipline or up-to-date knowledge needed to rejoin the present-day labour market. A fairly large element is older workers from other ethnic groups (discussed in chapter 11), while young women also run a higher risk of getting into WAO (chapter 10). All in all, it is a stressful situation for employers, workers and politicians alike. Moreover, it is feared that a similar process of erosion might befall the regular sickness benefit, but let's hope there is more alertness to the problem now.

Planning   Coming back to the time issue, a final aspect of this is planning. The Netherlands is definitely not a 'wait-and-see soci-ety'; the Dutch try to keep everything under control – even the future. In a stable, well-organised society this may not be as diffi-cult as it is in some others, but it still takes careful planning to achieve ...so the Dutch do just that. *'In Holland they prefer to deal with risk as a calculated risk.'* (Russia) The Dutch indeed have sever-al old expressions cautioning care: 'Don't skate on one night's ice', and 'Be careful, so the line won't break'. Additional proof is pro-vided by the fact that all companies and virtually all individuals[4] in the Netherlands have insurance for just about anything and every-thing that might go amiss in life.

In business, the procedure is to allocate realistic amounts of time and money for every part of the future plan and then – as one goes along – to check whether it fits in with the reality of the situ-ation. If it doesn't, the message is: 'Change the plan and reschedule.' Evaluation and analysis are important elements of this process because one can learn from them, especially when the outcome is critical, constructive and brutally honest. (Friendly feedback of compliments such as 'excellent', while polite in some countries, may make one feel good but doesn't really stimulate improvement, and the Dutch do not easily accept such flattery.) Critical and explicit evaluation, on the other hand, is carried out all the time – everywhere – and taken very seriously. In fact, an entire industry flourishes around this precept, with business consultants, policy advisors, interim managers, coaching and training bureaus feeding into it.

Obviously it doesn't always work, but still, the entire process of planning, establishing the exact criteria, monitoring, evaluating, reviewing and then planning anew is the preferred Dutch way. The term for this is *beleid*, an often-used word in companies and organisations alike. It translates as 'policy' but it encompasses not only the aim to reach targets, but also the underlying vision and the practical procedures needed to reach them. It is a very serious thing when in a company, for example, management is accused – whether horizontally or bottom-up – of having a wrong *beleid*, or none at all. This implies that either there is no realistic and/or inspiring vision for the future or, if there is, management did not think through all of its practical implications.

Companies and organisations are therefore encouraged to structure *beleid* and details of it 'pro-actively', i.e. to think in advance of every potential development or mishap that might influence the outcome, so that you can immediately react and adjust the plan to the new reality. The Dutch don't regard this as a particularly unusual procedure; it comes naturally to them. If foreign counterparts try speeding up business by regularly sending e-mails with 'a.s.a.p.' ('as soon as possible'), Dutch people may shrug their shoulders thinking: 'You didn't plan very well.'

Carrying this over to their private lives, the Dutch apply the planning principle by scheming, saving and taking insurance against all possible mishaps. All in all, with money to spend but little time to enjoy it, the concept of 'time is money' becomes 'time is much *more* than money'.

Of course things do go wrong sometimes and, given all the rules and regulations, people will immediately question mistakes. In the past, people simply accepted individuals' and organisations' apologies for mistakes. Nowadays, perhaps under American influence, they may start legal proceedings seeking compensation or damages, particularly if the other party is perceived as rich. But for the reader's peace of mind it should be said that, so far, judges here tend to grant far lower amounts of compensation or damages than their US counterparts do. Although the trend is for people to pursue higher compensations, most Dutch people still smile when they see all the overly cautious directions for use on some foreign products; and if someone trips over a loose carpet at a friend's house and breaks his leg, he or she rarely considers suing that friend for damages. But the tables are turning.

Some context   Overall, the Dutch try to balance countless social, economic, natural and legal aspects of life. Although they do appreciate some challenge and adventure, as will be discussed later, at home they prefer safety and cosiness (*gezelligheid*), full control of their own lives, and security. Living in a small country lacking in vast forests or mountains, there aren't many places where people cannot maintain a semblance of control. *'I don't like the flat scenery here; there are no surprises. You feel like God ... you can control everything and see everyone's activities.'* (Ireland)

Of course, with very few exceptions such as an occasional flood and climate change, the Dutch do have their natural environment under control. Keeping an area below sea level dry and arable implies quite a lot of organising of people, materials and funds, and even the floods are controlled for the most part by dykes and the Delta Plan, a masterful water-control project on the North Sea coast. Present-day water control in the Netherlands involves a mighty ministerial organisation (including regional and local subdivisions) with an annual budget of billions, and highly professional engineers with degrees from specialised universities.

Perhaps this explains how the Dutch became organised initially. One of Amsterdam's oldest buildings, now a popular café, used to be the municipal weighing-house, crucial for traders, where as early as the 17th century, precise lists and schedules were used in commercial activities. Present-day bureaucracy can be seen as a mere extension of this. Whatever the source, the Dutch do believe in control – in security. And government and business are not the only factions trying to achieve such security; individuals (consciously or not) make it their overriding aim – in their finances, their careers, their housing and their households. Dutch banks regularly supply the general public with booklets on how to best provide for old age, how to finance their children's education, and so on, and the Dutch follow their advice. Critically, of course...

Controlled 'irregularity'   So serious is the control issue in the Netherlands that even chaos is controlled here. For environmental reasons some formerly cultivated land is now being given back to nature, bulldozed back into deliberate wilderness. In some places, old river dykes have been broken open to allow the river to return to its natural meandering course and to create safe spillover areas – both of which lessen the risk of floods. Water engineers, biologists and others are involved in the careful planning and monitoring of such processes. It is estimated that between the years 2000 and 2050, on top of the normal budget for water control, the country will need an extra 11 billion euros and 60,000 hectares of land to make Dutch inland waters less threatening and more natural.

Bored by the rectangularity and sameness of suburban building and infrastructure, municipal architects are now creating 'spontaneously' meandering roads, and – oh, what whim! – houses with turrets and other irregular shapes. In new parks and natural areas, small hills are created to break the flat monotony. On a smaller scale, on some of the city's waterways, Amsterdam creates 'natural' rafts for bird, rare insect and plant habitats.

To people from other cultures, all this order may sound terribly boring and calculating (and some locals agree), but most Dutch people see it as a sound and sensible path to the future. And if you don't agree with them, they will point out to you how successful they have been by applying such precepts and procedures – and they have the facts to prove it. As a result of such foresightedness and planning, there is good and fairly cheap education for everyone, long (paid) holidays for most people, a very high rate of car ownership and yet good public transport, and the world's lowest percentage of teenage pregnancies, to name a few consequences. But, you might ask, at what cost? Well, yes, at the cost of detailed registration, specific procedures for almost everything, a host of permits and licences needed, an official stamp here, signatures there, and all the rest of the bureaucratic hassle. And of course, high taxation.

Not everyone likes this fact. *'The state is too strong here; it invades your life with so many rules. But everybody seems to happily obey and pay his or her taxes. I find this strange.'* (From Luxembourg, to my surprise, a country that can hardly be called a cradle of spontaneity itself. But they do have a strong bank secret...) And from a very different angle: *'The state is something big and heavy that lies on top of you here. A friend of mine is pregnant, and these health care people came 'round to inspect the house. She didn't like that, and I told her: "Just tell them NO."'* (Argentinean lady, not realising that in the Netherlands the preferred norm is to deliver the baby with the assistance of a professional midwife in the comfort of one's own home. Health authorities do indeed want to check whether both the mother's health and the general household situation allow for this.)

Given the chance, the Dutch set up private organisations in ways quite similar to those of the state, with plenty of structure, be it street committees, church organisations, charitable bodies or hobby clubs – they all have rules, a president, a treasurer and a secretary to take the minutes and possibly even a time plan with targets. Such meetings are also social occasions, of course, with chatting and always plenty of coffee.

Freedom secured: out of control   Again we come to a paradox, for even Dutch rules have their exceptions! In this (over?) organised country, you will see cyclists ignoring traffic lights all the time (I have to admit I'm one of them), and motorists often overtaking you on the right at a speed far above the legal limit (which I don't). You will see people throwing litter under a sign telling them not to, and dogs being allowed to relieve themselves on the pavement. Plenty are the reports of people cheating 'the taxman', or ignoring safety regulations. Are these the same rule-abiding Dutch people we just talked about? Is this a general decay of society, the breakdown of good manners, a disdain for the political decision-making process such as one finds in many Western countries ...or what is it?

'We (Russians) also have that combination of rationalism and anarchism, so typical in the Dutch. But with the Dutch, rationalism dominates and anarchism is deep down, while in Russia both anarchism and rationality are at the surface.' (Russia)

It may appear to some readers that bureaucracy in the form of rules and regulations is the main goal in life to the Dutch, but it's not, of course. It is, however, or should be, a practical means of achieving and maintaining the security to live the way they want. Once they feel that this freedom is secured, the rules can be set aside. If this doesn't happen officially, people will just ignore them and go their own way. This happens especially in situations where nobody knows you – where your peer group is not around – but generally not at home, not on one's own street, and not at work. This confuses foreigners. *'Some rules are broken; others are not. Why?'* (Britain)

In public, outside their own social box, the orderly Dutch can be quite anarchistic or even aggressive: in traffic, at railway stations, in supermarket check-out queues, in anonymous places which might be 'downtown' or only a few streets away from home. Perhaps it's just an outlet for repressed emotions and creative license. Just like everywhere else, whether people behave badly or not depends on personal temperament, the degree of inner civilisation, the day and age they live in, and many other factors. Many people from other countries (and with them the politer element of the Dutch population) certainly cannot appreciate this style of aggression. *'Dutch people never get out of your way; they are physically close by to you. I don't like that.'* (Australia) And: *'People are pushy here, more so than in Belgium or Germany. People in shops are downright rude.'* (USA) A survey[5] confirmed that in traffic the Dutch are the second rudest Europeans (after the British): 80% have experienced obscene gestures; a large percentage flash their headlights to signal others to move aside; and – what many find the most irritating of all – tailgating (driving much too close to the car in front) seems to be a national pastime. A German who just arrived from a long stay in Italy said, *'The Dutch have a southern way of driving.'*

Some more quotes on Dutch spatial behaviour: *'You cannot move a centimetre here or you run into someone. And all those masses of people, so many people. I sometimes feel like a fish swimming against the current, against all those swarms of people, while I want to watch everything at my ease.'* (Iceland). And: *'Driving is difficult here, with narrow streets and canals, and bicycles all over you.'* (Canada). Plus: *'Dutch cyclists seem to all have a death wish.'* (UK)

After first apologising for any aggression, may I hint at the potential difference in size and population density between the observers' countries and my own, and remind them that a 'comfortable physical distance' is also a culturally determined factor? May I also, without trying to excuse such behaviour, refer back to the paragraph on stress and work-pressure? But fair enough, one sees more and more examples of impolite and antisocial behaviour today, certainly in the cities. Clearly, they are expressions of highly individualistic and downright egotistic attitudes – a disregard for other people's comfort. If anything, the individual culprits would probably come up with vague excuses of 'urgent appointments' and 'stress'. To more critical reproach they may cynically answer, '*Pff*, there are so many things not allowed'. In later chapters we will explore the subtle borders between one's freedom and other people's annoyance in a densely populated country of individualists.

Norms and Values So far we've talked about fairly small-scale trespassing, but in recent years, larger scale ignoring of rules and norms has also occurred, such as the millions of euros of fraud due to silent price agreements among construction firms; some severe accidents as a result of neglecting industrial safety regulations; and numerous cases of employing ill-instructed and illegal foreign workers. This is civil disobedience at an inexcusable scale, combined with material greed and serious disdain for individuals and society at large. Needless to say, all this has led to public complaints by politicians, the media and the general public about the loss of decency and discipline. The Christian Democrats have called for a national debate on 'Norms and Values', referring to the tensions of the multicultural society – to be discussed later on – and also taking in the general concern about corruption, growing violence and worldwide terrorism. But other parties plead for more concrete measures, e.g. in the field of education, in stricter control of public finances and in standards of business.

Background Obviously, there is a background to the Dutch need for control. The major reason, deep down, may well be that the Netherlands is a successful and confident nation, so there is little incentive or stimulus for people to change their ways. And, of course, there's a history to it as well.

Remember the *waterschappen* discussed earlier? Lacking a central government, local inhabitants were forced to set up organisations to build and maintain dykes to keep the waters of the seas and rivers at bay. Everyone's contribution of work, money and materials was recorded in detail. Small-scale solutions were realised in regions where everyone knew everyone else. In drier areas, feudal landlords registered peasants' contributions (and shortcomings) while, in the cities, taxes were levied through equally precise methods. Organisations were in private hands and were basically interested in financial registration – business administration, so to speak – still a popular study today. Reports of meetings of all kinds and lists of contributions dating back to the late Middle Ages are still kept in Dutch archives and museums. The same is true of the cargoes carried by the United East India Company (VOC) and the West India Company, both founded in the early 1600s. Significantly, several Asian languages took their book-keeping terminology from the VOC, while Sri Lanka is still proud of having 'Dutch Roman Law'.

In a way, inhabitants created Dutch society without much influence from higher-up authorities, and apparently some people still sense this. *'The Dutch are very proud of their political culture, of their talent to get things done and to find negotiable solutions to their problems. They have a special feeling for practicality, based on self-confidence and trust in others, authority included. At the same time they know that authorities can make mistakes, too. This gives them a kind of tolerance toward other people's failures, and space to act for themselves.'* (Brazil)

As for civic behaviour, remember that the country was a federal republic. There was neither a royal court nor any other centralised authority setting the overall standard. The ancient nobility (where it still existed) no longer had much influence, and the rich merchants lived a life beyond other people's means so that they could not really set an example either. Cities and provinces enacted temporal laws to define and punish criminal and antisocial behaviour, but far more important than these 'earthly' laws were the norms and values of the Bible, which served as guidelines for most people. This left moral judgement largely to one's religious peer group, and to God, of course. Cleanliness was next to godliness, and this was reflected in the impeccable Dutch houses and an almost hysterical mania for cleaning, which foreign visitors were already commenting upon centuries ago. Even today the traditional open curtains of a Dutch home invite you to 'inspect' how orderly and decent the inhabitants are – a kind of voluntary social control. (Be advised that you may glance in passing, but you are not supposed to stop and stare!)

During these centuries the state was almost absent from people's private lives. Until about 1800 it was the churches that kept family registers. Then, under Napoleonic rule, the state introduced fixed family names and house numbers, and delegated the task of registration to the Town Halls. Gradually, more personal registration crept in. In the 19th century, the Dutch state was dominated by liberals who were against too much state interference, thereby leaving welfare to the churches. But by 1890 this had changed; industrialisation meant that working conditions, city housing and education had to be regulated. First Christian-democratic and then Social-democratic influence grew, and the first social benefits were set up to fight for workers' rights and against urban poverty. Soon, housing projects were set up by organisations affiliated with trade unions, and they needed data on the size of families, income, etc., in order to ensure a just allocation.

During the Second World War, the detailed registration of citizens' private affairs, including religion, made the persecution of Dutch Jewry very easy, with the effect that the post-war generation was very sensitive to too much government influence in this area. In the early 1970s, when the general mood among the intellectual elite was strongly anti-government, a census had to be cancelled because too many people openly refused to take part.

After the social changes which occurred in the 1970s, the political system adjusted and became more democratic. People generally began to trust the authorities again. Until recently, corruption was an exception in the Netherlands, and even now the country does very well in comparison. General wealth makes bribes unnecessary, the state annually accounts for all its expenditures, and anyone can see that benefits are distributed as fairly as possible. Despite all this, public cynicism has grown, partly also as a result of Pim Fortuyn's campaigning. Besides the aforementioned top salaries and bonuses that raised eyebrows, there have been cases of cartel-like fraud in the business world, while hitherto-respected politicians were seen to play power games instead of offering leadership during the profound social and ethnic changes the country is going through.

Further, quite a few people feel that 'other people' abuse their positions, whether as receivers of social benefits, well-paid functionaries or CEOs. Unfortunately, this motivates some to do likewise in order not to be left out of the game, giving the remaining population a rather sad impression of general greediness and lack of integrity.

Local 'abuse' is one thing, but, with increased immigration, there is public pressure on the authorities to combat immigrants' abuse of the social benefit system. Of course there is xenophobia and discrimination also, but don't forget that once foreigners are finally registered here, they also reap the benefits of this system.

All of this plays a role somewhere behind the bureaucratic controls and the distrustful approach from the immigration authorities, the aliens police and the banks, and I do understand the irritations that expatriates feel about all this. Yet it is strange how I never hear them complain about the generous child allowances they receive in the Netherlands....

This brings us to the next chapter, on tolerance and indifference in a pleasure society.

1. I should say: 'again', after a period of chaos in 2002, due to mismanagement and personnel dissatisfaction.
2. This name makes expats feel very far from home indeed, but it is older than the movie of the same title.
3. Wet op de Arbeids Ongeschiktheid.
4. Major exceptions are people from other ethnic groups and some fiercely orthodox Calvinists.
5. Sept. 2000, by Gallup International, interviewing 10,000 drivers in 16 European countries.

Chapter 8

THE PLEASURE SOCIETY
TOLERANT OR INDIFFERENT?

'Freedom = happiness.' (Dutch saying)

Cynicism? Business people who whiz from the airport to a business lunch, from a factory visit to a meeting, and then back to Schiphol airport may not notice the issues discussed in this chapter. But many business people take at least some time to see a bit more of the country they visit, to get a taste of the local culture. Other readers may have been recently posted to the Netherlands, and some may have lived here for several years already. Whichever, no expatriate can fail to notice some aspects of the local culture – in particular, the way the Dutch enjoy life, the apparently unlimited freedom and the liberal attitudes.

Although Dutch tolerance and the amount of freedom are still striking to many foreigners, things have changed a bit in this regard. In various corners of society there is a call for stricter rules, more control through greater law enforcement and, thereby, more orderly behaviour. Various factors play a role here: rising crime, diminishing social manners, fear of terrorism, and the uncertainties of a more and more pluriformous society with less social cohesion. The mood change even strikes the more seasoned expatriates, like this Brit: *'Sorry to say so, but I personally find that the Netherlands has become a less pleasant country. In every discussion on politics, a hard and aggressive attitude prevails, especially regarding minorities. The general picture of Holland as a tolerant and liberal society has disappeared.'*

Before discussing some of these aspects in more detail, let's look at general Dutch attitudes to authority, freedom and pleasure.

Authority As we saw in a previous chapter, Dutch people expect and demand to be able to judge matters for themselves and to make their own decisions. Such autonomous individuals dislike social obligations or any other claims that infringe upon their personal freedom. Financial debt is felt to do this, as do unannounced visits, social niceties and conventions about dress, and the possible demands that dealing with hierarchy might impose. The Dutch wish to be their own masters, only following authorities who have proven to be worthy of loyalty.

This is evidenced by the fact that, although there are more security personnel around than before, one still notices fairly few police officers in the streets and, outside of military barracks, uniforms can only be seen when soldiers travel home. In general, uniforms are felt to be pompous and slightly ridiculous, certainly for people without any real authority, such as waiters or clerks. (Remember: content is important in Dutch culture, not external appearance.) *'People here don't seem to feel much respect for police officers or for people in uniforms. They just talk to them or ask questions. It is all very simple and open, very normal.'* (Argentine) *'Especially Amsterdam is very liberal. But not just liberal, there is a simple logic to it. For instance: riding a bike on a one-way street against the traffic. In the beginning, when I saw someone do that, I thought, "How can you do that!" Now I know it is the quickest way. When I myself did it the first time, I felt rather wicked; a policeman saw me and the officer gestured towards me. So I started apologising, but he just said, "Look, we're coming from the right side, you from the wrong, so move over a bit." That was all! Just plain logical.'* (UK)

In recent years, the police are applying a harder approach, especially in the cities. Yet, Dutch authorities know that they are subject to critical inspection by the public and behave accordingly, i.e. with a low profile. If they can solve problems through calm discussion, they will usually do so, realising that the people with the problem will still be around afterwards. Crime prevention is considered just as important and effective as crime solving. The traffic police announce speed checks on the radio, for example, with the aim of persuading drivers to reduce their speed, as opposed to trying to catch and fine the maximum number of speeding motorists. The same goes for a campaign to persuade bicyclists to repair their bicycle lights.

Preferring to reserve their full powers for more extreme cases, police officers use violence only if absolutely necessary. Such measures are mostly restricted to dealing with violent criminals, football hooligans and the like. The Netherlands has far less police officers or private security guards per capita than many other western nations. Part of this might be attributed to problems in finding suitable recruits but, in my opinion, it also reflects the fundamentally non-authoritarian character of Dutch society. While the Dutch would prefer to keep it this way, they also ask for more frequent police checks on weapons, hard drugs and road behaviour. Under normal conditions, however, the police and other authorities leave people alone, and the Netherlands is a very free country, indeed. There are some limits, of course, but they are broad and determined by laws based on compromise, within which there is much room for highly individual behaviour, and little repression. *'I've worked in many countries – the Middle East, Asia, Australia, the USA – but I like working in Holland best. In no other country do you find so much personal freedom, both at work and outside.'* (Belgium)

Live your own life   In the cities, in particular, all kinds of lifestyles are openly practised, representing wide-ranging political views, artistic tastes, sexual preferences and so on. Such variances used to be more visible in public behaviour, in fashion, and in hairstyles than today, for with an increasingly market-oriented (and smaller) new generation, it seems one now sees less obviously unusual characters on the streets than before. Yet, catering for widely varied tastes, the country is booming with all kinds of parties, discos, festivals, clubs and other venues. Street posters announce wild party venues, but admission is generally linked to membership or restricted by high fees. In today's harder society, people perhaps withdraw more to the privacy of clubs and homes, since Internet makes it easy for people of the same lifestyle to find each other.

In response to people from a clearly different lifestyle, the Dutch may smile, shrug their shoulders indifferently or perhaps criticise sourly, but interference is considered 'intolerant' and is frowned upon. Also, unfortunately, after a number of serious cases of random violence, intervening between violent people and their victims is now considered hazardous. Luckily, there is an abundance of non-violent social and personal freedom most of the time. Comments differ. *'Here in Holland I have space to breathe. I can lead my own life. Nobody troubles me; I feel one among many. I love that freedom. Life here is as it should be. I like the way everybody here is independent.'* (Tanzania) But also: *'There is so much freedom and permissiveness here that sometimes it causes clashes between us and our children.'* (India)

Some years ago, the French *Le Monde* correspondent wrote, *'The Netherlands is not the modern country it loves to be, experimenting with social issues. But it is a country where you can feel free as a citizen on the condition that you can accept the pressure of social control, don't stand out too much and especially behave "normal".'* This social control has probably increased somewhat, considering that it is mostly expressed indirectly (for a change) by avoiding people that one does not like. Now this may sound rather hostile and anti-social, but it also implies the freedom to live your life within your social 'cubicle' – something that Dutch people value intensely.

Fun, fun, fun   As the Italian said, *'The Dutch have other ways of enjoying themselves.'* Indeed, they have. The 1990s saw an enormous growth of what we might term the 'fun sector'. There is a bit less money to spend now, but people still attend all kinds of spectacular events, both for business and pleasure.

Fairs, festivals and fun-parks are meant to attract families with children, but some events cater to quite specific categories of visitors, such as particular ethnic groups, 'techno' music fans or homosexuals. When the event is not quite their 'cup of tea', passers-by will watch with either amused smiles, curious looks or embarrassed glances, but making any overture or taking any action against people with a different lifestyle than your own is simply not done here. With the exception of certain football matches, events take place in a harmonious, non-violent atmosphere, observed from the sidelines by smiling police officers.

Amsterdam   In many people's minds, the very mention of 'Amsterdam' conjures up an image of sex and cannabis, as any Internet search will prove. Every year millions of tourists are attracted to the Dutch capital, with its unusual mix of old elegance and avantgarde lifestyles, and the freedom to enjoy both. *'I prefer Amsterdam to Venice. Venice is beautiful too, but Amsterdam is ALIVE!'* (New Zealand). Amsterdam's inhabitants are proud of their city to the point of chauvinism, while people elsewhere in the Netherlands see it either as an attractive place to do what they prefer not to do close to home, or as a dangerous place full of pickpockets and prostitutes. In Australia, there was even a warning given that Amsterdam is getting too dangerous, but this was felt to be quite ridiculous by the local Dutch. The city does take such signals seriously, however, with the result that increased controls to prevent extreme misbehaviour have led some residents to complain that the mood is less relaxed than before. Others observe that Amsterdam might be losing out to competing cities like Berlin and Prague. Yet foreign visitors still flock to this popular haven to experience freedoms – and culture – that they may not find back home.

With centuries of history as a very international port, Amsterdam offers just about everyone the chance to live the way they want. People from abroad don't always appreciate the 'buzz' here – an American woman in my programme used the term 'raunchy' – but most people are rather fascinated, especially by the widely publicised aspects of drugs and sex – the two aspects of the city's diverse lifestyle that receive the most attention. But if people can stay longer, they soon find out that there is much more to Amsterdam than just this: *'In Amsterdam they like art. ...I appreciate Amsterdam a lot; it offers me knowledge and culture ...it is a cultured city. It is easy for me to live and work here. Especially these last few years, the city is getting more international and I find that people must think internationally.'* (Hong Kong)

'No, coming from Tokyo to Amsterdam was not like coming to a village. Amsterdam has it, Tokyo doesn't. Tokyo is nice to look at, but in an artificial, superficial way. People there are interested only in buying things, clothes especially. Amsterdam may be more gross on the outside, not as sophisticated, but there is more culture ...it goes deeper.' (Japan)

Some of the Amsterdam brand of freedom has spread to other Dutch cities, and even to the countryside. Foreigners react in various modes of amusement and shock, reflecting very much what they are or aren't accustomed to at home. *'We see people at bus stops almost romancing each other. That looks odd to us.'* (Nigerian couple living in The Hague) And: *'A Dutch norm that the Japanese could adopt is the tolerance and openness. ...Seeing something new, the Dutch think, "Hey, that's nice ...maybe we can do something with that; let's take a closer look."'*

Political system: pluriformity   It is difficult to understand this tolerance, this freedom and these liberal attitudes (and this disdain of other people's feelings) without looking at the broad outlines of the Dutch political system.

After 1795, a centralised political system was introduced in the Netherlands, first still as a republic, but soon as a French 'puppet kingdom' under Napoleon's younger brother, Louis. The hitherto autonomous 'states' became provinces of a more unified state. After 1813 it emerged as an independent country again, under the now royal House of Orange-Nassau. By 1848, the role of the king was restricted under the dominance of the liberals, but after the 1880s, several Christian and socialist parties sprang up beside them, each representing a clearly defined section of the population. None ever attained an overall majority, and all governments were coalitions of two or more parties, with each party keeping in mind their own interests and weighing the pros and cons of every proposal. Compromise had to be reached before any action could be taken. Firmly stating one's own position, listening to the views of others, and finally adding 'water to the wine' became the norm. Nowadays, with more than 20 political parties participating in each national election, this is still the case. Some five or six of these parties play a major role at a national level, but locally, others may be important. Most people used to vote for a party that voiced their views but, in the current-day scene, individual politicians grow more important, and their private lives and income are revealed more to the general public. Still, being openly hungry for power is frowned upon. 'Act normal and use your talents,' remember? It's interesting to note that most Dutch politicians are highly educated people with more often than not a career behind them in the national bureaucracy rather than in the business world. This is also due to the large difference in income between the public and private sectors, even though top salaries in both are on the rise.

Pluriformity and diversity were given a fresh start with the rapid social changes that began in the 1960s. In just 30 years, the country saw the break-up of the former small-scale society. The existing, clearly defined groups, with a large degree of personal contact and internal control, gave way to a far more anonymous and mostly urban society where individuals followed very different and often opposing lifestyles.

This was not essentially unique, of course; it occurred in all western societies, but perhaps the effect was a little stronger in the Netherlands. One effect of pluriformity is that there is always at least one party prepared to annex any new social problem or a forgotten group of underprivileged people. They will bring the problem before Parliament and come up with proposals to solve it, trying to find support from the other parties. Then the Dutch carrousel of compromise is set in motion and, if agreement is finally reached, various amounts of money will be allocated to help fund the solution whereby procedures may be changed and committees set up to oversee the whole process. It is, of course, all very democratic and people from quite a few other countries express envy, but in the Netherlands itself it also leads to complaints about 'buying off problems'. Others merely find it 'boring', hopefully recognising a sign of good democracy when they see it!

Lifestyles and _in_tolerance   Individually, people living in the Netherlands can choose from a wide range of lifestyles, based on a combination of factors having to do with class and income, religious and political views, personal preferences and subcultures. People may also participate in all kinds of lifestyle-related organisations based on some joint activity or interest: a charity, some local issue, a hobby, or a particular course of study. Finally, on a more abstract level, many people have long-term subscriptions to a particular newspaper, linking them to an invisible ideological network.

The overall result is a patchwork society in which people half-consciously define themselves according to their affiliations, with covert, in-group feelings of 'us and them'. Under Dutch circumstances, all these groups are minorities, so they are forced to put up with each other. This means that as a whole, Dutch society may appear to be one of great tolerance, but with individual people this is not always the case.

For much of their lives, people stick to their group. Each group has its norms and values, its approved standard behaviour and its frowned-upon deviations. In public, Dutch people don't always openly comment on this, but in private they will certainly make known their opinion on groups they feel to be different from theirs. This is also done in the presence of foreign nationals, often to their surprise or dismay. It may strike them as outright intolerant, or at least inconsistent. _'They think they're liberal, but they are conservative really.'_ (USA) And the former ambassador of South Africa added, _'My personal experience in the Netherlands is that "tolerance" is a rather dualistic concept. On the one hand (and that is so confusing about Dutch society) there is an incredible amount of tolerance. Yet, at the same time people are very quick to jump to strong intolerant opin-_

ions.' Well, remember (from chapter 6) the rather unambiguous way of thinking of many Dutch people: this or that, yes or no, good or bad. It's fair to say that, on individual levels, people may indeed not be at all tolerant. It is only in the process of reaching compromise that tolerance and the ambiguity and vagueness related to it arise. As an American journalist said, *'The Netherlands is a conservative country ruled by liberals. When tolerance starts to hurt, people turn selfish again. ...Besides, it's Humanism; Dutch culture also has a conformist face. This may lead to doing as you're told.'*

An American book on European-American differences[1] states that Europeans define themselves through 'meaningful conversation'. That is certainly true of the Dutch, at least outside the workplace. When making the acquaintance of new neighbours or colleagues, the Dutch like to find out who the other party is and to make clear whom they themselves are by discussing fairly profound or personal subjects and finding out where you stand. This approach can sometimes shock newcomers because the inquisitiveness may involve religious or political subjects, ideas on life in general and the Dutch one in particular, philosophies on society and the modern age – literally anything and everything.

Some foreigners take this to be sheer nosiness – an unpleasant intrusion into their privacy. On top of that, they may see the Dutch as 'argumentative'. Yes, also in private the Dutch like outspoken opinions. After all, you only really get to know someone when you *dis*agree on a subject, don't you? So they use – and are accustomed to – firm statements, which will then be watered down in the ensuing discussion. The pros and cons will be balanced and a common standpoint reached – or, if not, there will be a clear picture of why they disagree. After such a discussion, the Dutch feel that they are closer to the other person than before, and the next encounter may be even friendlier. In many cases, it will take several such encounters before lasting friendship is developed. Perhaps this rather slow approach makes some non-Dutch people complain that it's hard for them to make friends with the Dutch. In return, the Dutch may complain that it is difficult to make really profound contact with non-Dutch people – who's to say?

Nonetheless, having opinions (and stating them) is a must in the Dutch culture. In spite of those 'strong and intolerant opinions', public life as a whole generally gives the impression of tolerance to all kinds of behaviour.

Freedom and non-interference Many factions may divide society, but Parliament and local councils set the overall rules, laid down after lengthy discussion and compromise. The effect is that there aren't really any rules for particular groups, rather a cocktail of differing ideas, respected to a greater or lesser degree by all. I have already mentioned tax evasion, bikers' anarchistic behaviour and the tendency toward pushing in queues and crowds. Other examples are far more serious and, in many cases, truly criminal. For example, sometimes the tolerant approach resulting from compromise is not to the public's liking and, calling it 'soft' and 'ineffective', they may take the law into their own hands. Specific instances include local actions against the establishment of a refugee centre for asylum seekers, and self-organised violent protest against real or perceived paedophiles in a particular area, as well as against drug users' hindrance.

On the flip side, there were also recent actions to *prevent* an asylum seekers' centre from closing down, since the locals began appreciating the newcomers, and felt sorry for them having to move to yet another area.

Taboos   In individual talks with the Dutch, few subjects are taboo. Exceptions might be one's **income** and one's voting behaviour, these being things that most Dutch people prefer to keep to themselves. Mentioning high or low income spoils the myth of egalitarianism, while the casual question 'Who do you vote for?' might be met with an open refusal to answer, since the question may easily be taken as an imposing enquiry about their lifestyle and philosophy.

On a national level, things are even more complicated. From the 1960s onward, one taboo after the other has been broken. Satirical television programmes and certain political groups made jokes about religion, sexuality, the monarchy and other hitherto 'touchy' subjects. At first this often caused scandal, but gradually it became quite normal. Until recently, however, making negative comments about jokes involving ethnic minorities – often in underprivileged positions – was just 'not done' in a society where underdogs are supposed to be supported (more on this in chapter 11). Generally speaking, any *public* remarks on underprivileged people of any kind will be met with some protest, but in more *private* conversations the Dutch are certainly not always politically correct. Even when critical themselves, many Dutch people may not much appreciate *foreign* criticism of the idiosyncrasies of their social and political system. They will easily conclude that 'outsiders' don't know or understand the finer points anyway.

These days, if there is an argument in a café or on the streets, few people will intervene, either out of respect (at best) or indifference (at worst) for the other norms of those involved. Also in recent years, several people just out for the evening have, for no apparent reason, been attacked and sometimes killed by young drunks. This 'senseless violence' has caused great protest and concern in Dutch society as a whole, but apart from demanding more police vigilance, nobody knows what the solution might be. An unfortunate side effect, however, is that, more often than before, people tend to turn their backs on any trouble they spot. The police even suggest that witnesses phone them rather than intervene.

So all this freedom and non-interference posture has a dark side too, and non-Dutch people, especially those from countries with strong local and family ties, notice it. *'Not everyone is like that* (stand-offish), *but most people are. The way of life here is very sad to me. I can't get used to it, no matter how long I live here. All this strong individualism ... everyone to himself.'* (Cameroon) *'The Dutch have a mind-your-own-business type of life.'* (Tanzania) And from a northern culture: *'The Dutch are not easy to get to know, but when you meet and make friends, they're OK.'* (Norway)

The Dutch seek their social contacts mostly within the group they feel they belong to, with people who share their norms and values, their tastes and preferences. This, in turn, may keep them from meeting outsiders, which of course doesn't feel very inviting to foreigners. In public life, they usually mind their own business. Still, people from western countries are sometimes happily surprised. *'Generally speaking, people here are friendly ... not like Paris, where you can live somewhere for five years without knowing the neighbours. Here, people sometimes suddenly ring your doorbell to ask whether you would like to come for a glass of wine. In other countries that happens only by previous arrangement, days beforehand.'* (Italy)

Luckily, I hear other positive stories from people with good neighbours or who have met helpful or friendly Dutch people, but I'm afraid the following observation from an Irish woman is just as typical, especially in cities: *'Here you don't just drop in to see a friend;*

you arrange a meeting and note it in your diary. But every time I do that, I wonder: will I feel like it that day?' And from another part of the world: *'People here are different, more business-like. I have only once visited a Dutch home, for reasons of work, but never for just a cup of tea.'* (Egypt)

Sexuality   In essence, Dutch society leaves you free to live the way you want to live, without much intervention by other people or authorities. On a summer afternoon on Dutch beaches you may see women sunbathing topless without anyone taking offence. *'Nudity is not a big deal here.' (USA)* No, it isn't, at least not in the urban western provinces. And there is more that the Dutch are liberal about. In a survey carried out in 2000, 77% of the Dutch said that they found homosexual relations normal and acceptable, a far higher percentage than in other European countries. In Parliament, a large majority voted to legalise homosexual marriage, and 62% of the Dutch were in favour of this measure. *'When ten years ago I brought Frank home with me for the first time, this caused quite a shock to my relatives in Argentina. The fact that two people of the same sex can openly live together in the Netherlands and might even marry is looked upon there as utterly ridiculous. The Dutch tolerance gives young people space to develop themselves the way they want. This enhances creativity. I notice this with myself. No matter what I do, Holland will face me open-minded. Non-conformism appeals to you people.'* (Argentine)

As further illustrations, childless couples having children by artificial insemination is now commonplace, and Amsterdam's Free University, originally founded by Calvinists, now offers psychological and medical support to people wanting a sex change.

Permissive society?   So many foreigners (including visiting journalists) see the Netherlands as a free, tolerant, and even permissive society. Depending on their own standards, they are amazed, pleased or shocked by the open attitudes. Some are downright critical of all this freedom. *'It is shocking for us to see so much nudity on television and on the beaches. I find this a problem with our children.'* (Malaysian expatriate) In some respects, I do understand their problem. Dutch expatriates in Muslim countries, for example, are also shocked by some things which are acceptable there but not to the Dutch ...so the pendulum swings both ways. Again, it's a matter of what you've been accustomed to in your home country.

Still, quite often the misunderstanding prevails that 'anything goes' in the Netherlands – that Dutch law is endlessly and inordinately tolerant. In reality, it doesn't and it isn't – there *are* limits. Many things may happen out in the open, but this doesn't always mean that they are legal. Often they are officially *illegal* but *tolerated* in practice. One might say that most matters concerning sexuality and nudity are not regulated by Dutch national legislation, since personal freedom is guaranteed in the constitution. Even so, certain kinds of pornography are definitely illegal (which is not the same as non-existent); municipal councils may allow nudity on beaches but not elsewhere; prostitution may be tolerated in some parts of the city but not in others.

The basic idea behind Dutch legislation in such controversial matters is that these phenomena exist anyway, indeed in many parts of the world, whether we like it or not. This being the case, the best thing, the Dutch are convinced, is to try and bring them out into the open and legislate them – to create a generally acceptable and practically applicable framework for dealing with them – a way of combining the ideal (these issues shouldn't exist) and reality (but they do).

Anything goes?   In an article on the European football championships held in the Netherlands and Belgium in June 2000, an International Herald Tribune columnist wrote, referring to British and Turkish soccer fans and Dutch society: '...*a strange match of potential nationalist breast-pounding versus a culture of carefully managed permissiveness, the non-confrontational environment here, may be seducing the street-fighting yobbos of European soccer into non-violence.*'

But the mood is changing. A series of incidents rocked the country in recent years. Drug-trading gangs have been killing each other's leaders, random violence to both other ethnic and Dutch people has occurred, and there were shocking signs of open discrimination both by Dutch people toward members of ethnic minorities, as well as violence and insult by other ethnic people to Dutch homosexuals, women and Jews. People have been saying more and more aggressive things about each other, and Amsterdammers are worried that the city's tolerant climate is eroding.

Witness the fact that in 2003, there was a shocking murder of a frail, female drug addict by a group of ethnic youngsters working in a supermarket who wrongfully suspected her to be stealing. Mayor Cohen gave a public address in which he said, *'To anyone in Amsterdam behaving or speaking in ways which are anti-Jewish or anti-homosexual, intimidating teachers or fellow students, molesting Jews and homosexuals and harassing women or behaving violently against women, I say: that is contrary to everything we stand for in this city.'* To that he added a short overview of the history of these groups in Amsterdam and Dutch society at large.

Drugs policy Suffice it to say that drugs are a 'hot' issue among expats, raising eyebrows and causing a great deal of worry regarding their impressionable teenage children. Granted, the Netherlands is known throughout the world for its lenient policy on cannabis and marijuana. Besides its reputation as a haven for users of these drugs, in recent years the country has also acquired the reputation of being a (or even *the*) major exporter of 'party drugs' such as XTC (ecstasy). Cannabis, marijuana and XTC are indeed easy to obtain in Dutch cities – from 'coffee' shops and street vendors, in discos and at dance parties – and foreign authorities do catch quite a few Dutch smugglers.

But contrary to what foreign media report, neither of these – nor any other drug – is officially legal. But if this is so, why they are so easy to get? Why is it that you never see the police arresting those street vendors or going into the 'coffee' shops?

In such matters Dutch policy is confusing to outsiders (and sometimes to insiders too), by combining legal prohibition with 'turning a blind eye' to users in everyday life. Indeed, there are some misunderstandings to be cleared up here.

Internationally known, this lenient policy applies to what the Dutch call 'soft drugs'[2] only, not to cocaine, heroine and other 'hard drugs'. So *dealing* in hard drugs is illegal and prosecuted, although the (understaffed) police prefer to concentrate on large-scale dealers rather than on petty street vendors, who are usually ignored, hard to control as they are anyway. And individual *users* of heroin and the like are considered medical cases rather than criminals, and they are guided into rehabilitation programmes or otherwise helped to survive in decent ways.

Without a doubt, production and large-scale dealing are not treated mildly at all. Every year the police destroy many small XTC factories and indoor 'hash plantations'. Dutch customs and excise officers confiscate large quantities of drugs, 'hard' and 'soft', and arrest producers and dealers if they can. This happens for the most part in Dutch ports and at border crossings, but also in the Caribbean islands called the Netherlands Antilles, officially Dutch, where there is cooperation with the US authorities in the 'war on drugs'. But Rotterdam is the world's largest port, the Dutch economy thrives on foreign trade, and those Caribbean islands are almost within sight of a number of major harddrug, producing countries. So there is considerable export and transit trade going on over Dutch territory. It was estimated that the illegal export of soft drugs alone from the Netherlands amounts to hundreds of millions of dollars.

When in the mid-1990s a diplomatic row developed between France and the Netherlands over the drug issue, Dutch politicians and newspapers came up with figures indicating the success of the nation's drugs policy in keeping the number of addicts low, in separating 'soft drugs' from 'hard drugs', etcetera. A French journalist living here then told a newspaper that drug use in France is considerable at all levels of society, but hushed up. He added, *'The Dutch reduce drugs to numbers, expenses, percentages. It is a materialistic type of consuming. The French are also materialistic but the Dutch are that in a harder way, without any wrapping. Dutchmen look at things in life in their full nakedness, they see themselves with all their mistakes. The French see themselves less sharply; they keep more of a distance; they soften things and embellish them.'*

Since then, French-Dutch debate and even police cooperation on the issue has resulted in a better understanding of the mutual viewpoints, but it may still be worth considering the quote, because it demonstrates a crucial cultural difference between 'Germanic' Netherlands and 'Latin' France. Remember the term 'Newtonian'? Indeed, the Dutch prefer to face reality, even when it's not pleasant to look at, and totally forbidden fruits may be more attractive than half-legal ones. Whether it's soft drugs, prostitution or euthanasia, Dutch authorities try to limit the problem by actively discouraging the practice, while not prosecuting those engaging in them.

This ambivalent and at times paradoxical policy is described in Dutch with the word *gedogen*, meaning 'allowing'. Unusual measures and experiments to find a balance have been tried; some have been more successful than others, some more accepted by the public than others. The (in)famous 'coffee shops' that may sell limited quantities of soft drugs only, the free testing of XTC pills at discos and house parties, and the relief centre for hard drug users in a Rotterdam church were a few examples, but in the present-day more restrictive climate, such experiments are under pressure or already abandoned. The 'coffee shop' system is under debate by national government, but some local authorities object, saying that forbidding them will only stimulate hard-to-control underground sales.

Dutch law is strict on hard drugs, but unlike dealers, users are perceived as pitiful creatures, more victims than criminals. While most people don't like having them around, the general idea is that they are human beings nonetheless, so they should be tolerated and helped. Welfare and church organisations are working together to help drug users and at the same time limit the spread of the use of drugs. But the efforts to help those addicted are hard to see from the outside, so people from abroad just observe the openness of the 'coffee shops' and the soft drug use, and are generally appalled. Perhaps they overlook the fact that under Dutch conditions, drug users hardly need to hide their habit, whether they are hard-core 'junkies' or teenagers in the try-out phase.

The generally humane approach to the drug user's problem is praised at international conferences on the issue, and most Dutch people are rather proud of this. They see it, basically, as a just and fair system, not flawless, mind you, but the best available, well-considered solution – the outcome of the democratic process and the precious art of compromise. A long-term Canadian expat comments, *'I'm really glad I raised my teenage children here because drugs may be widely available, but the pragmatic Dutch approach to the issue keeps teenagers from doing really dumb things. I'm sure that in another place, one of my kids would have gone much more wildly on drugs. Here they can experiment while they have all the information on the risks widely available, and without the exciting taboos that probably lure them into using them. I see similar positive aspects in the Dutch approach on alcohol and sex.' (Canada)*

Tobacco and tolerance   Far more widespread than any soft or hard drug use is smoking of cigarettes and 'shag' (self-rolled cigarettes). Foreigners were already complaining about this 350 years ago as they travelled through the Netherlands by the world's first public transport, in covered boats that sailed between cities at fixed hours. Some things never really change. A third of the Dutch still smoke, and foreigners[3] still complain about it, as do the increasing number of Dutch people who don't smoke. Statistically, the percentage of smokers rises as one goes down the social ladder. Also, until recently quite a few people in intellectual and artistic circles smoked, but this is rapidly changing due to less public tolerance, much higher tobacco prices and more anti-smoking campaigns. To the dismay of many, however – including expats – a great many youngsters still do start this bad habit, as can be seen in clubs and outside schools. Although smoking is forbidden in companies, in all public buildings and on public transport, the law does not yet include restaurants and cafés, as it does in some other countries.

Companies may still allow smoking in certain places and one-person offices, and you do see people ignoring the 'No-Smoking' signs in public places. Up until now, however, only one legal action has been taken by someone to secure a smoke-free work environment. The woman won her case, but her colleagues regarded her as 'intolerant' and 'fanatical' and she felt under pressure to leave her job. (The lawsuit triggered some public discussion on tolerance.)

My best advice is: if you can't stand the smoke in places where smoking is allowed, the best you can probably do is to either stick it out or leave. Asking the smokers if they would mind refraining could easily be met with disdain and strong words. Tolerance is not always two-sided.

Ethical issues   Dutch consensus usually has an element of 'having your cake and eating it too'. Many Dutch laws on issues like drugs and euthanasia (the so-called 'ethical issues') might be translated as: 'No, this is prohibited, unless conditions 1 through 4 are fulfilled,' or 'Yes, this is allowed, but only if criteria a, b and c are met.' This 'no but yes' aspect of the law may appear hypocritical to foreign observers, but the majority of Dutch people (with the obvious exception of religious fundamentalists) don't feel this way. Legislation and less official arrangements on such subjects are perceived as being finely tuned to the demands of the complexities of any modern society that reflects and encompasses widely different points of view. Dutch pragmatism also shines through. Concerned about potential abuse, researchers discovered that patients to whom euthanasia was administered would have lived, on average, only two – probably very unpleasant – weeks longer. One very critical American opponent of euthanasia offered the view that the whole arrangement was mostly meant to cut the cost of health care, but many Dutch people would term this a cynical view.

The social benefits system   The Dutch social benefits system is built on a rather positive relationship ('trust') between the citizens and the state. Dutch people generally consider the state to be a benevolent organism that is there to serve them. Good governance, incorruptibility and trustworthiness are taken for granted. Citizens pay their taxes and the government secures a good existence, be it smooth roads, a clean environment or good social benefits when needed.

The crucial role of the social benefits system has come up several times in this book. Let's take a closer look at its roots. First, a not-so-positive observation: *'In a society (like the Dutch one) where people can easily get social benefits, even for an unlimited period, indifference will prevail. This seems to me unfavourable, because in fact it means there is too little development in such a society. I also get irritated about the ease with which people on benefits can work "black". But I must admit that occasionally I do something "black" too. It is so tempting, you know.'* (USA) All I can say is: 'Aha!'

Obviously, the Dutch system of social benefits matches old-time Christian attitudes toward the weak in society, but it evolved through state institutions rather than through religious ones. It can be seen as 'mechanical solidarity', organised by and through the state, replacing the old-time 'organic solidarity' within families and church communities, between friends and neighbours. But even in the cities some of the latter also remains – small-scale and unpublicised.

With the industrial revolution (after 1880 in the Netherlands) growing state influence and the emancipation of the working classes resulted in protective laws against 'capitalist exploitation'. First, child labour was forbidden (1884). Soon after, restrictions were put on working hours, and basic assistance was organised for sick or injured workers. Protective laws covered more and more categories of people. At first, only employees of government and private companies were involved. But as a result of the severe economic crisis in the 1930s that brought unemployment and poverty to millions, people also outside the workforce were included, albeit under strict conditions.

After the enormous damage from the Second World War had been repaired, it was deemed necessary to do something to improve the lot of the weaker groups in society. A law passed in 1956 guaranteed a state pension for everyone over the age of 65. In the 1960s, more social benefits were established, especially under the Labour-dominated government of the early 1970s (remember the WAO case).

During those years the prevailing idea was that society is a human construction that could be perfected if people only tried hard enough. Anyone who faced problems, whether through unemployment, drugs or for some other reason, was considered to be a victim of circumstances beyond their control, and deserving of other people's attention and support. Welfare organisations sprang up for all kinds of people, paid for by government subsidies financed by increasingly high taxation.

Since the 1990s the social climate has changed. Society has become more individualistic and there is less emphasis on egalitarianism. There is more praise for 'winners' and less compassion for 'losers'. Many people feel that all these 'victims of circumstances' are 'cuddled to death' by too much welfare, and this greatly influences present-day government policies. People should work for their money, they say, and there is increasing irritation about social benefit abuse.

With the expensive social system being economically detrimental to the country, various governments have worked on reducing it, by economising, restricting the quantity and quality of benefits, bringing down taxation, privatising insurance, etc. Nowadays, the younger generations find it quite normal to make additional private arrangements to cover any future mishap, for old age and the like. The tax system introduced in 2001 will encourage still more individual responsibility, and the present government is heavily economising also on social arrangements which are *not* under public criticism, such as health care, old age pensions and education.

Yet, in spite of the hardening of official policy regarding social benefits, Dutch society will probably continue to be based on some form of collective responsibility for the well-being of fellow citizens for a long time to come. Quite a few Dutch organisations (trade unions, churches, people in education and health care) complain that government policy these days is too much focussed on economic issues, at the cost of the underprivileged and at the cost of general humanity.

With European integration, Dutch permissiveness is coming under increasing pressure from other countries, but when foreign critics cannot convince the Dutch of the superiority of their own approach, they dig their heels in. Criticism is fine, but the argumentation should be sound, unemotional and solidly based on facts. If it isn't, the Dutch will defend their views vigorously, making it a matter of national pride and emotional chauvinism, which are topics in the next chapter.

1. *American Cultural Patterns*, E.C. Stewart & M.J. Bennett, The Intercultural Press, Maine 1991.
2. A term for hashish and marijuana not recognised in many other countries
3. Depending very much on where they come from.

Chapter 9

NATIONALISM AND THE INTERNATIONAL OUTLOOK

'He who wants to be someone should not sit still, but put to sea.'
(old Dutch saying)

Some 700 years ago, Dutch traders were already sailing the seas around western Europe. Nowadays they are trading and doing business with countries in every corner of the world. For business and pleasure, the Dutch like going places. Their small country is home to a disproportionate number of multinational companies and banks operating worldwide, and vast investments are made on every continent. For example, the Netherlands is one of the top foreign investors in the USA. Once ranked third in the world in the field of international takeovers[1], many Dutch firms today export a large part of what they produce, now making this tiny country the world's eighth largest trading nation. As before, Dutch trucking and shipping firms are the great freight carriers of Europe. In banking and insurance particularly, Dutch companies are present all over the world. More than 200,000 Dutch people – not counting those who have officially emigrated – work abroad in countries ranging from neighbouring Germany to far away Papua New Guinea, although it must be admitted that, due to couples wanting dual careers, companies now have more trouble finding people willing to give up their comfortable life at home for an international job with uncertain career prospects.

With its open economy, the Netherlands was among the original founders of the European Union. Ever since, it has advocated further integration, although in recent years Euro-scepticism has set in just like elsewhere, but that seems to be related to the functioning of the EU rather than to the idea as such. People from other countries cannot fail to notice this international attitude. *'I don't know any other country that is so cosmopolitan, so receptive to foreign influences as Holland. It is a friendly, open country where a foreigner feels at ease immediately.'* (Switzerland). And from Japan: *'Dutch people are very open-minded. For instance, in shops one sees a lot of Chinese and Japanese food. It must also be because you speak English so well.'*

Think globally; act locally. That's the prevailing dictate these days. Even smaller Dutch firms are quite aware of the necessity of adapting their products, their advertising and the business behaviour of their representatives in order to meet the standards and the requirements of local markets. In response to these needs, governmental and business organisations in the Netherlands provide valuable export advice; culture and language training institutes cater to the business world; and literature and statistics abound on even the remotest countries.

None of this is new; it is merely the present state of an old tradition. As long ago as the 15th century, the Dutch were shipping merchandise between the Baltic and Portugal. In the wake of the 16th-century Spanish and Portuguese discoveries overseas, the Dutch trading empire expanded to Africa and the Americas, to the Arctic Ocean, to Ceylon and Indonesia, and even to isolationist Japan where the Dutch East India Company (VOC) held a trade monopoly for centuries. It was this first-ever 'joint venture' of Dutch merchants which discovered Australia, and founded Cape Town, South Africa. The West India Company (WIC) founded New York, under its original name of New Amsterdam. All over the world, remnants of this Dutch trading empire can be found – in buildings, in geographical names, in words absorbed into local languages, and in shipping terminology.

In the 17th century – the so-called 'Golden Age' – many foreigners came to study the achievements of the very cosmopolitan Dutch republic. Two famous admirers were Czar Peter the Great, who came here in search of the technology to modernise his navy, and the French philosopher Descartes, who studied and published in the Netherlands. People persecuted for religion in their own countries, such as the French Huguenots and the Jews of Spain and Portugal, sought refuge in the Dutch Republic. The English Pilgrim Fathers found shelter in the Netherlands for some time before they set sail for America. All these visitors and immigrants added to the international orientation of the republic.

At home the Dutch were smug, thrifty and careful, but overseas they found challenge and adventure. In the 19th and early 20th centuries, colonialism was the outlet for adventurous Dutchmen, while today it is international business, development work, military peace missions or international relief organisations that offer such wider horizons.

The world: a market and a holiday destination To the Dutch, the world has always been a potential market and, as everyone knows, to be successful you must know your markets well. Dutch schools spend many hours teaching foreign languages; and foreign programmes on Dutch television – of which there are plenty – are broadcast in the original language with subtitling, most of them in English, which greatly helps both understanding and pronunciation of this language. World geography is taught in all schools, and foreign news is reported in depth in the Dutch media.

Many Dutch people are also well-informed about foreign events in non-commercial ways – through personal contacts and special interest groups such as Greenpeace, Amnesty International and Médicins sans Frontières, each of which have far more members in the Netherlands than in surrounding countries. In an earlier chapter, I mentioned the large amounts of money that the Dutch donate worldwide to campaigns for disaster victims. One effect may be that many people develop a rather gloomy outlook on the international scene. *'Many Dutchmen know much more about Africa and my country than I expected. Unfortunately, they know mostly the negative aspects.'* (Nigeria)

On more official levels, the Dutch government is keen to play a global role, supporting international collaboration not only in the European Union, but also in NATO and various UN peace missions, as mentioned before. At the same time, however, we should not overlook the fact that this country is also the world's sixth largest arms exporter and one of the world's largest importers of tropical hardwoods (which, being water-resistant, is used both in the construction of housing, boats and port equipment).

Lots of leisure time *'This is ridiculous ... Holland is locked in summer. The whole economy comes to a standstill and you can't reach anyone!'* (USA) Yes, and the same is true between Christmas and New Year. Let's first look at the official labour arrangements concerning holidays, and then at how the Dutch like to spend them.

People with full-time jobs usually have 25 days (five weeks) paid holiday a year – an enormous difference from the US, but less so with other western European nations. In some sectors there may be a limit to the number of days that Dutch employees can take at one time – and of course parents must take their children's school holidays into account – but quite a few people can, and do, take three or four weeks off in summer, saving the rest for Christmas or perhaps a week's ski holiday. For people covered by a CAO agreement, a premium is withheld from their salary during the year to be reimbursed as 'holiday money', together with their May salary payment. Even people on social benefits receive an extra payment for a holiday.

'I was told that all construction workers here have to go on holiday at the same time. Why on earth is that?' (Switzerland). Quite simply, the answer is: because it is considered more efficient to completely close down building sites for a few weeks than to work throughout the summer with half of the workers absent. Most other people follow the rhythm set by the school holidays (the country is divided into three zones – each zone having a different, prescribed holiday period). Individual arrangements are made in consultation with one's immediate boss and direct colleagues.

On top of their regular holidays, employees under a CAO-regulated contract may have as many as 13 so-called ATV (Labour Time Reduction) days. This scheme was included in the 1982 agreement that triggered the polder model. Employers then agreed to have people with full-time jobs work 38 hours a week instead of 40, for the same salary. This gave workers a day off every four weeks – thus their 13 ATV-days a year. It was hoped that the accumulated millions of hours of 'work' would create new employment. In the end, as the global economy began to improve, this scheme did indeed help to create more jobs.

Theoretically then, people on full-time contracts can enjoy 38 days paid holiday a year, apart from weekends and bank holidays. Combined with the high degree of part-time work, this makes the Netherlands a country with a relatively low number of hours worked per person per year, which increasingly alarms local and international economic observers. It also leads people from other countries, as we have seen, to wonder whether the Dutch are a lazy culture.

As the labour market got tighter due to the success of the polder model, employers began wanting people to go back to working longer hours. So nowadays, to degrees that vary per sector and per company, people 'sell' this time back to the employer. They can also save up the days and use them later for 'sabbaticals' or for early retirement. For readers from countries that do not know this phenomenon, a 'sabbatical' is an unpaid, long-term leave – ranging from a few months to even a full year – with a guarantee of having your job to return to afterwards. Sabbaticals are mostly negotiated by full-time employees in more senior positions with a lot of work pressure, and are obviously highly appreciated. People may use a sabbatical for study, travel or other time-consuming private activities.

Employers themselves, and people with jobs higher than or outside CAO-levels, do not have ATV days, of course. But most of them still have – and take – far longer holidays than their colleagues in other countries. The only real exceptions may be farmers, people in small family firms, and the self-employed.

And now: let's travel! So how do Dutch people spend all their free time? As I've said, the Dutch do love to travel. The Saturday newspapers are full of advertisements for travel destinations, and you can be certain to encounter Dutch tourists and backpackers in the remotest countries. (But even adventure is well-prepared for by the Dutch, as an American observed. *'You guys always prepare your trips by reading a million guidebooks. We Americans don't do that.'*). Likewise, the Dutch are open to foreign influence at home as well, with interests ranging from exotic foods to 'world music' and international literature – read in English or other original languages.

As an English saying goes, 'no moss grows' under Dutch feet, as they tend to like going places and generally have the time and money to do so. With the lower economic tide, however, people do need to economise, and some use their holiday money for paying off debts, but two or three-week package holidays to Mediterranean beach resorts are still very popular today. People benefit from budget airfares and stiff competition from new tourist destinations like Turkey where low-cost deals lure travellers.

Typically, families with small children often hitch up the caravan and stay in the Netherlands or drive down to a campsite in France. People with more money and no children may want to travel to more exotic destinations, or to make several short 'city trips' a year. And while you will, of course, find Dutch people everywhere on earth, they remain very 'Dutch': a survey published in 2000 revealed that they spend about half as much money per holiday as other Europeans do – not always out of financial necessity. As one Belgian noticed, *'It struck me how in Holland even people like lawyers go hiking and camping out. Belgians prefer to drive around in big fat cars and enjoy luxury.'* Indeed, many Dutch people prefer to leave the beaten track to others, and such holidays to less-popular destinations tend to be a lot cheaper.

While I thought that this old stereotype needed revision, to my surprise a Dutch coach driver told me in 2001 that on his trips to Spain he, indeed, still sees quite a few Dutch people with caravans full of their own food, avoiding 'strange' dishes and saving money at the same time! The stereotype does carry some weight.

Whichever way they travel in the end, Dutch people relish the return to the comfort and snugness of home: 'East or west, home is best', as they say. But immediately they start saving for the next trip....

Anti-chauvinism   With all the country's international renown and economic power, one would think that the Dutch would be awfully proud of their country, but they don't really seem to be, certainly when talking among themselves. They love their country dearly, of course, but compared to many other nations, national pride is not as pervasive, at least not through emphasis on visible symbols such as the flag, national anthem, heroes or monuments.

Some years ago this observation was made: *'There should be more admiration for the good and beautiful things of Holland. This is such a small country and yet there are world personalities in the fields of art, literature, sports and film. Why aren't they proud of it? I am! The Dutch anti-chauvinism shocks and irritates me tremendously.'* (Argentine). Well, in recent years public pride of world champions and international stars *has* greatly increased, with festive Amsterdam canal trips and 'welcome home' parades. There is even a 'greatest Dutch person ever' contest going on (albeit a copy of foreign examples!) Yet the Argentinean's observation still rings true. Traditionally in the Netherlands, pride in one's own nation and culture was rarely strong, and not greatly stimulated by government, schools or the media. Only in the face of foreign animosity has this been different – such as during the Nazi occupation. But after the war, identification with one's own peer group took precedence again.

The Netherlands and Germany   As many foreigners soon realise, World War II has left the Netherlands with strong, bitter feelings about Germany, despite the fact that this large neighbour is its major economic partner by far. The saying even goes that 'if Germany has a cold, Holland sneezes'. After 1945, people obviously needed time to overcome their indignation about five years of brutal occupation. But even today, strong and easily voiced stereotypes about Germans still go around, such as that of being rigid, authoritarian and formal, and not having any sense of humour. These stereotypes easily survive among those who never encounter Germans, and indeed many Dutch people only see Germany from the *Autobahn* (the German highway) on their way to the sunny south, while upholding the myth that German language with its case endings is 'very hard to learn'. Many Dutch people especially treat older Germans in an unfriendly way, but anti-German feelings often come out stronger than that, not only in football matches but in childish jokes or unsympathetic behaviour aimed at young Germans as well. My guess is that such Dutch people need a 'mental opponent' for reinforcing their own self-assurance, with anti-German attitudes probably being the most socially acceptable *in*tolerance.

As you may have noticed, some of the Dutch reproaches toward the Germans are quite the same as those heard from other people about the Dutch themselves – but you'd better not say so in public, or mention the correct but unwelcome observation that Dutch and German languages have a lot in common. I have heard that German tourist and business guidebooks advise Germans to speak English in the Netherlands and, while I don't advise them against it, it should be said that the Dutch can usually hear the accent quite clearly. There may be no reason not to speak German, since the Dutch can always understand it even when they may be reluctant to speak it.

Surprisingly to foreigners, many Dutch people do not know the words of their own national anthem, and the Dutch flag is not overtly honoured. You may see cafés unceremoniously decorating their premises with the flag, and families flying it at private celebrations of birthdays or passed exams – and more so on Dutch national holidays – but the Netherlands is by far not a flag-waving country. As a result, such other nations' displays of nationalism are felt to be slightly ridiculous or even downright irritating. The Dutch tend to distrust countries in which the head-of-state's portrait hangs everywhere, where street slogans boast of national achievements, and where school children are forced to sing national anthems or perform flag ceremonies. It all seems a bit 'over the top' to them, reminding them of nationalism, a rather dirty word to the Dutch.

Listening to Dutch people grumbling about the imperfections of their society, one might even be tempted to think that they don't love their country. However, referring back to the Argentinean's irritations with 'Dutch anti-chauvinism', it is important to remember that in Dutch culture, criticism is an indirect expression of concern or appreciation. So, complaining about society or talking critically about certain conditions means that people care. People from other countries may not understand this. *'The Netherlands is constantly occupied with making itself smaller than it really is. That is the real "Hollanditis", a virus that has spread quite widely and that affects people in the street, the professor at university and the politician. Self-scoffing is an often-practised sport. The economy is the only field in which the Netherlands doesn't suffer from an inferiority complex.'* (France)

I would certainly have included football (soccer) in this last sentence, but indeed it seems that the Dutch are not proud of themselves – not even of football these days. But this may be just an appearance, as an American observer points out. *'I see a very strong Dutch identity, open to the outside world and in which individual differences are easily accepted.'* On nationalism he adds, *'In Holland it won't work to shout and wave flags. Even a demagogue needs to have a fairly intellectual level. That's why his movement collapsed when Fortuyn was gone.'*

Public negligence of official culture   While it may be difficult to notice, the Dutch do love their country. They are fond of its nature and proud of its waterworks; they care for its wildlife, its old city centres and its monuments ...including the windmills. Foreign eyebrow-raising has also made the Dutch more aware and proud of national accomplishments like their freedom and their highly humane society. Research proves that some 90% of the interviewed Dutch find the Netherlands a beautiful country where it is good to live, but only 25% named it 'the best country in the world', perhaps reflecting their international perspective and appreciation of other cultures. The number one aspect that generated national pride – in 88% of the people interviewed – turned out to be the struggle against water. Beyond that, each of the following had just a few percentage points less. Brace yourself, for this may astonish you. In second place came multinational companies; then 3) Dutch traditional food; 4) ice-skating; 5) the euthanasia policy; and 6) the legal possibility of homosexual marriage (63%!). Only then come more traditional items such as the flag, the royal family and the national anthem. Even the highly controversial drugs policy could still count on 33% enthusiasm. All this represents a love for practical things rather than for mere symbols.

But with previous successes fading, such as the 'polder model' and the welfare state, the political scene in turmoil, and now landscapes and nature being seriously threatened, this love may turn into gloomy concern and worry. Keeping the country as it was seems impossible. While millions are spent on restoring old houses and castles, and on saving vulnerable patches of woodland or swamp, the money certainly doesn't come only from the government. But the hunt for wealth goes on, and when the environment and the economy compete, natural and historical treasures usually lose out.

National pride? Some countries loudly trumpet their cultural heritage, not only abroad for tourist promotion, but also to their own citizens –in schools and the media, to raise awareness and national pride. Traditionally this never happened much in the Netherlands, geared, as it is, to international trade and pragmatic attitudes. Generally speaking, the Dutch school system tries to prepare students for today's society and careers, emphasising personal development and social participation, rather than making them memorise facts and figures about culture and history. In this view, national chauvinism is out of place in a united Europe and in a world striving for peace and justice for all. A doubtful result of this approach is that some years ago, members of the Dutch Parliament were jokingly tested on their factual knowledge of national history ... and most of them failed!

But things do change. Until very recently, the sensitivities of a multicultural society also played a role in treating Dutch culture in low-profile ways. In schools this is certainly still the case, but in public life and politics there have been calls for emphasising the norms and values of Dutch culture, immediately leading to a debate on what exactly these are. (More on this later).

Yet even now, Dutch upbringing and education produce citizens with a remarkable lack of pride in their own culture. Achievements in the fields of literature and the arts are no great source of pride to most Dutch people. It comes as somewhat of a surprise to them, for example, to hear that translated Dutch literature is very successful abroad.

Indeed, this country's rich past and present are taken for granted to a large extent. Although the intellectual elite organises successful exhibitions at home and abroad, the general Dutch public is not particularly interested in the international prestige of the Dutch arts. Many people are only familiar with the names of painters, composers, designers, inventors and scholars from the 15th century to the present day because they have streets named after them, and it comes in handy when playing in a TV quiz. Likewise, Dutch business people don't always fully appreciate or make use of the country's good image in fields such as the arts, or of its waterworks technology. Neither are they deeply impressed when foreigners use their own national glories to promote their business.

Be that as it may, the Dutch government spends much more money on promoting export and trade than on publicising Dutch culture abroad. Some years ago it took pressure from the much more language-conscious Flemish before subsidies were provided for the promotion of Dutch literature at the famous Frankfurt Book Fair in Germany. In 2000, only protest from intellectual circles prevented the government from scrapping the subsidy for a British university's Dutch language and literature department.

Dutch language   One can see how foreigners accustomed to symbolic or verbal expressions of nationalism may well think of the Dutch as lacking in patriotism. *'Hungarians have an emotional bond to their language. How come the Dutch awareness of language and history is so weak?'* (Hungary) I think one answer to that question can be found in the Dutch preference for self-attained status. It's not so much the things that ancestors or historical heroes did that count. No, what is important, what the Dutch can really be proud of, is their own efforts – what they have accomplished themselves. That is much more a source of self-confidence and pride than history and culture. Suffice it to say that the Dutch don't dismiss the old, but neither do they have a very strong attachment to it. They see their historical heritage largely as a pleasant background to present-day accomplishments. Thinking again in boxes, perhaps, rather than feeling a clear link between past and present, the Dutch tend to keep the two separated.

Another effect of this rather pragmatic attitude is that they are prouder of speaking foreign languages than of mastering their own. Many people are sloppy in their native Dutch, and many shrug their shoulders at other people's linguistic mistakes (if they notice them at all).

To most Dutch people, their language is a 'home, garden and kitchen' thing, an expression used to indicate its everyday, unspectacular but useful character. Few Dutch people become emotional about the qualities or the unique character of their language, or their literature. Foreign cynics may suggest that perhaps this is because it doesn't *have* any qualities. Well, you may not like the throaty sound of the Dutch 'G', but there *is* much poetry and world-class literature and there *are* excellent songs in Dutch, as well as plenty of good jokes and puns. If only the foreigners could understand them.

Foreigners speaking Dutch   From a Dutch newspaper interview with an expatriate: *'Dutch is not a language, it's a secret code for business people and they don't want foreigners to learn this business code. "Keep the knowledge of Dutch restricted, then we all make more profit." You don't find it relevant whether we (*expats*) can communicate in Dutch or not, for the accent needs to be flawless; otherwise we don't speak Dutch.'* (Nationality unknown to me).

The casual attitude the Dutch have to their language may also explain why foreigners learning to speak Dutch are looked upon with pleasant surprise, but not taken very seriously. One American lady comments: *'Now that I've taken it upon myself to learn and speak the Dutch language, the locals are more than flattered – they're shocked – that any outsider would make the effort to "bother" with such an obscure language!'*

Most Dutch people choose to switch to English rather than exercise the patience to wait for the slow beginner's answer or listen to their accent. In some respects, the Dutch are perhaps embarrassed for the struggling foreigner and simply revert to English to accommodate them. Many expatriates practising their newly acquired Dutch, however, get frustrated, like this Englishman: *'It is convenient, of course, that everyone speaks English, but they even answer me in English when I want to use my Dutch. How do they expect me to learn it if they don't give me the chance to practise?'* Let me pass on to the reader one Italian's solution to this problem: *'When they answer me in English, I pretend that besides some Dutch I only speak Italian!'*

But even in this field things seem to be changing. Some business people in my courses complain that all meetings at their office are in Dutch. *'There is little sympathy for non-Dutch speakers. They expect you to learn Dutch yesterday!'* (Australia) Most likely this refers to a work environment where non-managerial staff also participate in meetings, because among Dutch managers this would not generally be the case. It might also be a side effect of increasing public impatience about the frequently slow integration of immigrants into Dutch society.

A few more things should be said about the use of English in the Netherlands. In my courses, some newcomers complain, *'In shops, everything is in Dutch'*, or *'Information, magazines and books are mostly in Dutch.'* In my view, these people obviously don't realise to what extent English is used here compared to other countries. The use of English in the Netherlands – in education, in business, in advertising, in everyday life – is increasing at a faster rate than it is in Germany, Belgium or France, let alone in Italy or Eastern Europe. All this is intended to evoke an image of cosmopolitanism, of global culture. For example, in Dutch-language job advertisements, English job titles are frequently used: 'chief technology officer', 'human resources director', 'key account retail manager', 'strategic tariffing manager', 'recruitment consultants', 'legal advisor/employee benefits' – for which there are perfectly good Dutch equivalents. Terms like 'win-win situations', 'not-for-profit', 'best practices', 'competencies' and many more can be heard and read, although they could easily be translated into Dutch.

After decades of exposure to American and English pop music and television programmes, and years of hard-to-translate computer terminology, English usage while speaking Dutch has become common practice, although regretted by some. Companies frequently use English to evoke a more international image, and advertising in newspapers, and on the radio and TV is full of English terminology and American slang. English is, after all, becoming the universal language, as is evident here in the Netherlands as well. An official government policy against this, like the French objections to 'Franglais', is unlikely to come about here, however. On the contrary, the use of English is stimulated in Dutch education. Traditionally, it was taken for granted that students and academics were able to read books and articles in English, German *and* French. Now, increasingly, they are being stimulated to also *publish* in English, thus linking Dutch academia to the dominant Anglophone world. At the same time, fewer and fewer Dutch people speak good French and German. In a test carried out by a language institute a few years ago, the telephone operators of several companies became so nervous when called by a French-speaking customer that they simply broke off the connection.

Nationalism after all? Discussing these issues in a training programme, an Englishman objected. *'Come on, what are you saying? The Dutch are super-nationalists! Look at those crowds in orange! We even saw shops full of orange decorations, orange cakes, and orange custard!'* He was right, in a way. Contrary to the public negligence of *official* culture, but consistent with their 'act normal' attitude, the Dutch can be quite chauvinistic when it comes to more mundane achievements.

With a bit of luck, if one values the spirit of nationalism, you may encounter celebrating crowds of youngsters waving the national flag, wearing bizarre orange-coloured outfits and wigs, and shouting (for once) 'Holland, Holland!' They are sure to be celebrating a (now rather rare) national football victory. Sports, and football in particular, bring out stronger nationalistic feelings in the Dutch than probably any other facet of the culture, and over recent years this was stirred up by extensive – and increasingly commercial – media coverage. During international championships, many motorists drive around with orange decorations and shops sell orange-coloured food and souvenirs, while cafés and private houses are decked out in Dutch flags and orange banners. For major events like the European Cup, some people may even go so far as to dye their grass orange in the front garden!

This illustrates the increasing nationalism not fuelled by the state. Dutch media analyse what they call 'the Orange-mania' more as an expression of a kind of tribal collectivism than as an outburst of nationalism. (There is also a certain link to class and education involved here, and the not-so-fanatic Dutch keep quiet while the other half goes crazy.)

Related to European Unification, there is an increased national self-awareness all over the continent. In the rapidly expanding EU, the Netherlands is now merely one of many small nations (albeit one with a large economy that has always been a loyal net-contributor). In broad outline, this country remains firmly rooted in the European Union and the world community, with an open eye to all sides, balancing the commercial interests of the economy with the humane ideals of peace, development and equal opportunities for people everywhere.

Yet at the same time, as we have seen, there seems to be a more narrow-minded outlook. Under public pressure, the policy for admitting asylum seekers has hardened in recent years (more on this later). And with the enlargement of the EU toward Central Europe in 2004, the Netherlands was one of the countries trying to protect its labour market by keeping out workers from the new member states for the first two years. Further, European elections result in low participation. Instead of enthusiasm about a new start for this old continent, there are petty (in my mind) concerns about finance, employment and safety close to home. In relation to this, we will discuss in a later chapter what has been termed 'the closing of the Dutch mind'.

---

1. Spending some € 21 billion on this in 2001, sharing the third place with Switzerland.

Chapter 10

ON GENDER, GENERATIONS AND PERSONAL RELATIONS

So far we have discussed the main stream Dutch business world – the culture of ethnic, male, white Dutch, most of who live and work in the Randstad, the highly urbanised western part of the country. But only half the population of the country is male, a little over half of them live outside the Randstad area and many people in the Netherlands are not white. It is time to moderate the general picture painted in the previous chapters.

Women in Dutch society   In the Netherlands you will encounter working women in all sectors – but not often in managerial positions. There are exceptions, indeed, but the fact is that women in business mostly function at midlevel and in administrative jobs. Among men, 21% of employees hold a management post of some description, while among women this is only 5%. As far as government employees are concerned, the situation is not that much better. Only in health care, education and other traditionally female jobs are women over-represented, taking up more than 50% of all jobs. Yet even in these branches, at managerial levels there are more men than women.

Some years ago a Hungarian woman remarked, *'If I had known about the position of working women, I would never have come to Holland.'* Since that remark was made, Dutch women's economic position has improved, but even today some expats express amazement at the low presence of women in management. In fact, in a 26-country American survey on the issue, the Netherlands shared the last position with… Pakistan! Partially, this is attributed to the rather narrow Dutch definition of 'the board', as in 'board of directors', which excludes the many vice-presidents but even so. And among the very few women one does find on Dutch boards, there is a noticeably disproportionate representation of *foreign* women.

Although at more mundane levels, gender differences in degree of education are decreasing and more and more Dutch women participate at all levels of political and social life, foreigners still experience less progressiveness in the position of women than apparently they had expected. Many Dutch women seem to be content to work part-time and perhaps settle for less than the topmost jobs. A newspaper article[1] on the issue produced statistics indicating that Dutch women are not highly ambitious: of those women with higher vocational and academic education, only 22% found promotion chances important. This is less than Dutch men (32%) and less than their female counterparts in the culturally similar Scandinavian countries (but of which, unfortunately, the article did not state the figures).

Women at work   Up until just a few decades ago, women's overall participation in the Dutch labour market was low (1981: 30%). Concurrently, so were their incomes, and their legal status was downright old-fashioned, with restricted financial and legal independence from their husbands. Although the legal aspects have much improved – partly due to EU pressure – women's participation in the Dutch job market today is still merely average compared to that of other EU member states, and most of these jobs are part-time, certainly when considering *married* women. On average, Dutch women are paid only 77% of their male colleagues' hourly salaries. That may sound terrible, but this rate is actually a little above the world average. (Compare: USA 75%, Australia 91%, Britain 70%, and Bangladesh 42%). This male/female difference in salary no longer springs, scientific researchers say, from legal discrimination, but reflects the average Dutch working woman's younger age and her shorter work experience or – if she is older – her outdated job experience due to career interruptions for child-raising. Many would differ with this perspective, I'm sure, but regardless of the reason, the fact is that the average income of a 35-year-old Dutch woman is only half that of her male counterpart.

As most working women in the Netherlands are fairly young – between the ages of 25 and 35 – they statistically tend to run a higher risk of burnout and stress. It is estimated that women in this age group are four times more likely to receive a 'WAO' (Labour Disability) benefit than their male colleagues in the same age group. The causes of this are not completely clear yet, but it may partly have to do with the kind of work that women do. Many of them work in health care, for example, which is not an easy job, either emotionally or physically. Suffice it to say that both in this sector and in other strongly 'female' sectors of the economy, pay is relatively low, there is a great deal of psychological pressure and career prospects are poor.

These factors, of course, also affect job satisfaction. Researchers say that women may also be more sensitive to unpleasant working conditions and, therefore, likely to give up their job sooner than men. An additional factor may be that women simply have a harder struggle to be taken seriously in a still male-dominated economy, so they may have to work harder to prove themselves. A 'glass ceiling' is certainly still present in quite a number of Dutch companies.

This relatively low labour participation of women is not exactly in line with the Netherlands' generally progressive image. Dutch observers cite various reasons, but virtually all point to the shortage of childcare facilities ...but since the availability of these facilities has been improving over the years, there must be more to the equation than that. Until three decades ago, most women did not work outside the home, which means that the concept of childcare facilities is relatively new here. Although the inordinately strict hygienic, pedagogic and safety standards have been somewhat relaxed, it is still difficult to start such a centre as a private initiative. Therefore, they are limited in number and often overbooked, with waiting lists as a result. While this is still a major hindrance to female employment, the fact that is that Dutch family life (in the sense of the nuclear family) is quite strong, and there is still an element of the 'stay-at-home-mom' at play here, although it is diminishing somewhat. It may be useful to take a closer look at it.

Individualists or collectivists? How expatriates experience Dutch family life depends very much on their own cultural backgrounds. Foreigners particularly notice how parents and children generally make it a habit to eat together and enjoy their leisure time as a family unit, and it is not only Americans who tell me they are impressed with the Dutch family orientation. But people from other countries, such as those in the tropics, see elderly people going into nursing homes and hear about young people ignoring their parents and often comment on the Dutch as being 'strong individualists', or even 'cold'.

From an international perspective, the Dutch indeed rank among the more individualistic nations, but less so than the Americans. The Dutch perceive themselves as individualists, and it's easy to get that impression in public where 'going it alone' is held in high esteem, with quite a few people eating, walking and travelling by themselves. This makes outsiders think that the Dutch are, overall, highly individualistic. But both in private life and in the workplace, the Dutch definitely also have a collectivist tendency. Committees and community centres are commonplace here, although people with lower-level incomes generally frequent the latter. Permeating Dutch society is a strong Social-Democratic (Labour party) tradition – its effects being the social benefits, the collective labour agreements and the housing associations. Also a collectivist aspect, in a way, is the fact that many people are members of clubs or other organisations and have long-term subscriptions to ideologically or religiously based newspapers or magazines.

Privately, perhaps, the term 'particularistic' is more appropriate. Socially and emotionally, people tend to cling to their peer groups, i.e. people with similar incomes, education and lifestyles. Such contacts often last a lifetime, even when people move away from the neighbourhood. Although dining or some outdoor activity may be involved, the personal contact through 'meaningful conversation' and 'good times' is more important than that. The Dutch word used for such occasions is *gezellig*, meaning 'cosy' or 'sociable' and implying a certain in-group comfort. It is also associated with *koffietijd* (coffee time) and even certain arrangements of furniture (typically in a circle) and room decorations are involved. This may all contribute to a general feeling of 'us-ness' – us here in our little box –as opposed to 'them out there'.

Also at work many people appreciate a certain togetherness with their departmental colleagues – their team – that may easily extend to the canteen. Foreigners are particularly struck by the way in which birthdays are celebrated at work, with ritualistic get-togethers around coffee and cake. *Gezelligheid* plays a role even there.

The borrel *and other company occasions*   In a
way, companies and organisations are seen as families. Although
the social bonds are far more limited than in Japanese companies,
for example, the Dutch also try to create a sense of togetherness
at work. People appreciate a good atmosphere in their workplace, perhaps with family photos on desks and potted plants on
windowsills. Some employers, fearing an image of not being
business-like, may limit employees' attempts at making their
work domain look all too *gezellig*. Among close colleagues, the
need for a group culture may extend to joint lunches at one
table, and to out-of-work contacts or outings, such as a bowling
or 'bar tour' evening. Occasionally, such activities may also be
part of a company's team-bonding efforts, either as a separate
event or as the end of a one, two or even three-day conference
for designing new policy. Specialised conference centres are
often located in nature areas, so sometimes people jokingly
speak of 'a session on the moors', even when it actually takes
place in a city hotel.

Also, smaller office celebrations may involve more than the
traditional birthday coffee and cake. Management may throw an
after-hours party for employees at all levels on occasions such as
a colleague leaving to take up another job or retiring, to cele-
brate good results, or to mark festivities such as Christmas and
New Year. The Dutch word for this is *borrel*, which basically means
'a stiff drink', but is also used to refer to a 'sociable gathering'
where, of course, other drinks (and snacks) are available, too.
Such parties are valuable times for in-company networking and
for revealing who you are on a more personal level. I recommend
that foreign employees attend such occasions because they offer
a good opportunity to build social contacts with their Dutch colleagues – and to learn Dutch!

The nuclear family   Dutch family life is rather restricted to the
'nuclear family', which may strike people from other cultures as
being odd. *'I find it strange that the concept of family here has such a
limited meaning. Family here is dad, mum, brother, sister and sometimes
grandpa and grandma, but that's it.'* (Cameroon) For the most part,
the 'extended' family seems to have vanished from the Netherlands centuries ago, but 'nuclear' family life is quite strong. Dutch
people prefer to raise their children without undue interference

from extended family or others. As such, nannies and boarding schools are almost non-existent here. Until children are about 16 years of age, most families dine together, go out together and go on holiday together, so many foreigners find the country positively oriented toward children (witness the prevalence of children's activity corners in Dutch car dealers, banks and the like). *'They seem to have a very intense family life, and a very active social life.'* (Britain) Given this general pattern, the Dutch don' t have a concept such as 'quality time', although the phenomenon of children enrolled in day-care centres, or placed in the care of au pairs and babysitters, is on the rise in circles of young, ambitious couples.

Nonetheless, in couples with children, only 6% both have a full-time job, while in 46% of the cases, one of the pair has a full-time job and the other works part-time. Yet only 19% of the Dutch are of the opinion that male/female roles should be traditional, and only Scandinavian countries are less traditional in this respect.

Housewives and part-time work   Until the 1970s, it was assumed that housewives – 'stay-at-home-fathers' hardly existed in those days – had time to do their shopping in the daytime, and this assumption still has its effects on society. Opening hours for government organisations are often from 9 to 5 only and, outside of city centres, shopping hours are mostly from 9 to 6. (The same is true for service people coming to your house.) This makes foreigners, particularly in smaller towns, complain that they cannot handle the required bureaucratic procedures or even spend their money due to limited hours. *'Everything is open when we are working but closed when we are not!'*

Most people are happy that, in 1996, legal restrictions were relaxed and many shops and supermarkets can now remain open until 9 or 10 in the evening. At first, a majority of the Dutch said that they did not care for longer opening hours, but some years later now, evening shopping is a huge success, accounting for 11% of all sales. At the same time, some municipal authorities also introduced other opening hours. Outside the centres of larger cities, however, particularly in small towns, virtually all shops still close at 6 p.m., to the annoyance of people from the US and other countries where all-day and evening shopping – even 24-hour – is common. Even shopping in the Netherlands takes planning!

The editor of a leading women's magazine gave an interesting but hard-to-prove view on non-working women. According to her, Dutch women are quite content to be housewives because, after centuries of women running the household in the absence of their seafaring husbands, that 'position' has a higher status in the Netherlands than it does in other countries. Housewives in former days were not only managers of the family but also of the farm or the shop, and responsible for the workings of the entire household and budget.

Perhaps a more plausible explanation can be found in the Dutch tax system. Dutch taxes are not only high but also 'progressive', meaning that the higher the income, the higher the tax percentage. So, unless a couple explicitly states that they want their incomes to be taxed separately, joint income will be taxed at the higher level. Needless to say this doesn't encourage married women to work outside the home.

As a result of all this, only one in seven married women works full-time – representing one of the lowest percentages in Europe. One can look at this phenomenon in two ways: negatively, in the sense that they may be unable to find a full-time job, or positively, in the sense that they deliberately choose to devote more time to their family, simply choosing not to have a career. A survey conducted in 1997 revealed that 70% of working women were content with the number of hours they worked, and that 15% would prefer to work fewer hours. Of Dutch married couples (with or without children), only 14% both have a full-time job. In 37% of the cases, the husband has a full-time job and the wife works part-time; in another 28% of households, the husband has a full-time job and the wife doesn't have a paid job at all.

Statistics also show that the Dutch labour market has the highest percentage of part-time jobs in the western world (39%), with 8% of *men* working part-time in the Netherlands. This is made possible because part-timers also profit well from the high wage levels and relatively good job security, much to the liking of those involved but not to those parties considering the national economy and international competition. Some years ago the Dutch Parliament discussed working part-time as a legal right for all workers, but this was voted against (with just a meagre majority), obviously to the relief of employers, who find it difficult to accommodate such employees in the workplace.

Companies feel the same about another recurrent trade union hobbyhorse: the four-days-a-week job. These days it is most unlikely to ever become official policy, but in fact it already does exist on a more individual and un-official basis. In fact, quite a few senior people have successfully negotiated a workweek consisting of four 9-hour days.

Luckily for the employers who find it difficult to manage the parameters of part-time staff, part-time workers are still the exception. The average worker in the Netherlands is still a married man with a 38-hour-a-week job and a wife that works part-time. Yet, in the larger cities, a different impression might emerge. One sees both scenarios previously described – plenty of working women, and shops full of customers during evening opening hours.

Double earners and living together   Among the younger generation, especially in the cities, the phenomenon the Dutch call 'double earners' – that is, two people in one household, married or living together, having a full or part-time paid job – is widespread. After years of increasing by more than 100,000 couples annually, such cases involving both marriages and partnerships (as opposed to our figure above for married couples alone) now make up some 50% of all households, with only 15% still having just a single breadwinner in the traditional way.

As I have implied, 'double-earners' are not always married. For some years now Dutch law has given couples (of mixed gender or the same sex) living together in a so-called 'registered partnership' virtually the same legal status as officially married couples. Since this law came into force, many people have decided to 'live together' in a permanent, or at least long-term, relationship. To some people from non-western countries this comes as a shock. *'How about this living together; doesn't society find it a disgrace?'* (Tanzania)

Indeed, it *was* considered a social disgrace before the 1960s. In those days, living together was a revolutionary thing among urban intellectuals and artists, that only later spread to all levels of society. Nowadays, even among people with religious affiliations, few have objections to the practice of living together outside of marriage. The main reason seems to be that people value mutual trust more than a legal bond. The concept particularly appeals to those who don't intend to have children. Nowadays, almost all couples that marry have already 'lived together' for a period of time. Living separate while 'officially' engaged is now deemed to be rather old-fashioned in this country. Engagement parties and rings are a rare phenomenon in most circles. (In a way, this is another example of the Dutch not caring very much about authority, the state or the church.)

'Living together' might be one factor explaining why Dutch women are 'world champions' at having their first child at a relatively late age: on average in the Netherlands this only happens when they are 29 years old. *'In Japan it is far less accepted when someone in her thirties like me is not yet married and does not have children. The Netherlands is much freer in that respect.'*

Easy consumers   Since couples living together – as opposed to being married – are found mostly in the cities and, interestingly, are often higher educated than married couples, they earn higher average incomes. For tax purposes, as I mentioned, they can choose to keep their incomes separate or joint, depending on both partners' income and on their relationship. Typically hard-working and without children, they are an attractive target group for companies that market timesaving devices and luxury products. Lured by flashy ads for loans with 'easy' repayments, for example, such couples may not only invest in a house or apartment with a high mortgage, but also go for a second car, expensive furniture, a boat, or other high-priced items. A growing number of such people run into financial trouble, as is the case right now, when debts pile up because of some economic mishap.

Sexism and emancipated men   The general picture, then, is still an under-representation of women in the Dutch labour market and, as a matter of fact, also in politics and other important sectors. Over the years many Dutch women, with or without feminist sympathies, did not like their situation, discussed it, and protested against it. Their protest has resulted in quite radical changes in recent decades. As in other countries, there have been campaigns for reversal of discrimination against women, and campaigns encouraging girls to take on traditionally male studies such as technology, the sciences and mathematics. These had some results, women say, but as we all know, changing the law is one thing but changing attitudes another. However, it seems that the 1990s polder model – one of its effects being job creation – has had more effect on bringing women into the labour market than any official campaign.

Sexism exists in the Netherlands, too, but it is slowly waning as more and more women enter careers in companies and organisations. Working women in the Netherlands, including those from other countries, complain of men's subtle discrimination or, in rare cases, open harassment toward them. Practical and legal measures have been taken against the latter, but the more subtle negative attitudes are always more difficult to change. Some men still tend to 'joke' about women and overlook female talent and capabilities but, fortunately, few people laugh along these days. With the younger generation, any difference in treatment seems to have virtually disappeared. For American readers, it bears saying that 'political correctness' is less of an issue in the Netherlands than in the United States.

By not appreciating women's talents, such men and organisations lose a lot, according to this Argentinean (male) observer: *'The personality of Holland is female. Women here are more intelligent, more attractive, stronger, and more powerful than men. I admire them very much. They are better managers; they will give you an honest answer, and you can trust them.'* (Argentine) But there is also this observation from a Canadian woman working here: *'I quite often notice how Dutch women in higher positions, instead of supporting each other, play nasty power games on one another, especially outside the business sector. I find that a very sad situation, not exactly stimulating a change in male attitudes!'*

Foreigners also observe that Dutch men seem to be quite emancipated, as one sees them regularly shopping for food, pushing prams, and taking the kids for a walk. Especially among urban, well-educated 'double earners', men do some of the household chores; quite a few regularly cook dinner also. *'It is surprising to see so many men doing the domestic tasks.'* (Philippines). Not everyone thinks they do enough, however: *'Men in Dutch society depend too much on the women'* (Denmark)[2].

This may still be true in more traditional families, but among young urban couples the division of household chores is coming closer and closer to a 50/50 split, although some households are relying more on the help of hired housecleaners. Socially, such

Dutch couples leave each other quite free to pursue not only their careers but also their leisure time pursuits, accepting that their partner or spouse may have different interests and different friends. *'Here I have freedom. It is perfectly normal for a married woman to have friends of her own, to go dining somewhere without her husband. You can do what you like here. We don't have children, although we've been married for four years. In my country everybody wants to know why not. They think I'm crazy; everyone there has two children because that's the way it should be. Luckily, here they don't.'* (Czech Republic) But not everyone likes the treatment resulting, perhaps, from equal gender roles – the 'every man (or woman) for him(her)self'[3] attitude. *'I find the Dutch selfish and impolite when going through doors or using elevators, especially men vis-à-vis women,'* said a lady from Hungary. I'm afraid that in this old-time merchants' republic, 'courteous' manners were never highly developed in the first place.

Children and youngsters Although not a subject related to business, I would like to say something more about children and age in general because so many visitors, particularly from Africa and Asia, wonder, *'Where are the children?'* or *'How come I see so many old people?'* For one thing, the birth rate in the Netherlands is low. It is known that birth rates generally decline as countries develop. Children are not considered as they once were as a means of providing extra income for the family or for taking care of their elderly parents, and child mortality rates are low. This means that just a few children 'will do'. This is a quite recent phenomenon, however. In past decades, the population of the Netherlands increased very rapidly – from just 8 million around 1920, to 12 million in the 1960s, to over 16 million today.

From the 1970s onward, however, the average Dutch family has had just two children, although there is something of a baby boom going on at present, with some families having a third or fourth child. Moreover, children of ethnic groups in the Netherlands, reflecting their more traditional lifestyles, take up a large share of the birth rate. In some areas of cities such as Amsterdam and Rotterdam, school classes consist mostly or even exclusively of 'other ethnic' children (see chapter 11).

As they reach secondary school age, Dutch children begin to negotiate more freedom from their parents – first the freedom to choose their own clothes, to go to parties and to come home late. A few years later they 'demand' to be allowed to drink beer and to go to dances and discos, and to go on holiday with their friends rather than with their parents. Gradually, their independence gets stretched more and more. Money isn't generally a problem for Dutch youth, as parents tend to be generous with pocket money, and many have part-time jobs or scholarships. (Although with low birth rates the Netherlands may not be the best market for children's products, the young share in the general prosperity and spend a lot of money on fashion, music, electronic gadgets and entertainment). Many Dutch children go to school camps at an early age; a few years later they may go on special youth holidays. As parental control decreases, independence sometimes gets out of hand. At weekends especially, there are frequently problems with groups of drunken youngsters, and of course there is drug abuse. But note that they are the exception, however, and the main interests of the majority of young people in the Netherlands seem to be study and a career. The phenomenon of 'school dropouts' does also exist here, but not to an alarming degree.

Obviously, to compete successfully in the present-day, market-oriented job market, a good education is needed. On average, Dutch children study up to the age of 18, but many study longer. And while most Dutch youngsters trust that if they study and work hard enough, it will be easy to find a satisfactory job and a good position in society, they tend to want more out of life than just a decent job and a fixed salary. Surveys have revealed that Dutch youth find personal development, a good work atmosphere and friendly relations with colleagues at least as important as money. *'Dutch youngsters love challenge. If I have a technical problem, they rush in to solve it. Everybody has good ideas. But they lose interest when a solution is found. In fact you should give them something new every day, because they don't like routine.'* (Morocco) A rather gloomy view comes from the Belgian journalist/author quoted before: *'Dutch education is very good for children's assertiveness up until they're about ten years old, but it has gone too far. Dutch teenagers are awful, they don't respect anyone, they will not take "no" for an answer and don't respect age or experience. This is bad for society in the long run also; it creates arrogant civilians and an aggressive and restless society.'*
In many countries, young people prefer to set up their own companies, and this is not uncommon in the Netherlands either. There

are starters' subsidies and tax allowances but, as we already saw, all kinds of legal requirements do make it complicated. Self-employed people receive less legal protection than employees and, certainly after a recent wave of bankruptcies, many Dutch young people avoid taking large risks. There is quite some concern about this in entrepreneurial circles.

Older people   With low birth rates and – in spite of its shortcomings – good health care, there are more elderly people in Dutch society than young people. The baby boomers of the 1940s and 50s have reached the top of the labour market, but here I want to focus on *their* parents and grandparents, the oldest generation.

The 'greying' or aging of the Netherlands is under way, although at a somewhat slower pace than elsewhere in Western Europe. On average, women can now expect to live up to about the age of 80 – men a little less. (Quite a few Dutch people live to see 90 or even 100, and the officially oldest living person on earth right now is a Dutch lady of 114.)

For society in general and business in particular, this age dynamic requires a general restructuring. A higher percentage of older people means that there is an increasing demand for specialised health care and more money is needed to provide pensions. Further, as the working population decreases, tax revenues decrease, and in the future this may present problems in financing the needs of large non-working groups of people. In 2000, newspaper reports said that over the next fifty years, European countries will need many *millions* of immigrants in order to pay for old-age pensions, to replace retired workers, even to keep the population stable or growing. The Netherlands is small and cramped already and, with growing concerns about the multicultural society, other solutions may be more appropriate. Government and financial institutions are urging people to make private provisions for their old age rather than depend on state pensions, and also to work longer.

Real problems are foreseen, however, for the years after 2010, when the 'post war baby boomers' will reach retirement age. But that raises the question, what *is* 'the retirement age'? Officially it is 65, when the state pension, 'AOW', payments begin (irrespective of income and financed by monthly contributions from all people working). But, as one American observed, *'I have the impression that virtually nobody here works until the age of sixty five.'* This observation is quite correct. Many people strive for early retirement, through private savings, special arrangements with their insurance companies, or by taking the 'freedom-with-less-money' option. The pensionable age of government workers has been made flexible, and in companies, too, arrangements can be made, although at considerable cost to the person involved.

There is also another, quite contradictory, trend: with an ageing population and the lack of local skilled workers, parties like employers, the government and the Central Bank call for people to work *over* the age of 65, rather than retire early, perhaps offering bonuses to those willing to do so. But pointing out the higher average age, or warning about competitive labour costs in China and India makes few people change their plans. In a March 2000 survey, most Dutch people said they would prefer to retire at age 59, and after a few years the government gave in a little and allowed arrangements to retire at 63, be it at one's own expense, of course. In European perspective, Dutch men do effectively stop working early. (I did not find statistics on women). On average, this occurs at 61 years of age, but when including the involuntary inactivity of sick or unemployed people on welfare, it goes down to age 58.5.

Again, I suspect readers of having the word 'laziness' in mind, but let me assure you that most senior citizens in the Netherlands, although they don't work, are quite active – in pursuits such as charity, sports, travel or studies. Most Dutch people live comfortably to a ripe old age; for many, real physical restrictions only start around age 78, 80 or over.

Old age provisions   As in many western countries, there are good provisions for the elderly in the Netherlands, but foreigners do not always understand the Dutch perspective. *'I was extremely shocked to find that this (Dutch) family I visited had sent their own mother to a home for the aged, while having a dog sit on the sofa as if it were a family member.'* (Tanzania). At first, most Dutch people will react with smiling surprise (or guilt feelings) but, in retrospect, will agree that it must look strange. Things are apparently also different elsewhere in Europe. *'The Dutch have lost the contact between the generations. You never see a grandmother here living with her daugh-*

ter or son. Older people are put away somewhere; there is no family feeling anymore.' (Ireland) It must be added that Ireland is still among the more traditional European countries in this respect, but it is true, indeed, that Dutch grandparents usually live elsewhere (see below), and are not often directly involved in their grandchildren's upbringing. But there is a story behind this.

In the Dutch nuclear family, the children have a lot of freedom, as I have said – their own room, their own music, and usually their own TV set and computer, as well as a great deal of social independence. But Dutch houses are not large and grandparents don't want to be bothered by loud music or impinge upon their adult 'children' in such tight quarters. They often prefer to stay in their own homes as long as possible; and the government, through subsidised organisations providing meals, cleaning services and basic medical care, encourages this independence of the older generation. *'I'm full of admiration about (*the Dutch system of*) home care, who try to assist people as much as they can in the comfort of their own surroundings. Please don't economise too much there; home care is part of a civilised society.'* (Northern Ireland)

Indeed, many older people prefer this independence, and there is a long tradition in the Netherlands of that generation living apart from their children, even if only in a separate part of the house. As early as the 17th century there were homes for the elderly, run by either churches or municipal authorities, and such homes are still an important part of Dutch society today.

If circumstances no longer allow the elderly to live in their own houses, they can move into such homes where they can live independently but with varying degrees of household and/or medical assistance. If their health deteriorates too much, there are special homes for the disabled elderly that provide full care, including recreational and medical facilities. It has to be said that there have been quite some economisations in this area too, and after negative media reports, more and more people prefer to stay away from such homes as long as possible. (Thence the previous, Northern-Irish quote)

If their condition permits them to live at home, they will require a mixture of support from grown-up children, friends, neighbours, homecare and, depending upon their condition, all kinds of mechanical and electronic devices to make independent living easier. To people from countries where family members support each other through thick and thin (even if the overriding reason is a lack of social benefits), this organised old-age care is perceived as cold and impersonal – as 'mechanical solidarity'. This quote comes from a Pakistani businessman who regularly visits the Netherlands: *'I was shocked by the treatment of aged people, by the living together of non-married people, and by the loose sexual morals.'*

Indeed there are cases when the situation is very sad – for example, for old people without children who totally depend on outside assistance from (an economising!) government or charitable organisations. Unfortunately, the following observation is correct: *'There are many people here who feel alone. You read more and more about elderly people found dead in their homes. When recently I heard about a woman who gets money just to visit an old lady, I was happy to be Turkish. With us that is different.'* Hard as it may be to explain to non-westerners how it feels from the Dutch perspective, it needs to be said that among migrant communities from such countries the same trend is developing, since they now share the general Dutch conditions of housing and workload.

Personal independence *'People are nice here, but they don't make an effort to get in touch with you. They leave you alone too much. In the apartment where I live, they helped me when I locked myself out, but afterwards they were at a distance again.'* (South Africa)

Yes, Dutch society, like other western cultures, is 'atomising' … individualism is increasing, and it shocks people from more 'collectivist' cultures. *'I think Dutch people don't want to get involved with each other.'* (Iran)

Most people here quite like their independence and become uneasy when they feel that it is threatened. Many Dutch people live alone: single, divorced and widowed people represent some 35% of all households nationwide. In the larger cities, sometimes more than 50% of households are single-person. Living alone, of course, is not always the same as being lonely. Just like their married or cohabiting counterparts, single people have their friends and colleagues, their hobbies and sports clubs – their own lifestyle. A single person's leisure time is often highly structured, not by the family, as it were, but by an individual routine.

Regardless of household status, the separation of work and leisure time is important to the Dutch. Small wonder this observation was made: *'It is very hard to get your Dutch colleagues to go for a beer after work, at least I haven't succeeded in that yet.'* (Finland). In the current, more adaptable economy, many Dutch people try to negotiate flexible work hours in order to arrive at an optimal balance in their private lives – sharing childcare, for example, with their partner who also works. Quite a few employers accede to requests for such arrangements. Also, some experimentation with 'tele-working' has started in branches such as insurance, where people can work at least part of the time from home.

An increase in one-person households obviously has consequences for 'the market' – they also want essentials such as furniture, refrigerators, microwaves and other appliances. Also as a result, more and more one-person portions of food and other products are being sold. When marketing or selling in the Netherlands, business people may want to keep this demographic trend in mind.

Hospitality   One last aspect of individualism should be mentioned, as it affects visitors from other countries. Being quite individualistic, the Dutch assume that everyone is like that and prefers to be left alone – free to make his or her own choices. In fact, the literal translation of the Dutch word for hospitality, *gastvrijheid*, is 'guest-freedom'! So colleagues from abroad are not always given the kind of hospitality that they themselves might extend to guests at home.

In the Netherlands, invitations are given for set evenings or weekends. Typically, the Dutch hosts will cook a good meal, set the table nicely, select music to please their guests, take them somewhere that they feel will interest them, etc. In short, they do their best to make things *gezellig*. Guests receive 100% of the family's attention, and anyone dropping in or phoning will be put off – remember that the Dutch are 'monochronic'. But this shower of attention lasts only as long as that particular dinner party or that particular one-day excursion. Western visitors have little problem with this aspect of the Dutch character. *'I always found Dutchmen very hospitable. All right, you must make an arrangement to visit them and I had to get used to that. But once the arrangement is made, they receive you very well.'* (Iceland) And: *'Our neighbours are friendly, they have invited us twice for tea and they give us good advice on how to do things for example, in finding a hospital for childbirth.'* (Japan)

But a lady from India commented, *'In India we had Dutch expatriates for neighbours. We went to their house to say hello, welcomed them with a dinner party and offered our help. When we moved to Holland, we expected the same in reverse, but nobody came. I had to go and ask them in. Only then they came. That was very disappointing to us, but I must add that later they were very nice to us.'* I can imagine the initial disappointment, but readers should be reminded that privacy is a major priority in the Netherlands. Dutch neighbours are reluctant to intrude upon people who are still settling in – perhaps cleaning up their new house or apartment, arranging their furniture and, in general setting up their household. Remember the section in this book on charity: the Dutch are sensitive to anyone who needs help, but they also respect people's privacy. Help is almost always given – but only if asked for.

In essence, the Dutch consider themselves to be very hospitable, always doing their best to please their guests. But given their sense of privacy and their family orientation, Dutch hospitality does not imply a non-stop welcome at any given time – access *is* restricted. To expatriates from countries where the door is always open for anyone to drop in, this may be disappointing: *'People here are different, more business-like. I have only once visited a Dutch home, for reasons of work, but never for just a cup of tea.'* (Egypt)

This brings us to the position of migrants in the Netherlands.

1. All figures mentioned in this chapter were found in articles in *NRC-Handelsblad* newspaper.
2. True or not, it does hold for quite another aspect: a 2004 survey showed that in many Dutch households the wife arranges the payments for rent, electricity and the like!
3. To my experience, perhaps for pragmatic reasons, Dutch women seem to have less objections to using only 'he' in phrases like this one.

Chapter 11

ON ETHNIC ISSUES AND
MULTICULTURAL SOCIETY

Already for some years now, the multicultural society – or its failure, some say – is the hottest issue in the Netherlands, both in politics and in the everyday life of people, particularly in the cities. As
a result, this is the chapter that most urgently needed to be
revised for this new edition.

Visiting business people and expatriates living in the Netherlands cannot fail to notice that they are not the only ones of foreign descent. Rotterdam leads in this aspect of demographics, with
the largest percentage of foreign residents, ranging from harbour
workers to generally well-paid expatriates. In this chapter, I will
focus not on expatriates but on people of non-western origin who
are permanently residing in the Netherlands – the non-western
migrants (quite a few of them of recent arrival) who make up over
10% of the total Dutch population, estimated to be 15% by the year
2020. In large cities they already make up 1/3 of the population or
more; and of those below age 15, they are even the majority – a
factor that obviously has certain consequences for education.

Foreigners, aliens, migrants, guest workers or
allochtonen? '*I was shocked to find they have a special word
for everyone not born here.*' (South Africa) To begin with, the Dutch
never quite know how to refer to the immigrants here. Yet clear
definitions are required for legislation, certain tax deductions,
educational arrangements and the like. What exactly should be
the criteria? Is it one's place of birth (but then, what about former
colonials?), the passport one carries (what about double citizenship?), the official residence (how about people retired in Spain,
for example?), and what about the second or third generation?

It is estimated that some 10 – 15% of the present population of
16 million were not born in the Netherlands, or at least one of
their parents was not[1]. This last aspect is the official criterion for

defining *allochtonen*, a Greek word meaning 'born elsewhere', used by the Dutch to indicate the widely varied group of more or less permanent immigrants here. About half of the *allochtonen* are people from former colonies (Indonesia, Surinam, the Netherlands Antilles) who already had Dutch citizenship when they arrived. Exact figures on this segment of the population are not known because of the differing degrees of residence in the country and a legal prohibition, after 1945, on registering race or descent (unlike foreign nationality). In 2004, Rotterdam municipality announced that it will no longer use the word *allochtonen*, but – when necessary – terms like 'Rotterdammers of Turkish origin'.

Needless to say, the presence of so many migrants in Dutch society is a very touchy issue, with both political correctness and pleads to ignore too much sensitivity, with strong mutual feelings on both the Dutch and the non-Dutch side, and with incidents, insults and sometimes injuries from both sides.

In 2001, besides the shock of 9/11, the Netherlands also experienced the sudden and fierce political debate by Pim Fortuyn and his followers on the limits of migration and multiculturalism. Fortuyn's assassination in 2002 made him a martyr to some, and it kept the debate open-ended, certainly when his following mostly fell apart soon after. But what Fortuyn left behind – in the media, the political scene and among the wider public – was an even stronger degree of outspokenness on the issue, experienced by some as a refreshing lack of political correctness but by others as a dangerous venue for opinions verging on the edge of racism. As a result, there is more public pressure on national and local authorities to restrict the influx of foreigners, or at least to apply stricter criteria and checks on them.

Proposals to keep 'people with poor chances' out of the Netherlands and to attract the potentially successful – as Rotterdam with its locally-strong Fortuyn party did – were not shocking only to foreign ears. But in Dutch culture with its tradition of directness and critical opinions being open for debate, people are perhaps not as easily offended as elsewhere. The idea is: 'If you don't agree, speak up!' And indeed, both the national government and several more left-wing parties and organisations did object, leading to ongoing debate.

The aliens police   *'Dutch bureaucracy is incredible; it took us seven months to get the right permits to come to Holland!'* (Indian manager)

In the Netherlands, registration and residence permits for immigrants, including all expatriates who may be here for only a few years, are arranged through the so-called 'aliens police'. (In Dutch, its name – *vreemdelingenpolitie* – does not sound quite as strange as this literal translation.) Realising that Dutch residence with its related benefits and freedoms is a very attractive option for scores of people from less privileged countries, the aliens police is the instrument to restrict membership, particularly of those who may be 'unwanted'. Dutch authorities know very well how some people from abroad pay enormous amounts of money to be smuggled into the Netherlands. With reports on smuggling, false marriages and such, there is a lot of mistrust. *'When I applied for a visa at the Dutch embassy in Moscow, they treated me really badly.'* (Russian management trainee)

Expats tell me how appalled they are by the aliens police's bureaucratic and distrustful procedures, although this may greatly differ from one municipality to another. Although not aware of this, they encounter more or less the same procedures by the Dutch immigration policy as those people seeking permanent residence, including asylum seekers and refugees. Given the Dutch view on equal treatment for everyone, so far the aliens police have not been permitted to distinguish between different categories of applicants. All have to take a number, sit down and wait their turn.

Already for years, companies needing foreign workforces have pleaded for faster procedures to allow their employees legal access for work, but only in 2004 does it look as if the authorities involved will finally expedite this.

Describing the present-day complex situation of ethnic issues in the Netherlands is not easy. Let me try to present some Dutch views, because even more than on other subjects in this book, there are 16 million views represented here.

In the background, there is of course the Dutch 'box-society' which leaves people all the freedom they want but which also leaves them to themselves. Another aspect is that the Dutch press and media are perhaps a bit too voluminous for the size of the country, with journalists eagerly chasing scoops, over-exposing incidents, sometimes manipulating people into saying unwise things and recycling all this a few times over. As such, bad and shocking news always draws more attention than good developments – including on multicultural issues. In all Dutch cities, one can see hard-working, successful shopkeepers of other ethnicities, but yes, some of the telephone shops indeed appear to be cover-ups for illegal activities. Most young people from those groups eagerly study to make their way in society, as do many of their Dutch friends but, indeed, some of these immigrant youth really misbehave, first provoking other people into hostile reactions and then complaining about being treated with disrespect.

Dutch city people have become accustomed to most aspects of multicultural society, and one notices many mixed friendships and love relations. Ethnic music, literature and food are quite popular these days, and yet Dutch society in general is not quite multicultural. For example, although quite unique in Europe, there are subsidised national television programmes in the Netherlands for various ethnic groups, but a rather low presence of other ethnic people on regular Dutch television programmes. It should be said that it is not only the native Dutch who tend to stay in their 'boxes'; some groups of immigrants prefer to stick to their own communities and media, particularly the more conservative Muslims. And there we come to the core issue.

In terms of religion, the Dutch usually have a relaxed attitude, as this immigrant notices: *'I experienced the tolerance toward other people's faith as a relief. I think it's wonderful how fundamentalist Protestants, Catholics and non-believers can live next to each other in peace.'* (Northern Ireland) But that observation has to do with varieties of Christianity. It's a different story with non-western religions, or rather, with Islam, since the presence of Asian religions never causes any concern. As it stands, there are almost a million Muslims in the Netherlands now. The majority of them are not fanatics, but as with any faction, the more conservative and intolerant among them draw the most attention. In general, the Dutch don't object to Islamic – or any other – traditions, such as the wearing of headscarves for women. *'Nobody at university minds me wearing a headscarf. Quite the contrary: my fellow students admire me for it. People in Turkey could hardly imagine the combination of a female student and a headscarf. That alone proves that the Netherlands is where I want to be. I'm too attached to my freedom. That doesn't mean I don't value Turkish culture, of course.'* (Dutch student of Turkish descent)

I'm not going to deny, however, that most Dutch people do oppose full veiling and burqas, and their opinions were adversely influenced by reports of certain gangs of 'ethnic' youngsters terrorising teachers, attacking bus drivers at night and harassing women in swimming pools. More than once the media has reported how conservative imams fiercely preach against homosexuals and women's rights, in languages incomprehensible to outsiders. This is visibly upsetting to the Dutch and a real problem of integration for the Muslims.

Remembering how most of the Dutch abandoned the churches in the 1960s and 70s and how religion became a totally private and socially invisible issue, Dutch people are definitely not pleased to see grim preachers enter the scene again, even from another culture, sometimes explicitly warning their followers not to mix with non-believers – with 'immoral' Dutch society. This mood change is all the more striking since, for decades, it was quite 'taboo' to express any negative feelings about the immigrants, for they were considered to be underdogs – a category of people that, by Dutch standards, one should go easy on.

From my experience, direct or hard statements by Dutch individuals on this issue can be quite difficult to understand for some people from abroad. Indeed, quite extreme, sometimes shocking views are openly expressed nowadays and, depending on the kind of debate that foreigners are accustomed to back home, the reaction varies. *'I hear well-educated middle-class people saying things about Moroccans without any hesitation, which would be absolutely unacceptable in Britain. Bashing minorities is widespread. I can imagine that some groups start feeling excluded in Dutch society.'* (UK journalist)

For decades, Dutch society had an image of endless tolerance, and it still is as liberal as always on most lifestyle issues, but now suddenly there surface these harsh opinions on some other ethnic groups. Understandably, people from the cultures under debate may feel personally offended, while citizens of countries where immigration was the very basis of their existence – the USA, Canada, Australia and a few others – might be shocked by the explicit tone of such remarks. In these referenced countries, where virtually everyone considers him(her)self or the ancestors as immigrants, mechanisms and procedures for integrating newcomers into society are well-established.

But Europe is, by and large, the continent of those who stayed. Many Europeans have strong feelings that 'this land is ours; it always was'. In Europe, minorities traditionally had their own regions, their own areas in towns, their economic niches, and their separate social channels. In this regard, the Netherlands is no exception, although any negative feelings were only verbally expressed. Here also, newcomers were felt to be outsiders, tolerated as long as they accepted their minority position and did not grow too large in numbers or influence. Throughout Dutch history, people of different walks of life have always dealt with each other economically but kept apart from each other socially. That may be the case even today. *'What strikes me is how little curious the Dutch are. And vice versa, they also don't seem to appreciate it when others are curious. For newcomers to this country this is bad. Without curiosity there is no real communication. Curiosity makes contacting people much easier and more pleasant.'* (USA)

Luckily, there are also more positive views from immigrants from other cultures, as this Cuban dance instructor expressed, *'We (Cubans) move from our heart and that is hard to copy for the "sober" Dutch. Of course I like it that Latin-American dance and music become more and more popular in the Netherlands. This country is open to new influences; it is good in selecting exactly those foreign elements that add colour to its own culture. Aerobics to exotic music and with a tropical sauce, for instance; that's what the Dutch really love.'*

In my opinion, two Dutch characteristics are involved here: first, the tendency to restrict social life to one's own group and not be inquisitive about someone else's, and second, the pragmatic approach – is there anything useful or pleasant that I can pick up from that new culture?

Some historical and psychological background It should be noted that the Netherlands was an all-white country up to the 1920s, since even people from the Dutch colonies hardly ever made it here. So without any restraint, the 19th century national anthem began: *'To those with Dutch blood in their veins, free of foreign* *taint...'* (In 1890 this anthem was abandoned for a 16th-century hymn, now still in use.)

Granted, there had been religious refugees from other European nations in the 17th century (mostly Spanish and Portuguese Jews and French Protestants), but by 1930 that episode was long forgotten and their descendants almost invisibly integrated into Dutch society, having created their own niches. Then the first group of non-westerners arrived – Chinese shipping personnel from the steamboats connecting the Dutch East Indies to the Netherlands who lost their jobs in the 1929 economic crisis. Consistent with the Dutch compassion for underdogs, they were welcomed and helped. The same applied for the people expelled from Indonesia around 1950, often of Dutch or half-Dutch descent, and familiar with Dutch mentality at least to some degree. The humanitarian (but also somewhat paternalistic) principle of 'helping the underdog' was at first also applied to the migrant workers from Mediterranean countries arriving in the 1960s, the decade in which mass immigration to the Netherlands by people from vastly different cultures really began.

'Guest workers' By the mid 1960s, after Marshall-aid and postwar reconstruction, the Dutch economy boomed and the nation could afford to offer its young people a good and extended education. This resulted in a serious shortage of blue-collar workers and, as in surrounding countries, work contracts were given to unskilled labourers from poor rural communities in Morocco, Turkey and, to a lesser degree, from other Mediterranean countries economically far behind Western Europe. With an apparent lack of skills for city life, the hard-working young men evoked some sympathy, but, living in cheap pensions, were generally left to themselves in the 'live and let live' structure of Dutch urban society.

In the initial years of their stay, both these 'guest workers' and their hosts expected them to soon return home with their earnings, so neither party felt the urge to further the acquaintance. In the strongly socialist-inspired political climate of the time, the mood was to give social assistance to these underprivileged people. It also allowed them the freedom that the Dutch were so eagerly exploring (or disapproving of, depending on the perspective) in the hippie era and during the student revolt: 'Do your thing and don't bother anyone else; all you need is love.'

But the guest workers were neither hippies nor students, and their love was not for the alien hippie culture but for their own wives and children left behind in (Turkish) Anatolia and the (Moroccan) Rif Mountains. As years went by and saving their money turned out to be harder than expected, labour contracts were prolonged – as was the loneliness among the men, prompting them to ask permission to bring their families to the Netherlands. In most cases, such permission was granted. Thus, not only the number of migrant people rose, but also the opportunity to live their social life in their own circle, quite in line with the already existing Dutch system of social segregation.

Meanwhile, Dutch attention was drawn to a new wave of immigrants. In 1975, more former colonials arrived in a rather dramatic exodus from suddenly independent Surinam, a former Dutch colony[2] in South America with politically rivalling ethnic groups of African and Indian descent. They were soon followed by Caribbean people, migrants from the Netherlands Antilles – again, many of them speaking Dutch to some degree. After considerable initial problems, their integration into Dutch society was reasonably successful. The two groups together now number some 400,000 people[3] and social relations between them and the local Dutch are generally quite positive.

Emigration *from* Holland   All in all, immigration and integration went smoother for people with some familiarity with Dutch culture, but was more difficult for groups from cultures farther away. It should be realised that the Netherlands never really perceived itself as a country of immigration until the 1970s. In fact, already since the 1880s emigration had occurred *from* the Netherlands. Around 1950, in the bleak, post-war years when the Cold War cast an uncomfortable shadow across the whole of Europe, some 300,000 Dutch people left to start a new life in countries such as Australia, New Zealand, the USA and Canada. Then the economic tides changed and immigration began. After decades of an immigration surplus, in 2004 the trend reversed, with more people leaving from the Netherlands than arriving here. They are not only returning migrants, but also ethnic Dutch themselves, some of whom leave for economic reasons, others in search of wider horizons.

Although more people immigrate than leave, it was only in 1998 that the government officially recognised the fact that the Netherlands is a great draw to immigrants. The effect of this belated acknowledgement was that – unlike the true immigration countries mentioned – the Netherlands had never developed an official policy or procedures for mass immigration. No introduction programmes had been set up, no obligatory language classes, and no nation-wide strategy for providing housing, education and jobs to newcomers. There seemed to be no need for this when immigration started circa 1950, since the first immigrants spoke Dutch and were familiar with Dutch culture. Indeed, most of them silently and successfully integrated into Dutch society.

When the families of the Turkish and Moroccan workers left their rural surroundings and came to live in urbanised Netherlands, they often found housing in the dilapidated, cheaper blocks built during the industrial revolution of the 1880s. The same blocks from which, if they could afford it, Dutch working class people were moving away to greener suburbs. Likewise, the decaying suburbs from the 1950s and 60s also became increasingly 'ethnic'. Naturally, the immigrants opened shops to cater to their needs, and organised places of worship and community centres. Gradually, all the larger cities of the Netherlands saw the rise of ethnic groups with quite different cultures, many of them living in the working class areas surrounding the old city centres.

Integration   Up until the 1980s the Dutch economy generally thrived, and there was little competition for jobs from the 'foreign' workers. But then things changed. Unemployment rose among the Dutch, but it rose much more among the immigrant workers. When on international television fierce-looking groups of extremists started violently advocating Islamic revolution, irritation in the Netherlands about the foreigners' cultural habits, their women's scarves and even their Muslim beliefs, was voiced more and more openly. Authorities and individuals alike began to worry about potential ethnic violence. All kinds of municipal and welfare organisations, official and private, developed preventive activities. Although all of these initiatives were subsidised by the government, there still was no overall policy, thereby resulting in a confusing patchwork of small-scale solutions. Only in the 1980s, when permanent ethnic minorities started forming from these groups (in an unfavourable economic climate with high unemployment), did the need for a more consistent policy become urgent.

However, the introductory citizenship and language programmes then set up proved not to be very successful. At first, newcomers were merely advised to follow them. By 2002 they were made obligatory for attaining permanent residence. But with fixed quality standards and a shortage of teachers in regular education, there are not enough people today to facilitate them, resulting in waiting lists. There is also confusion as to what is useful content for the programme: how much should one know about a society, its history, and its habits? Moreover, suddenly making such programmes obligatory as well for those people who arrived long ago is difficult to accept, certainly after having been neglected for years and allowed to settle without such requirements.

There are now an estimated 350,000 people of Turkish origin and 300,000 of Moroccan descent living in the Netherlands. (Given the confusion on definitions mentioned before, these figures are quite uncertain.) Most of the 'first generation' migrants have retained their original nationality, since dual nationality is either legally impossible or considered undesirable in their country of origin. Lacking a better word, people still call members of immigrant groups *allochtonen*, although there are more and more objections to the term from the people involved, for instance with sarcastic jokes such as: 'Do you speak Allochtonian?'

Many Turkish and Moroccan families in the Netherlands still live mostly in their own circles. There are few social contacts outside their own religious and ethnic groups, let alone marriages. Ongoing marriage-immigration from the region of origin, with so-called import brides, has a negative effect on the position of the groups as a whole, adversely affecting their offspring's cultural adaptation, language capacities and economic chances. Pressed by radical politician Pim Fortuyn's ideas, in 2003 the government introduced much stricter requirements on admitting such marriage partners to the country. Fierce protests against this policy from other corners was not to much effect.

Asylum seekers   So far I have focussed on the groups that arrived as labour migrants. But at the same time, the influx of asylum seekers from countries all over the world also demanded action. Ever since the 1970s, Europe has witnessed an increase in the number of legal and illegal refugees, arriving from countries all over the world, requesting political asylum. Authorities around the continent try to distinguish between real (political) refugees and mere fortune seekers and are under pressure from various sections of society. People fear abuse of the social benefit system, the loss of the established peaceful social order, religious fanaticism or even, in the case of the Netherlands, still greater over-population. Exact figures are hard to give, since people come and leave across the EU's semi-open borders – both legally and illegally – but estimates are in the 100,000's. Countries from which large groups of asylum seekers have arrived include Afghanistan, Iraq, Iran, former Yugoslavia, Somalia, Sudan, Angola and Sierra Leone.

Until recently, both in absolute and relative figures, the Netherlands received the second highest number of asylum seekers in Europe, after Germany. (With open borders and people entering illegally, once more, exact figures are hard to give.) Under public pressure, policies were severely restricted, and the number of arrivals has considerably gone down, both in absolute and relative figures. Even so, the immigration police department set up to check the validity of these people's stories – deciding which are genuine and then channelling these legitimate cases into Dutch society – is grossly overburdened.

One result is that people not yet legally admitted are made to endlessly wait their case in special centres, where they are neither allowed to work nor to even learn Dutch, since that might falsely indicate permission to stay. Only their children up to age 16 go to school. Tragic stories of depression and loss of self-respect are received by the Dutch media. Many people protest against expelling ('deporting') people who have to wait so long that their children are now fully integrated in Dutch schools. But at the same time there is increasing pressure on the authorities to crack down on what are seen as 'bogus' asylum seekers. It also didn't help the asylum seekers' case when it was found out that some had had their young daughters circumcised, at times even during a visit to their supposedly unsafe country of origin.

With stricter criteria, the Netherlands hopes to deter people from coming here, but the country's prosperity and good human rights reputation mean that people continue to arrive. When finally admitted, asylum seekers are supported by job mediation and integration programmes.

Perhaps in line with this issue, other immigrants including expatriates fall victim to the growing suspicion of 'foreigners' in general. *'I got so angry when this police officer told me: "This cannot be your car!" Just because I look a bit different and speak Dutch with an accent!'* (Serbia) After the opening up of Eastern Europe, the Netherlands faces an increased influx of immigrants from those relatively nearby countries. With some very violent criminal gangs active here but originating from those countries, in 2004 the mood in the Netherlands on the new EU member states and labour migration from there is averse and conservative.

Social issues among immigrants   Among the migrant groups in the Netherlands, unemployment is three to four times higher than among the locals, and salaries are on average 22% lower. This can be partly explained by lower levels of education, a lower average age (of workers) and a higher share of part-time work, but selectivity and outright discrimination from the side of employers obviously also play a role.

When a few years ago it became known that almost half of the 'ethnic' workers above forty years of age now receive a WAO (Labour Disability) benefit, debate ensued in the Dutch media. It was argued that the basic reason for this was the harder physical labour of these workers, but that it probably also signalled a less satisfactory relationship with colleagues and the employer due to cultural differences.

This brings us to other social problems, in the field of health care and education. In general, people from the ethnic minorities have more health problems than the native Dutch. At the same time, communicating these problems to Dutch doctors and institutions may be more difficult for them, often requiring translation by their children. This is also true when dealing with municipal authorities and similar bodies. In spite of advertisements and information brochures in Turkish and Arabic (but not necessarily English!), there are quite a few cases where *allochtonen* do not reap the social benefits or subsidies they are entitled to, due – in no small way, it seems – to illiteracy or unfamiliarity with the Dutch system. School attendance of young immigrant children also lags behind, sometimes due to the parents' cultural or religious beliefs, while lack of knowledge also leads to more obesity and more teenage pregnancies in these groups.

Coming generally from poor backgrounds in their native countries, the majority of first generation Turkish and Moroccans in the Netherlands have only finished elementary school. Among their children, who were either born in the Netherlands or brought here at a very young age, secondary school participation is growing fast, but even so, a much higher percentage of these children leave school without a certificate than is the case among the locals. One result is that, in the dip that the Netherlands is going through, unemployment rates are rising more strongly than average. Whatever was gained during the 1990s boom is lost again. A few figures: unemployment among Dutch youngsters between 15 and 24 was 7% in 2003, but among youngsters of Turkish and Moroccan descent, 17% and 18% respectively. Many of these immigrants follow the lower types of education such as basic vocational training, and there are quite a few school dropouts, whose public behaviour often causes concern among authorities from all sides. *'Our social hierarchy is different. Out on the streets those boys behave differently than at home. Nobody likes the way they behave, but society is hard, and it is everyone for himself. Those guys don't know anymore what solidarity means. They don't know what is expected of them and how things should be done. Perhaps they feel forgotten, overlooked so they pester back.'* (Turkish representative of the Dutch Islamic Society for Senior Citizens.) Campaigns are set up to better inform and involve parents in their children's school career, but this is not an easy task when those parents hardly have any experience of school themselves.

Luckily, the majority of these youngsters do finish their education and they don't do badly at all; in fact, more and more people from Moroccan and Turkish descent work in mid-level and high-level jobs. There are also an increasing number of 'ethnic' people in media, the arts and literature and the political scene, but just as with women, representation could always be better. As elsewhere in Western Europe, immigrants and their offspring are more often found at the lower levels of society and business. Statistics show that they tend to be cleaners, factory workers and supermarket personnel rather than intellectuals or managers.

Multicultural society   In the previous edition of this book I quoted a young waitress of Turkish descent who said, *'The thing I like most about the Netherlands is the level of tolerance. Regardless of*

*whether you're black or white, man or woman, hooker or stewardess –
no one gets in your way.'* I am not sure if she would still say so now,
as the social climate has hardened, and tolerance has decreased,
especially toward Muslims. It has been said that Dutch tolerance
has bitten its own tail, that the liberty in lifestyles may have decreased the necessity for ethnic minority groups to fit in, leading
to more mutual *in*tolerance. The hardening of Dutch opinions on
immigration and on Muslim culture in particular sometimes also
increases uncertainty and feelings of not belonging, of not being
accepted, among various other categories of migrants, including
non-Muslims.

Yet, to people from other countries, and certainly to well-educated expatriates moving here, Dutch society is still quite open-
minded and welcoming. For them, the following quote still holds:
*'Generally speaking, there is an atmosphere here of tolerance, equality
and equal rights. In other so-called developed countries, the locals act as
if they're superior and they behave dominantly. Of course, here too there
are some people who act strangely and discriminate in subtle ways, but
the majority is tolerant and hospitable to foreigners.'* (Cambodia) And:
*'Children here don't sit up at all if a new kid in class looks quite different,
but we didn't know that before we came. My kids expected to be in a
school full of pink children with white hair.'* (Japan)

Racists?   All the stories and statistics published in the press and
all the debate leads parts of the general Dutch public – perhaps
those less educated and living in areas where the ethnic mix is
strongest – to feel rather overwhelmed by the changes that immigrants and multicultural society have brought. Conservative and
chauvinist about the accomplishments of Dutch society, they
often feel threatened by what seems to be a never-ending flow of
people who all want to come and live here. Quite a few fear that
these immigrants – sticking to their own culture and religion – will
not truly blend in. Some complain quite loudly, and former politician Pim Fortuyn gave a venue for this discontent. But with his
political movement mostly eroded now, many people grumble in
the privacy of their own homes. In this vein, there is also a great
deal of silent opposition from people withdrawing into the shelter
of private life and closing off from society at large. In contacts
with other groups, such people behave neutrally, never saying bad
things but also not reaching out.

'Dutchmen pretend to be the conscience of the world. But you only need look about you or read the newspapers and you see a whole lot of discrimination. Here too, people are not treated equally.' (South Africa)

Yet, in my opinion, the vast majority of Dutch people are not really racists in the sense of distinguishing people on the basis of colour. Granted, they may be conservative and not half as tolerant as their reputation goes, but on the streets and on television you can see quite a few ethnically mixed friendships and marriages (and 'living together', of course). By far, most Dutch people accept such relationships. People of different backgrounds also happily work, study and party together. In a comparative survey of European racism, the Dutch were found to be no more racist than citizens in surrounding countries (but indeed, not less either). So in most circles, skin colour is not a big issue, but what *does* matter to the Dutch are signs of religious intolerance and disrespect of people's personal freedom and lifestyle. The risk is, of course, that the attention drawn by Muslim fundamentalists or violent youngsters negatively affects the reputation of their communities at large.

In the debate on multicultural society, pleas are made to keep open the lines of communication, to remain on speaking terms, and to prevent the kind of socio-religious *apartheid*[4] that ruled much of Dutch society until not so long ago. But like the Dutch majority itself, many people from the other ethnic groups seem to prefer living their lives within their own groups and not mixing with people from others. This is obviously not favourable to social integration, and migrants may have a hard time climbing the social ladder as a result. *'People from Turkey or Morocco can only marginally participate, not in leading positions or in politics. Within Dutch organisations, foreigners get very few chances. People still think that if they can't speak Dutch exactly like us, their knowledge will probably be less also.'* (Turkish businesswoman)

The housing situation also keeps people separate. Expats are guided into in an almost separate market of very expensive houses, but the local housing market for the wider public is more complicated; and with limited space and large demand, housing prices have greatly increased over the last few years. Dutch people do not move house easily, and in the larger cities many apartments are municipal properties for rent, with a system of allocation and waiting lists based on family size, income and urgency. The overall effect is that there is an increasing segregation between the Dutch living in newer and mid-market areas, and migrants in the older, cheaper areas. It should be said, however, that even in those less expensive areas, housing conditions are by far not as bad as in the poorer areas of most other countries.

As happens in other countries, 80% of the Dutch think that residential areas deteriorate when there is a high percentage of other ethnic people living there. Likewise, more than 50% of the *allochtonen* think the same, and many try to avoid schools where too many children don't speak Dutch properly, since this negatively affects the learning process. Half of them also say that there are too many other ethnic people in the Netherlands already.

All in all, the social gap and geographical separation between Dutch and non-Dutch citizens leads to a continuation of stereotypes and prejudices about each other's cultures. It keeps people in different 'boxes', and even expats notice this. *'The Dutch have a silo mentality.'* (Russia) And: *'It shocks me to hear the Dutch openly say negative things about whole categories of ethnic people. In the UK, racism happens on a more personal, individual level; here it seems to be generic.'* (Britain)

Without trying to deny this, I want to point out to readers that in 'the olden days', Dutch people easily spoke the same about other religious groups, knowing that – in a country without a clear majority group – in the end all lived in freedom. Since generic terms were not felt to be greatly insulting or dangerous, could that be why the Dutch still readily use them?

Ethnic dividing lines cán, of course, easily evoke attitudes of 'us' and 'them', in spite of campaigns on television and street posters designed to help overcome such feelings. The limits of tolerance are stretched by minor everyday irritations triggered by such sensory reminders as exotic-smelling food or the neighbour's native music, or the local shop with its array of foreign products replacing the Dutch merchandise.

More personal contact and communication are probably the only way to overcome such prejudice and discrimination. Given the tendencies on both sides to cling to one's own group, this may be difficult to bring about; but people should nonetheless try – keeping in mind that integration is a two-way process. With a long tradition of living with 'people who think differently'[5], the Netherlands has always had several social mechanisms to keep a balance between togetherness and separateness in a small playing field.

But the players have changed, and so did the game. Dutch society and the world as a whole have hardened. Under public pressure, authorities set stricter rules and apply them more relentlessly, while organisations from other corners of society defend the people affected. Most parties want to prevent conflict, try to be humane and do justice on both sides, but interpretations differ greatly, and it is clear that in certain areas tensions are growing.

Finally Dutch society, the same as all others, has become much more complex in recent years. With increasing individualism and pluralism against the backdrop of worldwide tensions, disintegration of the social fabric might surely turn benevolence toward other groups into indifference and intolerance. Social dissatisfaction is on the increase, and youngsters especially may be tempted into lawless and antisocial acts ranging from vandalism and harassment to violent crime, thereby causing widespread annoyance, fear and outrage from their victims and the general public. This is true of *all* ethnic groups, including the Dutch. The police may produce decreasing crime figures, but reports of hooliganism, violence – particularly against older people, children and animals – theft, drug abuse, and so on, do nothing to appease the general feeling that society is heading for even harder times.

Yet outside the spotlights, there are also good things happening. Mixed marriages occur increasingly often, with people of all backgrounds meeting in their places of work, in schools and shops, at sports clubs and in other organisations. Second and third-generation immigrants blend in much more successfully than their parents. Speaking Dutch fluently, they reach higher education levels and find better jobs, thus coming into closer contact with their Dutch peers. Cultural bridges will be built and will grow naturally.

Unless economic disaster or worldwide cultural clashes occur, there is still a fair chance that in a few decades people with unusual family names will go just as unnoticed in Dutch society as those with French or German names are now, that Asian or African features will become as 'socially invisible' as Indonesian ones are now. The process is already underway. Perhaps we're just too impatient.

Having explored the issue of cultural variety over the last decades, let's now turn to some regional varieties in Dutch culture.

1. Excluded from this figure are people from other European Union member states, who number some 300,000.
2. Since 1954 an autonomous part of the kingdom.
3. Being Dutch citizens, they are not separately registered.
4. Probably the Dutch word best known internationally, through the South African variety of Dutch called *Afrikaans*. It literally means 'separateness'.
5. This term is one word in Dutch, *andersdenkenden*, an old expression used for people of another religion.

Chapter 12

REGIONS AND RANDSTAD

Netherlanders and Hollanders: regional diversity in a small country

In the introduction I already pointed out that Holland, the Randstad, refers only to the dominant western part of the Netherlands. But, contrary to international perspective, there is much more to the Netherlands than the Randstad, both in area and in cultural variety. In this country of formerly, somewhat isolated areas with poor internal communication and a history of decentralisation, there is still a distinct flavour of regionalism in some areas – however minor it may be. This may result in outsiders – whether Dutch people from other provinces or people from other countries – having a hard time being accepted into local communities. As such, they may still be nicknamed 'import' many years after arrival!

Geographical mobility   People's sense of distance is related to the size of their country. To the Dutch, 200 kilometres is 'far', and they are quite averse to travelling more than one hour to work. In this small country, the accepted average commuting time is 38 minutes, and people are not keen to travel much more, even if doing so would mean a higher salary. Besides the risk of long traffic jams or train delays, again, it's the quality of life that counts. What may play a role also is the fact that Dutch people tend to have their long-term social contacts (relatives, neighbours, clubs) in their immediate area, and many towns still have quite a distinctive 'feel' to them that people don't like to give up.

The bottom line, of course, is the fact that the Dutch economy and the comfortable social benefit system do not force anyone to chase a job and move to another location if the previous job is lost. With private savings or a social benefit, most people can stick it out until they find a suitable new job closer to home, thus avoiding the process of moving house and leaving friends and family behind.

Let's take an in-depth tour of the various provinces of the Netherlands, beginning from north to south, before returning to the cosmopolitan west.

The northern provinces: Friesland and Groningen   Regionalism is quite strong in the northern province of Friesland. To the Dutch the province evokes an image of milk, black-and-white cows, lakes, ice-skating, dark-sailed ships and quaint old villages on manmade hillocks (*terpen*). Among themselves, Frisians speak their own language, Fries, or as they say *Frysk*. It is not a dialect but a separate Germanic language related to Dutch, English and Danish.

With a distinct history and identity, Frisians have a drive for cultural autonomy and probably the country's strongest folklore traditions. In 1996, they succeeded in having the name of the province officially changed to *Fryslân*, and local media are popular. Towns have names posted in both Frisian and Dutch, and primary education is taught partly in the local language. Frisians are said to be hardworking and, once you have gained their trust, very loyal, but watch out ...with a touch of anti-authoritarianism they are reputed to easily lose their temper if provoked.

Culturally, the province of Groningen enjoys a less distinctive image than Friesland, but economically it is very important because of the enormous quantities of natural gas found there, providing resources not only to all of the Netherlands, but also to large parts of Western Europe. Focussing on the area around the provincial capital city of Groningen itself, the more coastal parts of the province have always been fertile and prosperous farmland, but the east was poor, subsisting on peat digging (for fuel) and potato growing. With the profits of the natural gas production going to the national government and not to the province as such, Groningen rather lags behind the rest of the country, with a somewhat lower average income and more unemployment than elsewhere. Yet it is home to a state university, attracting students from the northern provinces and beyond. In a major effort to invite new investments, promotions highlight its spaciousness and the quality of life in its lively capital city, with a hint of its northernmost position on the map: 'There is nothing above Groningen!,' as they say.

The eastern provinces: Drenthe, Overijssel and Gelderland
Generally speaking, easterners are felt to be less outspoken and sociable than people from the western part of the Netherlands. Their reputation is one of being somewhat shy and introverted, of 'not using one word more than is absolutely necessary'. Those from the Randstad may disapprovingly call this 'surly'. This may reflect their earlier largely agricultural orientation, and – even today – the less intensive exposure to the speedy pace of modern-day business life and foreign contacts.

The image of the provinces of Drenthe, Overijssel and Gelderland is mostly based on wooded, hilly areas – although to some foreigners, the Dutch idea of a hill is no more than a bump in the road. Drenthe is relatively flat, so any variances in landscape can primarily be seen in certain – but not all – areas of Overijssel and Gelderland.

All three of these provinces are popular for holidays and among retired people from the Randstad looking for 'somewhere else to live' away from the hustle and bustle. Indeed, there are many charming old towns in this eastern region, and the pace of life is generally slower than in the west. Besides farmland, there are also more industrialised areas, such as can be found around the city cluster of Arnhem and Nijmegen. The eastern industrial area called Twente, once home to the textile industry, focuses on the twin cities of Enschede and Hengelo. Both conglomerations boast universities, which play a role in stimulating innovation and technology, while the Agricultural University in the small town of Wageningen (Gelderland) draws students from across the globe. Logically, business in these areas has convenient connections to the German border and areas beyond to Central and Eastern Europe.

In the mid-1990s, the Gelderland river area called Betuwe received international media attention when it was threatened by potentially disastrous flooding. And although dyke improvements, known as 'the River Delta Plan', have since been made, both locally and further afield people regret the disturbance of the charming river landscapes that this brings about.

The Bible Belt   *' "To Sodom and Gomorrah", said a compatriot when I left from Ireland to Holland ten years ago. But I found a totally different world in the Betuwe countryside, where Sunday rest is still normal and hard work the everyday standard. Our neighbours there were expecting their twelfth child and groups of girls in neat frocks biked past* *on their way to the secluded world of the Calvinist schools.'* (Northern Ireland)

Although not a province in itself, there is a narrow band of land that stretches diagonally through the country from northwestern Overijssel down to the islands of Zeeland and has a very particular variety of Dutch culture. Known as the Dutch 'Bible Belt', this largely rural area has a high proportion of orthodox Calvinists. Social life in this area is still strongly dictated by fundamentalist interpretations of the Bible, such as frequent church attendance and absolute observance of Sunday as a day without work. Both insurance and vaccinations may be considered as opposing God's will, and these Calvinists abhor the modern aspects of city life, including television. On the basis of different interpretations of the Bible (hard to follow for outsiders), this group is subdivided into various denominations, political parties and related institutions such as schools, etcetera. Referring to their stern, sombre manner of dress, the Dutch call them 'black stocking churches'. It was from these circles that, in 2000, a draft amendment that gave workers the right to refuse to work on Sundays was presented to the Dutch Parliament. Employers and their favoured party, the VVD, voted against this amendment, but all other political parties – albeit for various other reasons of their own – supported it.

In the Dutch debate on restricting the fundamentalist Muslim influence in religious education, there are references to the comparable but better-known Bible Belt fundamentalists, who refuse any such curtailing by the state. *'To foreigners, Holland is little more than Amsterdam, a country full of progressive liberals, where anything goes. But going into the provinces, you find people with closed-minded and biased views, strongly religion-oriented. I wrote an article on the outbreak of foot-and-mouth-disease in Kootwijkerbroek, a deeply Calvinistic area. I met people there who saw the crisis as God's punishment.'* (British journalist)

Flevoland   Before turning to the south, something should be said about an area almost without any image at all: the newest province, Flevoland, only officially inaugurated in 1985. For centuries, this area was part of the Zuiderzee, a large body of seawater in the heart of the country. After devastating floods in 1916, it was decided that it should be enclosed and partially reclaimed. Flevoland is the result of decades of hard work by thousands of people, a high-tech province designed in straight lines. *'This is incredible! Isn't it amazing to realise that all of this is not just nature but man-made land!'* (USA) As new land still needing support for development, the EU subsidises some elements of its economy and infrastructure.

Obviously, it also takes time for cultural identity and natural beauty to develop, but it's worth remembering that below all this modernity there *is* a past after all. Long ago, before disappearing under the waters of the Zuiderzee, this area was dry land, and recent excavations have brought to light graves dating from about 5000 BC. Such things might make you think twice about a question I was asked – with some hesitance – on a programme I presented at the Royal Tropical Institute (KIT) in Amsterdam for young African health care workers: *'With all this taking land from the sea, aren't you Dutch afraid of nature taking revenge?'*

The southern provinces: Noord-Brabant, Limburg and Zeeland

This is the part of the country 'beyond the big rivers' of the Rhine, Waal and Maas, with the exception of the province of Zeeland. In contrast to the rest of the nation, southerners are felt to be somewhat more outgoing – enjoying life's pleasures more and being less strictly business-like. Interestingly, in 2003 this so-called 'Burgundian' lifestyle was given as a likely explanation for elderly southerners suffering health problems a bit earlier in life than their more sober compatriots from other provinces. Also, southerners are reputed to be slightly less individualistic than people from the Randstad, and more oriented toward relatives and people from their hometowns.

Clearly, some of these perceptions may be stereotypical, but they do contain a grain of truth. Both outsiders and the southerners themselves point out that all this is related to the fact that the area was never Calvinistic. After the 1500s it remained Catholic when the rest of the country became Protestant. Possibly as a result of the stricter feudal and Catholic hierarchy, people in these southern provinces also have the reputation of being more respectful to authorities such as their boss, the church authorities and political figures.

Professor Geert Hofstede[1] suggests that this Catholic part of the Netherlands might, culturally speaking, be classified as the northernmost part of Latin Europe, while the rest of the country could be called the southernmost part of Scandinavia. Indeed, southerners are also felt to be less openly critical or blunt – perhaps a touch of this Latin mentality. In the business world this leads to more attention to 'representation', e.g. attendance at lunches and dinners, slightly more formal manners such as dressing up for business occasions, and taking more time to get to know each other better.

Nowadays, the large province of Noord-Brabant is highly urbanised and the most industrialised area in the country. But to the Dutch it still evokes images of a slightly Latin ambience that includes carnival celebrations in February, and large, sociable families enjoying food and drinks together. This image reflects the past, a feudal society of rich and noble families owning sandy and infertile land worked by poor peasants, such as the 'Potato Eaters' painted by Van Gogh as late as 1885, along with other images of grinding poverty. A bit of the old pastoral charm still lingers in some villages here, but 'immigration' from other provinces has virtually erased this aspect of life. Around the same time (1890) industrialisation was triggered by the northern Philips family investing heavily in this low-wage area, soon turning the village of Eindhoven into a prosperous industrial city focussed on light and electronics products. To this day, Philips has a very significant presence in the Eindhoven area, including a high-tech campus devoted to major research. The city of Tilburg also has a university.

Speaking of a Latin feeling, it is even stronger among people from the province of Limburg. Its extreme southeastern geographical position and the strange shape of this province suggest that it might easily have become part of Belgium or Germany had history taken a slightly different turn. Indeed, its character is in no way 'typically Dutch', especially in the southernmost part. There one finds (real) rolling hills, a different type of farm and village, a distinctly different lifestyle and a strong dialect, barely understandable to northern ears. Its most distinctive feature is the so-called 'soft G' (also heard in Noord-Brabant), a rather more pleasant way of pronouncing this letter than the 'hard G' in official Dutch.

Limburg's provincial capital city of Maastricht can be called the most Latin city of the Netherlands. *'Sometimes I go to Maastricht. It is more formal there than in Amsterdam, but I like being there. People are happier, more open; they are not Calvinistic. I feel related to them.*

Calvinists are even more religious and stern than the Irish.' (Ireland)
Maastricht became known internationally when it hosted the
1991 EU Treaty carrying its name, and in the 1970s a single medical faculty in the city was extended into a full-blown university.
Limburg hints at its un-Dutchness in tourist advertisements and
it promotes its 'Euregion' character, with German and Belgian
industries nearby, in a bid to attract international business and
investors. Its business culture is also a bit Latin – a less down-to-
earth behaviour than northerners generally have – more ceremony
and more time for initial contact. But over the years, a number of
incidents exhaustively reported in the regional and national press
also proved some less conventional business practices: there were
hints of nepotism and local corruption.

Finally, we turn to Zeeland, the only southern province that turned
Protestant, and therefore, culturally speaking, belongs to the west
rather than the south. But Zeeland has a distinct flavour of its
own. The province has many water-related connotations: islands,
waterways, beaches, oysters and mussels. Until the 1960s this
island province was not only isolated from the rest of the country,
it was also isolated internally – which explains the differences
between islands and villages as well as the low population density.
Zeeland has also suffered from regular flooding. Only after the
devastating floods of 1953, in which more than 1800 people died,
did the rest of the country realise that something should be done.
The Delta Plan was soon underway – a plan that envisaged a complex of huge and ingenious dams designed to keep out the sea
from between the islands, and connecting the islands to the main-
land. This Plan changed the entire character of the communities in
the province, even before the final dam closed off the inland waters
from the North Sea in 1985. Then Dutch and later German tourists
discovered the beauty of the islands, and people from Zeeland
began to commute to work in and around the Rotterdam harbour,
reinforcing the area's 'western' mentality.

Randstad   So that leaves the Randstad. People from overseas
might still wonder, what *is* the Randstad? I already briefly mentioned a few times how the Randstad is the dominant western area
of the country. Here I will add something about its geographic,
economic and cultural makeup.

The word *Randstad*, meaning 'ring-city' or 'edge-city', was coined not that long ago for the cluster of cities in the west which encircle a rather unpopulated agricultural area in the provinces of Noord-Holland, Zuid-Holland² and Utrecht. It includes smaller cities such as Dordrecht, Delft, Leiden, Haarlem, Zaanstad and Hilversum and four main centres: Rotterdam (agglomeration: 1.1 million inhabitants), The Hague (700,000), Amsterdam (1.1 million) and Utrecht (600,000). Together, these cities and the adjoining towns and villages form a metropolis of more than six million people. The economic and cultural activities taking place in the Randstad make living there attractive to many, and further growth is expected (and feared). Several cities proudly host universities, with the one in Leiden being the oldest in the country (1574) and the one in Delft internationally famous for its technology oriented studies.

When travelling between all these cities, people from other countries experience the Randstad as one large conglomeration with a few blotches of green in between. The Dutch still perceive separate cities, and critics say that this hinders a badly needed master plan for the infrastructure. With increasing mobility in recent years, a kind of shared urban identity is growing, but individual cities and villages still boast their own dialect, mentality, history, traditions and culture, although these are fast disappearing. Let's look at the major cities of the Randstad:

Rotterdam, the busy economic heart of the country, is the most modern Dutch city, being continuously rebuilt since the 1940 Nazi bombing raids destroyed the old city centre. Rotterdam is home to many important economic and scientific activities, and its Erasmus University is closely (but not exclusively) linked to them. Its port areas stretch for over 30 kilometres to the sea and are home to shipping and shipping-related companies, huge oil refineries, and Europe's largest cargo storage areas. In fact, Rotterdam is the main harbour for the German Ruhr region, with which it is connected by excellent inland waterways, the Rhine and Waal rivers. In terms of mentality, Rotterdam's inhabitants are known to be very pragmatic, hardworking, money-minded and somewhat chauvinistic. Its business circles, closely linked to the harbour, are said to combine all these traits, generating a certain pride even in being described as 'rough and tough'. As mentioned before, Rotterdam is also the city with the highest number of non-Dutch residents.

Den Haag (The Hague) is the residence of Queen Beatrix and it is the country's political centre, and yet it is *not* the official capital; Amsterdam is. This city is home to the Dutch Parliament and its ministries, to the foreign embassies, the International Court of Justice, and the International Criminal Court. Royal Dutch Shell's headquarters are also here, as well as numerous national organisations. In spite of the many activities that take place here, it has remained a quiet, green city where many foreign expatriates choose to live. Some Dutch people like the 'chic' atmosphere of the city, while others may not appreciate the Hagueners' slightly formal lifestyles, accusing them of 'window dressing'. Of course, the city also has some less well-to-do areas east of the centre.

Amsterdam is the official capital and home to the Netherlands' cultural elite and to thousands of non-conformists (see chapter 8). Amsterdammers are fiercely chauvinistic about their city's avant-garde position and even of its somewhat doubtful reputation. They are the most extroverted of all the northerners, and the city's proverbial humour and dialect still reflect the city's former Jewish subculture. But Amsterdam's reputation often makes people forget that the city is also a booming business centre. It is home to the age-old Dutch stock exchange with its AEX index, to the head-quarters of a number of Dutch and international banks, the diamond industry, and a number of graphics industries, including national newspapers. In the field of ITC, Amsterdam is one of Europe's leading centres. It also houses two universities, a smaller Calvinistic one and a larger general one.

Schiphol, the international airport of Amsterdam, strives to be the 'Gateway to Europe'. A reclaimed lake from the 1860s, it is almost a city in itself now, home to hundreds of companies that provide the myriad of services that Europe's fourth busiest airport demands.

Utrecht, the hub of the Dutch railway network (including its headquarters), is a historical city that boasts the country's largest exhibition and fairgrounds (Jaarbeurs) and its biggest shopping mall (Hoog Catharijne). Utrecht is also the traditional capital of the Dutch Catholic Church, as well as a number of other denominations. It is home to the country's largest university and, therefore, a sizeable student population, which helps in making it a lively city with many cultural and commercial activities.

The Green Heart   The areas between these major cities, the so-called *Groene Hart* (Green Heart), and the surrounding areas of the two Holland provinces are still relatively sparsely populated, but new development threaten its open spaces. Until the 1970s it was largely agricultural: idyllic pastures with cows, straight ditches for draining, meandering rivers, old farms and quaint villages and towns – some of which still exists. But the region is under increasing pressure from the surrounding cities to take some of the overflow from their burgeoning population, with new towns and rather monotonous suburbs springing up in designated areas. Particularly in the Green Heart, new highways and railway connections (including international high-speed links) disturb the rural calm, and the huge volume of traffic creates jams all around the cities. Furthermore, the increase in Schiphol's air traffic and number of runways is causing friction with surrounding towns and villages, as well as with environmentalists, some of whom plead for declaring the area a huge Central Park so as to better protect it from further development.

So far, people visiting or coming to live in the Netherlands can still admire 'typically Dutch' scenes of green meadows, canals, windmills and tulip fields. Yet it remains uncertain how much of it, in the long term, can be saved from urbanisation and economic pressure.

Now that you have (almost) finished reading this book, you should be ready for dealing with the Dutch yourself. I'll conclude by summing up some of the advice given, together with some hard facts about the country, its people, its economy and its history.

1. The Dutch 'guru' of cross-cultural studies, who wrote *Culture's Consequences* (Sage, London 1984) and several ensuing publications in this field.
2. Around 1800 the former 'State of Holland' was split up in two separate provinces, North and South Holland, in order to diminish its dominance.

Chapter 13

DO'S AND DON'TS

Here follows a summary of the advice given throughout this book – the major do's and don'ts in the Dutch business world. Obviously, not everything is pertinent to every reader, as it depends very much on where he or she comes from.

When working or doing business with the Dutch:

Do's
- Do come well-prepared, with detailed and practical information on your products, needs and capacities;
- Do come to the heart of the matter quickly, within a few minutes at most;
- Do try to present yourself as punctual, modest and practical;
- Do try to give a positive but realistic and not 'overdone' presentation of you personally, your product and your company;
- Do concentrate seriously on the matter in hand, making only occasional small talk or jokes, until the business itself is over and done with;
- Do state your opinions clearly and without too much emotion;
- Do consult your Dutch colleagues on all levels (but don't take up too much of their time!);
- Do be prepared for criticism and learn to deal with it calmly;
- Do be critical and outspoken about the Dutch too – they expect and appreciate it;
- Do be open to compromise during any form of negotiation;
- Do take initiatives and don't worry about losing face by being creative or by asking questions;
- Do bring up alternatives when something is said to be impossible;

- Do ask Dutch colleagues their opinion on your performance (but be prepared for very honest answers, and remember that they indicate involvement!);
- Do tell Dutch colleagues your views on their working environment and ways of doing things; 'constructive criticism' will be appreciated;
- Do ask subordinates for their opinion also, and show interest in their personal backgrounds;
- Do tell your colleagues and subordinates about your own personal background without bragging unnecessarily;
- Do participate in company rituals such as birthday 'coffee and cake', the 'borrel', Christmas celebrations, etcetera;
- Do try to learn to speak Dutch, and do practice it even when the Dutch speak English, or another familiar language, to you;
- Do read and ask questions about Dutch history and society; this will help you to understand the Dutch better;
- Do try to keep yourself as well as your colleagues from generalising and stereotyping.

Don'ts:
- Don't bring (or expect to be offered) expensive business gifts;
- Don't, during the introduction, boast about academic degrees, influential family connections, or relationships with important people;
- Don't overdress; see what other people are wearing, and when in doubt, ask Dutch advice;
- Don't ask direct questions on income and personal political views;
- Don't assume that everyone is married and has children;
- Don't expect lavish meals or sightseeing tours in town. (But if you *are* offered them, it is obviously a good sign);
- Don't, as an in-company visitor to Dutch headquarters, expect to be booked into the very best hotel in town (and don't feel compelled to do that for them either when they come to visit you!);
- Don't expect intensive personal coaching by people from the host company outside of working hours (and when they visit you, ask them if they perhaps prefer to be alone);
- Don't, when working with Dutch people, be 'bossy' to subordinates;

- Don't expect the Dutch to come for a drink after work, but *do* continue to ask ...one day they will come;
- Don't, when selling, forget to mention any environmental advantages of your product;
- Don't expect (and certainly don't ask for) personal favours outside of a transaction;
- Don't shower Dutch people with compliments; it makes them uneasy; try to keep mind and emotions somewhat separated during working hours;
- Don't begin long discussions on philosophy, literature, art, etcetera during introductions, business lunches or during working hours.

Appendix

THE NETHERLANDS:
FACTS AND FIGURES

General The Netherlands lies in northwestern Europe, with Germany to the east and Belgium to the south. Across the North Sea, to the west, is Great Britain. The Netherlands is quite a small country – only 120 km from the beach at The Hague to the nearest German territory, and the maximum distance from north to south is a mere 400 km. The total area is 41,870 km² (15,772 sq.miles), including the Waddenzee, IJsselmeer and other lakes. The land area is 33,800 km² (12,731 sq.miles).

Climate The temperate maritime climate has winters with day temperatures around freezing point, often with strong winds. Snow and day-time frost occur in rare severe winters. Summers can be hot and sunny (30+°C in the day-time, 20 °C at night), but may also be disappointing with much cooler, cloudy weather. Rain and humidity can occur in all seasons, which makes winter days very chilly and summer days sticky.

The Dutch weather is changeable and unpredictable, which might explain its importance as a topic of casual conversation.

Scenery The country is mostly flat, with much man-made land (reclaimed lakes and swamps) below sea level. This is generally true for the northwestern half of the country, where water is to be seen almost everywhere: rivers, canals, lakes, estuaries and the omnipresent ditches that drain the low grasslands, giving them a neatly carved-up appearance. The lowest point, near Rotterdam, is some 7 metres (21 feet) below sea level.

The east and south of the country are slightly higher and drier. There you can find sandy elevations, areas of forest and heather, and in some places 'hills' some 100 metres in height. The highest point of the country (321 metres or 1053 feet) is in the extreme southeast, in the province of Limburg.

Although the country is densely populated, strict building controls safeguard open spaces. The Netherlands has areas of outstanding beauty which are popular with natives and visitors alike.

Natural resources The main assets of the Dutch economy have always been its fertile soils and its favourable location on the rivers and seas of western Europe, which has stimulated trade for centuries. The Netherlands was always regarded as being quite poor in natural mineral resources. Up until the 1970s coal was produced in quantities that did not allow export; there was small-scale exploitation of oil and iron ore, and of clay and gravel for construction. But in 1960, enormous quantities of natural gas, and further oil reserves, were discovered in the north of the country and in the Dutch part of the North Sea.

Economy Over the last 200 years, the Netherlands has had a strongly agricultural image abroad. However, milk, cheese and tulips by no means represent a realistic picture of the country. The Dutch economy is predominantly industrial and service-oriented, with a strongly international orientation based on its long trading tradition and colonial past. Even agro-industry is much more varied than the above products, with an export-value second only to that of the USA. Just over 2% of all working people are employed in agriculture itself, reflecting its high degree of mechanisation and automation.

The Netherlands is home to a disproportionately high number of multinational companies such as Ahold, Akzo-Nobel, DSM, Heineken, Philips, Shell, Stork, Unilever and Wolters-Kluwer/Reed-Elsevier. Its financial organisations like ABN/Amro, Aegon, ING, KPN and Rabobank are well-known abroad, but not always identified as being Dutch.

The oil industry, machinery, electronics and other high-tech production, the large and varied agro-industry, together with transport and other trade-related facilities like banking and insurance make up the bulk of the economic output.

The carefully managed exploitation and export of the Netherlands' large reserves of natural gas have given a sound basis to the Dutch economy ever since the early 1960s.

Activities such as tourism and the breeding of oysters and mussels for foreign markets may be eye-catching but are in fact marginal when compared to the size of more conventional activities. Few people realise that the banknotes of many countries are printed in the Netherlands, or that their CDs may have been produced in Holland, or their booming ports expanded or modernised by specialised Dutch building companies, or their ships-in-trouble saved by Dutch maritime services. They may enjoy Dutch beer or ice cream, cook with Dutch dried spices, and feed their babies on Dutch milk powder, and enjoy a large variety of Dutch candy. And they may of course have Dutch flowers in their vases and Dutch-printed posters on the wall. And this list is far from complete!

On a more abstract and culture-related level, Dutch economy can be described as a mixture of free-market economy and government control, although the latter is gradually decreasing. A deeply felt need to have everyone share a decent standard of living has led to a system in which, more than in most countries, national wealth is distributed to all.

One far-ranging aspect of state control are the rules and regulations imposed on enterprises. These concern matters such as safety, hygiene and other labour conditions, salary levels, workers' rights, environmental protection, all kinds of limitations on building, and many others. Yet, the Netherlands has much to offer to foreign investors: a highly-educated workforce, an excellent coastal position at the heart of the world's largest trading block, nearby emerging markets, very good infrastructure and, in spite of the otherwise high taxation, favourable tax rates to foreign investors.

Spread of population and economic centres With 16.3 million inhabitants, the Netherlands is very densely populated. Only a few countries have more people per square kilometre. The spread of the population and therefore of economic activities is quite uneven. The less populated areas are to be found in the northeast and the southwest. Nearly half the population lives in the west, the so-called Randstad.

Language Dutch, a Germanic language like German and English, is spoken throughout the country, although there are various regional dialects. The province of Friesland in the north has its own language, related to Dutch.

Religion   The Dutch became Christians in the 9th century. From the 1500s on, Calvinism, a rather strict Protestant denomination, dominated the region north of the three major rivers which cut through the middle of the country, while in the south the great majority have always remained Catholic.

In the 1960s, church-going quickly declined. Nowadays only some 20% of the Dutch regularly attend church services. Among the ethnic minorities, Islam is the most widespread religion.

Education   Education in the Netherlands, organised in the continental-European tradition, is good according to international standards, albeit with little integration of theory and practice. Both state and private schools are government-funded and, therefore, nearly free up to age 16. An extensive state scholarship system helps people over 16 to partially finance further studies, regardless of parental income.

State control has resulted in fairly even quality throughout the country, including the universities, although some faculties may enjoy a particularly good reputation. For careers in the business world, MBA studies and HEAO (a sub-academic training) are widely popular nowadays.

School attendance is obligatory up to the age of 16, but a substantial percentage of students continue into higher education. Some 7% of the population has completed an academic education. For students from overseas there is a broad range of schools with a British, American, German or Japanese curriculum.

Basic history

40 BC – 4th century AD   Areas south of the river Rhine are part of the Roman Empire, with fortified towns like Utrecht, Nijmegen and Maastricht guarding its borders. To the north are tribal areas.

5th – 8th century   The southern areas of the Netherlands are part of the Frankish, Merovingian and Carolinian empires. The north is 'Free Frisian' territory.

8th – 10th century   Charlemagne conquers the Frisians; from 870 on, the Low Countries (including Belgium and Luxembourg) form part of the East-Frankish Empire and, from 962, of the Holy Roman Empire.

11th – 14th century   Feudalism is the dominant system in the higher-lying areas. As the population increases, low-lying marshlands in the west come under cultivation. Peasants and fishermen build dykes to protect their property and lives, creating *waterschappen*, organisations for the construction, maintenance and repair of dykes and sluices. In the west of the country, towns like Amsterdam, The Hague and Rotterdam are founded. In the 1400s, towns in the eastern areas develop maritime ('Hanseatic') trade with other European lands.

15th and 16th century   By inheritance, the Low Countries become part of the Burgundian empire; later they are ruled by Habsburg Spain.

16th century   Reformation gains many followers in the Low Countries. Reacting to oppression by Catholic Spain, the Protestants rise up and declare independence in 1581, forming the Republic of the Seven United Netherlands, a federation of northern provinces dominated by the state of Holland. The Princes of Orange-Nassau are in power but not as royalty. Calvinist religion comes to dominate; Catholics need to be very low-profile. By 1590 the rebellion has been won, but formally continues until 1648. The south remains Catholic, partly occupied by the Dutch Republic, partly still under the Spanish. In the 1800s, the latter areas become Belgium.

17th century   Pursuing the Spanish enemy and its ally Portugal, the Dutch Republic develops a highly successful and worldwide maritime trade empire, ranging from the Arctic to the East Indian archipelago, now Indonesia. The Republic enters its 'Golden Age'. Many people prosper, cities expand, art flourishes, many lakes are reclaimed and the Republic acquires widespread international prestige. A national identity gradually develops.

18th century   Stagnation of Dutch maritime trade in the face of British competition.

1795 – 1813 Anti-Orangist regime based on French revolutionary principles, followed by French occupation. Napoleon's brother Louis becomes the first king of this vassal state (1806).

1813 Restoration of independence, reunification with Belgium. The Prince of Orange becomes King. Belgium industrialises, while the north remains mostly agrarian. North-south antagonisms increase, and Belgium separates in 1830. The name 'Netherlands' is increasingly used for the new country. By 1854, Catholicism can officially surface again.

1880s After a period of stagnation, the country begins to industrialise and modernise. In Indonesia, colonial rule and exploitation are intensified and bring the Netherlands great profit. Various religious and political groups set up their own political parties, organisations and education systems, leading to social compartmentalisation.

1914 – 1918 The Netherlands remains neutral in World War I. The 1916 floods lead to the closing off and reclaiming of the Zuiderzee in decades to follow.

1920s Modest prosperity, increasing industrialisation and modernisation. Radio is introduced, organised into separate socio-religious broadcasting organisations.

1930s Severe economic crisis. Government increases its grip on the economy in an attempt to solve massive unemployment.

1940 – 1945 Nazi occupation, 100,000 Dutch Jews perish in concentration camps, another 100,000 people in acts of war and repression. Enormous economic damage ensues. From 1941 on, Japan occupies the Dutch East Indies. In the face of the German occupation, social compartmentalisation is temporarily overcome.

1945 Liberation of the Netherlands by Allied forces. After liberation from Japan, Indonesia declares independence. For four years, Dutch forces unsuccessfully fight against this. Colonial functionaries and the military are expelled by newly independent Indonesia.

1950s   With US aid ('Marshall aid'), the country slowly recovers its prosperity. Hard work, thrift and acquiescence to leadership are emphasised. The 1953 flooding in the southwest (1850 people die), results in the Delta project, closing out the sea and linking the islands.

1960s   Beginning of the welfare state, made possible by the discovery and exploitation of large quantities of natural gas. Student protests against the old-fashioned education system lead to a youth revolt and vast social changes after 1965. This results in more democratic relations and the loosening up of religious bonds. Gradually, the old-style system of social compartmentalisation dissolves.

1970s   More prosperous than ever before. Under strong social-democratic influence, social benefits and taxes grow to the highest levels in the world. Labour immigration from Turkey and Morocco, and people from former Caribbean colonies create ethnic minorities.

1980s   Under liberal/Christian-democratic government the country is faced with economic recession, growing unemployment and persistent state budget deficits. There are attempts at cutting back on welfare and other state expenditures. The 1982 agreement between trade unions and employers leads to the foundation of the 1990s' 'Dutch economic miracle' also known as the 'polder model'. Some ethnic tensions emerge in the cities.

1990s   Economic recovery leads to unprecedented prosperity. After 1994, two consecutive liberal/social-democratic governments stimulate self-employment and further 'deregulation'. This leads to the creation of many jobs and to economic growth higher than in surrounding countries. Large infrastructure works are started up: cargo railroad Rotterdam-Germany, high speed trains, and further expansion of Schiphol airport.

2000 and after   Soon after the beginning of the new millennium, both the international and Dutch economies are affected by a general slump and the terrorist attacks of 9/11. After the economic miracle, Dutch growth suffers stagnation and even recession. Unemployment rises. In the 2002 election campaign, radical politician Pim Fortuyn's oppositional movement comes to a sudden halt with his assassination. A liberal/Christian-democrat government ensues, cutting back state expenditures and emphasising more discipline. These developments plunge the country into a somewhat gloomy mood.

ABOUT THE AUTHOR

Jacob Vossestein (1949, Utrecht) studied human geography and social anthropology and has visited more than 60 countries. A staff member of the Royal Tropical Institute (KIT) since 1979, he developed 'country briefings' for Dutch expatriates-to-be. Since 1988 he has also been responsible for KIT's 'Understanding the Dutch' training programme for foreign managers living in the Netherlands, and for programmes on globalising business teams. Such training programmes are organised for companies such as Shell, Unilever, ABN/Amro Bank, Philips, DSM, Quest, and others. As a cross-cultural trainer, Jacob Vossestein also does introductions to Dutch culture for foreign students and academics.

His book *Dealing with the Dutch* was first published in 1997, with a Dutch translation in 1998. A revised and updated English edition appeared in 2001. Also in 2001, he contributed to the *Expat Handboek*, a Dutch-language manual for expats-to-be. In 2003, *Vreemd Volk* ('Strange Folks') was published, a book for a Dutch audience on the systematics of people's behaviour in other cultures. All these books were published through KIT Publishers. (www.kit.nl/publishers).

ACKNOWLEDGEMENTS

I would like to thank my colleagues at KIT who have helped me define the changes going on around us, in particular my fellow trainers on the 'Understanding the Dutch' programmes: Anne Henry, Els de Jong, Wilfred Ploeg and Jeanne Visser 't Hooft.

Needless to say, I am pleased that KIT Publishers is interested in publishing once more a revised edition of this book.

And, of course, where would I be without the interesting and often funny observations that the participants of the programmes have shared with me. Their comments contributed much to the success of previous editions and I have no doubt they will do the same for this one.

Finally, I would like to invite readers – foreign or Dutch – to send me their comments. I am always on the look-out for new quotes and insights, either supporting my ideas or disagreeing with them, and I welcome your reactions. You can reach me by e-mail at j.vossestein@kit.nl

INDEX

A
Academic titles 39
Advertising 73, 91, 102, 160, 170-171
Agendas 121, 124
Art 28, 31, 41, 51, 73, 91, 93, 107-108, 111, 141, 143, 164, 168, 221, 227
ATV (Labour time reduction) 162-163

B
Banks, Banking 19, 29-30, 43, 45, 52, 72, 89, 99-102, 106, 114-115, 117, 131, 133, 138, 159, 162, 178, 186, 217, 224-225, 231
Bankruptcies 19, 117, 185
Building (industry) 18, 41, 108, 118, 131-132
Bureaucracy 7, 25, 53, 89, 114-117, 120, 131, 133, 144, 193
Burnout (see also Stress and Labour disability) 126-127, 174
Business lunch (see also Food) 139, 221

C
Calvinist backgrounds 12, 17, 20, 26, 42, 56-57, 81, 89-90, 103, 138, 149, 212-215, 217, 227

CAO 63-64, 70, 126, 162-163
Catholicism (see also Religion) 57, 228
CEOs 9, 40, 52, 68-69, 108, 122, 137
Children 13, 22, 25, 29, 38, 91, 96, 100, 106, 113, 124, 131, 141-142, 149, 151, 153, 162-163, 166, 175, 177-178, 180-181, 183-184, 187-188, 198, 201-204, 206-207, 220
Church (see also Religion) 20, 56-58, 89-90, 133, 137, 153, 155, 157, 181, 187, 195, 212-213, 217, 226
Clothing (see also Dress) 63
Coaching 67, 130, 220
Colleagues 7-8, 36-38, 44, 51-52, 70, 83, 98, 102, 115, 117-118, 122, 126, 146, 154, 162, 174, 176-177, 188-189, 219-220,
Collective Labour Agreement (CAO) 63, 70, 126, 162
Commuting 209
Company council (OR) 61, 86
Competition 14, 16, 19, 38-41, 43, 53, 59, 63-64, 70, 84, 119, 163, 179, 199, 227
Compromise 8, 16, 76-77, 88, 90, 122-123, 141, 144-147, 153, 219

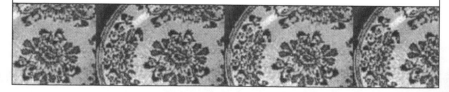